RBF.M

Operation Sealion

Operation Sealion

Hitler's Invasion Plan for Britain

David Wragg

Pen & Sword
MILITARY

First published in Great Britain in 2018 by
Pen & Sword Military
An imprint of
Pen & Sword Books Ltd
47 Church Street
Barnsley
South Yorkshire
S70 2AS

Copyright © David Wragg 2018

ISBN 978 1 47386 738 3

The right of David Wragg to be identified as Author of this work has been asserted by him in accordance with the Copyright, Designs and Patents Act 1988.

A CIP catalogue record for this book is
available from the British Library.

All rights reserved. No part of this book may be reproduced or transmitted in any form or by any means, electronic or mechanical including photocopying, recording or by any information storage and retrieval system, without permission from the Publisher in writing.

Printed and bound in England by TJ International Ltd, Padstow, Cornwall.

Pen & Sword Books Limited incorporates the imprints of Atlas, Archaeology, Aviation, Discovery, Family History, Fiction, History, Maritime, Military, Military Classics, Politics, Select, Transport, True Crime, Air World, Frontline Publishing, Leo Cooper, Remember When, Seaforth Publishing, The Praetorian Press, Wharncliffe Local History, Wharncliffe Transport, Wharncliffe True Crime and White Owl.

For a complete list of Pen & Sword titles please contact
PEN & SWORD BOOKS LIMITED
47 Church Street, Barnsley, South Yorkshire, S70 2AS, England
E-mail: enquiries@pen-and-sword.co.uk
Website: www.pen-and-sword.co.uk

Contents

Acknowledgements vii

Introduction ix

Maps xi

Chapter One	The Unstoppable Hun	1
Chapter Two	After Dunkirk	21
Chapter Three	Lessons of Invasions Past	29
Chapter Four	The Germans Prepare Their Plans	41
Chapter Five	The Battle of Britain	63
Chapter Six	The State of the Navies in 1940	79
Chapter Seven	Woe to the Conquered – German Occupation in The East	91
Chapter Eight	Woe to the Conquered – German Occupation in The West	107
Chapter Nine	The Lessons of Crete	135
Chapter Ten	Barbarossa and Deliverance	141
Chapter Eleven	What Would German Occupation Have Meant?	167
Chapter Twelve	The Lessons of Normandy	175
Chapter Thirteen	Was a Negotiated Peace an Option?	199
Chapter Fourteen	Could The Germans Have Invaded?	203

Appendix A	The Invasion Barges	209
Appendix B	Specialised Equipment	213
Appendix C	New Equipment	217
Glossary		219
Bibliography		225
Endnotes		227
Index		231

Acknowledgements

In writing any book, an author is grateful for the help and assistance of many others, and especially those who have placed on record their wartime achievements, many of them in the invaluable Imperial War Museum Sound Archive.

No work on something as vast as our wartime navy can cover every inch of ground, and for those whose appetite has been whetted by this book, I hope that the bibliography at the back is helpful. This book concentrates mainly on the German plans to invade the south of England in autumn 1940, after the fall of France and when the British Empire was all that stood between the Axis powers and their domination of Europe.

David Wragg

Edinburgh

August 2017

Introduction

The British Isles had not been invaded since 1066, but in the summer of 1940, Nazi Germany seemed unstoppable. The German army and air force had swept through Poland, paused for the winter, and then invaded Denmark and Norway, in the latter case landing from the sea and the air, before turning their attention to Belgium, the Netherlands and then France. Even before the Second World War had started, Germany had annexed Austria and taken Czechoslovakia. Hitler had secured his eastern flank through an alliance with the Soviet Union that not only provided security, but fuel, food and raw materials so that a British blockade would not have the same devastating effects that Germany had experienced during the First World War. Germany after all had far more modern means at its disposal for an invasion than had William of Normandy in 1066.

The Mediterranean was closed to merchant shipping other than in convoy and the Suez Canal then became part of a roundabout route from the UK to Egypt and Cyprus via the Cape of Good Hope, the Indian Ocean and the Red Sea. In the Mediterranean and North Africa, Italy's belated entry into the war as an ally of Germany threatened the British colony and base of Malta and the Suez Canal, the vital link to the Persian Gulf, as it was then known, and India, Australia and the Far East.

As the British adjusted to this new state of affairs, realising that they were on their own and being thankful that at least most of the personnel of the British Expeditionary Force had been recovered, albeit without their transport and heavy equipment, a new threat emerged: invasion. Aerial reconnaissance discovered invasion barges being gathered in the French and Belgian channel ports. While the RAF bombed the barges, efforts were made to improve the equipment of the Irish Free State's armed forces in case a German invasion came via Ireland, thinly populated and weakly defended.

These were preparations for the invasion of England, a plan known to the Germans as *Seelöwe*, Sea Lion.

Just how realistic was the German threat of invasion?

Maps

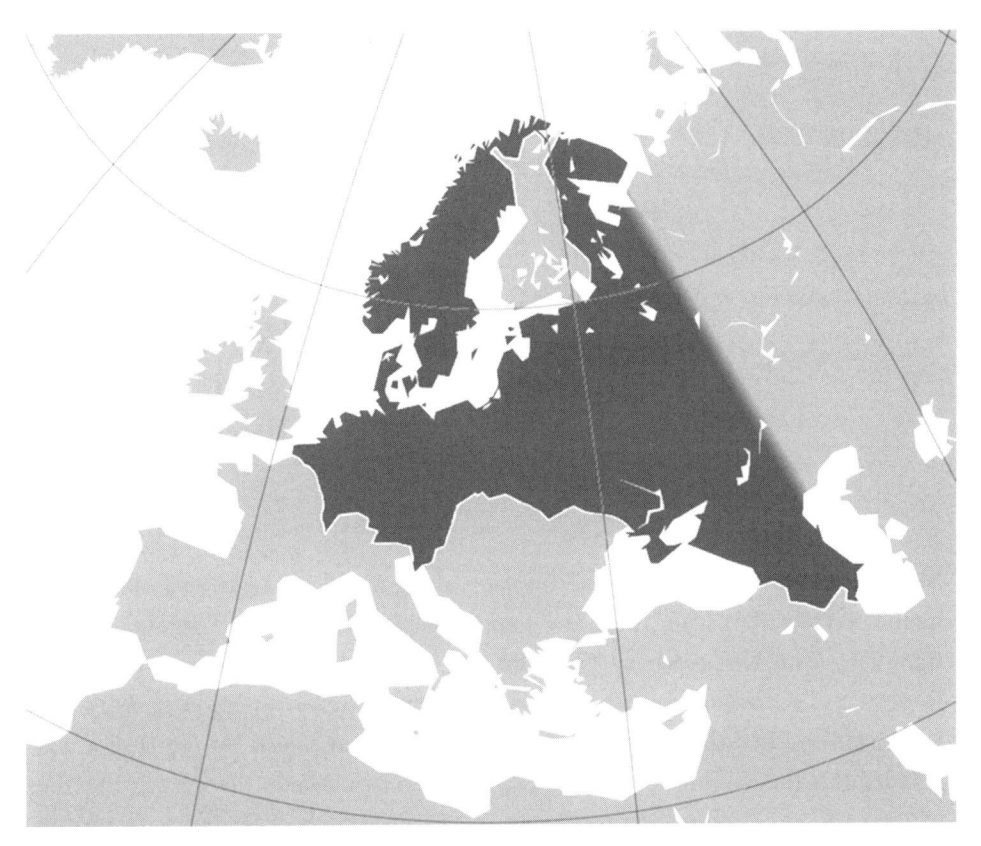

MAP 1: Hitler's plan for a 'Greater Germany' designed to provide the Lebensraum or 'living space' that he felt the country needed. Norway, Denmark and the Netherlands were seen as countries that had Aryan populations. On the fringes and in the east, those who also had this characteristic would be welcomed, while others would be moved further east into inhospitable territory.

xii Operation Sealion

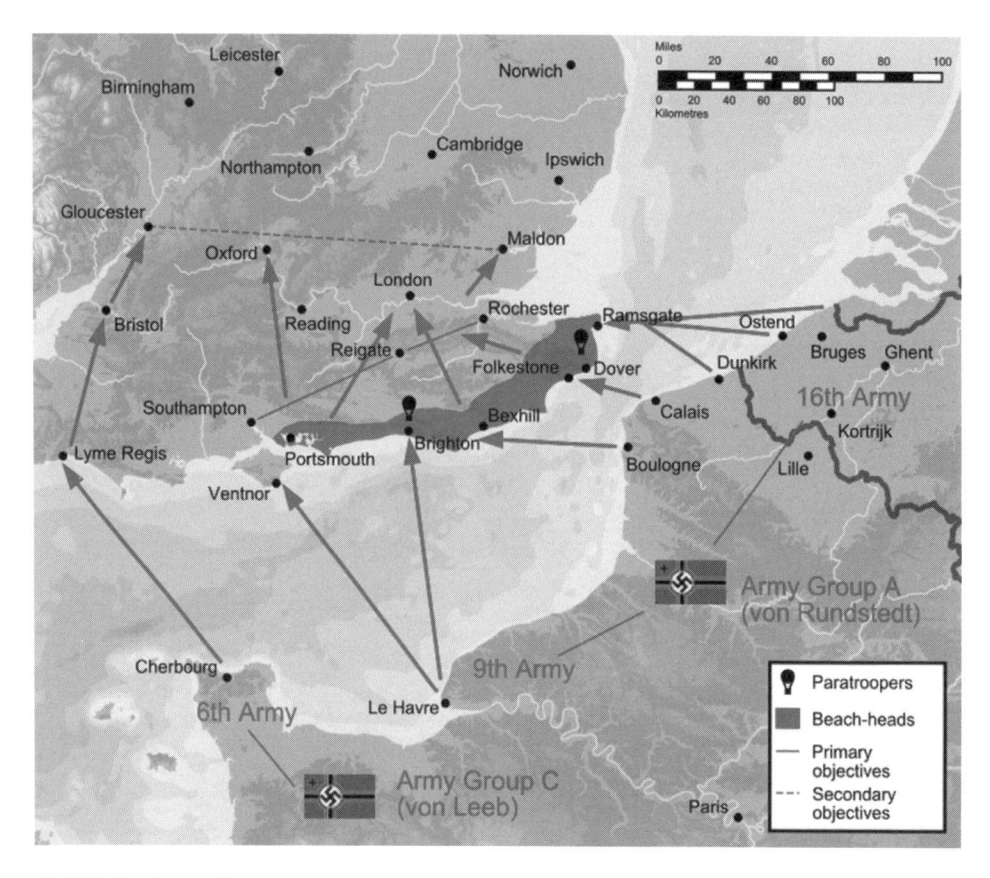

MAP 2: An early proposal for an invasion along a wide front from Lyme Regis in the west to Ramsgate, with the main beachheads between Portsmouth and Ramsgate. The Kriegsmarine regarded this as being far too long and difficult to protect the invasion force and the subsequent resupply operations, while the Luftwaffe opposed the alternative assault through East Anglia. In the end, it was decided that the landing zones would be between Brighton in the west and Hythe in the east, some miles west of Dover and without high cliffs, but with terrain much of which was marshy.

Chapter One

The Unstoppable Hun

On the night of 15/16 September 1940, Guy Gibson, later to be the most famous of the Royal Air Force's bomber pilots, was flying a Handley-Page Hampden bomber over the port of Antwerp in German-occupied Belgium. It was the biggest raid on the port at that early stage of the war.

'It was the night of the full moon; many barges were sunk, many blew up, destroying others around them,' recalled Gibson. 'They were full of stuff and we could see, there and then, there was no doubt about it, the Germans were ready.

'Flying low over the docks that night we could easily see the tanks on board, the guns on mountings at the stern of each invasion craft, the tarpaulins over sinister objects on the docks. "Der Tag"[1] was drawing near for the Hun, and September 15th was, perhaps, the day when they realised that it would be no use.'[2]

What had brought the RAF to bomb barges in a Belgian port? Indeed, why were barges being gathered in northern France and Belgium?

France had fallen on 21 June, less than six weeks after the German invasion had begun after nightfall on 12 May. The evacuation of the British army, as well as many French soldiers, from Dunkirk had been completed on 3 June, leaving most of their equipment behind them.

France and the United Kingdom had declared war on Germany on 3 September 1939, after Germany had ignored an Anglo-French ultimatum for Germany to withdraw from Poland, which been invaded two days earlier. It seems that the Germans did not expect the United Kingdom and France to act upon their ultimatum, indeed both the head of the German Navy, or *Kriegsmarine*, Erich Raeder, and his U-boat commander and eventual successor, Karl Dönitz, were taken by surprise and had to temporarily excuse themselves from meetings when the news was passed to them. After all, there had been no Anglo-French intervention during the Sudetenland crisis almost a year earlier, and a look at a map showed that neither of the two allies was well-placed to intervene in Poland, with Germany, the most populous and largest country in Western Europe, sitting firmly between France and Poland, and able to control the natural approaches to the Baltic, the Skagerrak and Kattegat.

It was not just this, for during the intervening period, Germany had completed the occupation of Czechoslovakia with little fuss. Germany had earlier, in March 1938, absorbed Austria into the Third Reich, but not without the support of many of that country's population. Germany and what had been at the time the Austro-Hungarian Empire had been allies in the First World War. Post-war, plans to call Austria *Deutschösterreichische* were banned by the Allied Control Commission, determined not to see the creation of what might be called a 'greater Germany' from the ruins of what had been the costliest and bloodiest war in history. Nevertheless, the dream of a united German people lived on, with many yearning for an *Anschluss*, or 'joining together' of the two countries.

Germany's ally, Italy, had also been expanding across the Adriatic into the Balkans, and, more controversially, had nearly started a European war with its invasion of Abyssinia, present day Ethiopia, in October 1935.

The British and French governments' policy of appeasement had been highly acceptable for most of the British population. In 1939, Mass Observation, the official public opinion polling organisation, had found most people were keen to avoid war at almost any price with memories of the First World War still vivid. In Germany, the invasion of Poland was supported by many as simply being a case of Germany regaining territory lost in the First World War, when Poland's boundaries had been extended westwards by the Treaty of Versailles. Germany did not complete the occupation of Poland until the launch of Operation Barbarossa, the invasion of the Soviet Union, in summer, 1941, and in the meantime was content to allow the Soviet Union to occupy the eastern area of the country. Trade between the Soviet Union and Germany continued right up to the start of the invasion as Germany was heavily reliant on Soviet supplies of food, raw materials and, most important of all, oil. The traffic was not one way as the Soviet Union also needed German machinery and vehicles.

While much attention has rightly been given to Hitler's demands for *Lebensraum*, 'living space', for Germany's population, the other important factor was that Germany was heavily dependent on imports, with few natural resources other than coal. Even agriculture was only viable with massive imports of fertilizer.

Poland was invaded on the pretext of what might be described as a frontier provocation – but Poland was in no state to invade Germany. In 1939, the country was one of the most backward in Europe, with poor roads and communications, less than 100,000 lorries, and the armed forces were using obsolete equipment. The Poles fought valiantly but were overwhelmed by strong Germany forces.

It should not be assumed that the Germans were completely superior to the other countries in Europe, or their armed forces. There were serious weaknesses in the German armed forces. The air force, the Luftwaffe, was the best equipped and had been the favoured service since the Nazi take-over. Yet even the Luftwaffe lacked heavy bombers with long range and had developed as a force to operate in close coordination with fast moving ground forces, with assaults spearheaded by armoured formations, and this combination of close air support and tanks, the famous *Panzers*, was the basis of the concept of *Blitzkrieg*, 'Lightning War'. The Luftwaffe also lacked transport aircraft to compare with the American Douglas C-47 Dakota, or Skytrain, the military development of the DC-3 airliner. The German Junkers Ju52 was an older, slower and less capable design, originally designated as a 'bomber-transport', but obsolete as a bomber during the Spanish Civil War, and as a transport by 1939. No less important, the absence of full-time transport squadrons and aircrew meant that the bomber training schools were raided for pilots when an airborne assault was required, interrupting training of bomber pilots while their instructors were away.

The German army, or *Heer*, had fast-moving Panzer units, but the supply units had not been mechanised between the wars, unlike those of the British army, and so there was an almost complete dependence on horses to pull supply wagons and field artillery. This meant that German advances were held up by the slower pace of the horses, with the tank units risking becoming isolated from infantry and artillery, while the supply of fodder for the horses was an added burden, being bulky and much more difficult to transport than fuel, and of course, much more of it was needed.

The German navy, or *Kriegsmarine*, 'War Navy', after a change ordered by Adolf Hitler from the post-Great War *Reichsmarine*, 'State Navy', lacked aircraft carriers and was short of destroyers and battleships. The so-called 'pocket battleships', a term coined by the British and American media for the *Panzerschiffe*, 'armoured ships', were no match for a battleship, and while their diesel engines gave them considerable range, they were much better suited to commerce raiding rather than naval battles, and slower than a contemporary battleship or cruiser. In 1939, there were plans to develop a strong U-boat arm, but at the outbreak of war there were few ocean-going submarines actually in service.

Overall, despite ambitious rearmament plans, in 1939 Germany was short of manpower for its armed forces and heavy industry, and too short of fuel and raw materials to build the armed forces that had been planned. It was just that the early opponents were much weaker in manpower terms and equipment. The delay of almost a year after the Munich Agreement and the outbreak of war had been put to good use by the British, while the French response had been hampered by nationalisation of the aircraft industry. The problem for the British was that they were already running out of money. It has been said that in 1939 'Britain could only afford a short war, but could only expect to win a long one'. Nevertheless, Germany was also in all practical terms bankrupt by this time, with armament plans that could not be afforded.

Germany Strikes North

Denmark was one of the countries that placed their faith in neutrality in the years after Hitler came to power. Neutral since 1815, the country had lost Schleswig and Holstein in 1864, and from this time increasingly fell under the influence of Germany, a process that accelerated after Hitler's rise to power in 1933. That Denmark was within what might be described as Germany's sphere of influence was widely recognised not only by her neighbours, Norway and Sweden, but also by her main trading partner, the United Kingdom. Alone amongst the three Scandinavian countries, in spring 1939 Denmark accepted Germany's offer of a non-aggression pact. Despite this, on the outbreak of war there was no attempt to interfere with Danish trading links, and up to the invasion in 1940, the country continued to trade with the United Kingdom.

A good indication of Denmark's agricultural importance was that after the invasion, the country provided Germany with ten per cent of German consumption of butter, eggs and meat.

Denmark was neutral in the fullest sense. Pacifist policies were widely advocated, and the armed forces did not have the same public and political support as in other European countries. It was not until 1937 that new legislation led to modernisation of the armed forces. Despite this, in April 1940 the army had just 14,000 men, out of a population of 3.85 million, of whom no less than 8,000 had been conscripted during the previous two months. The small navy depended mainly on coastal defences to protect Danish waters. It had only two coastal defence vessels, one of which dated from 1906, fifteen torpedo boats, of which five dated from before 1920, and eight small submarines, with 4,000 men. Between them, these two services had just fifty aircraft, mainly obsolete.

While details of the planned German invasion were leaked to the Danish military attaché in Berlin as early as 4 April 1940, the reports were not believed initially (the head of the *Abwehr*, the German military intelligence and counter-intelligence organisation, Admiral Canaris had released some details intending to embarrass Hitler, against whom he had considered a *coup d'état* in 1938). It was not until 8 April that any attempt was made to strengthen Danish forces near the border with Germany. The next day, at 0415, German forces crossed the border against brief resistance from the army, while the navy, which had not been placed on alert, did not fire a single shot and a German troopship entered the harbour at Copenhagen unchallenged. At 0500, German paratroops attacked the unarmed fortress of Madneso, south of Zealand, and an hour later Copenhagen was occupied. At this point, the Danish government declared a ceasefire and, under protest, accepted that Germany had occupied the country. Even so, the Danish government continued to maintain that the country was neutral until as late as 29 August 1943.

Apart from its agricultural output, Denmark was important to the Germans as a stepping stone on their way to Norway, Operation *Weserübung*, and once that was achieved as a secure means of communication with Norway. With both countries occupied, Germany also controlled the sea approaches to the Baltic, the Skagerrak and Kattegat.

Norway was also intent on neutrality, as in the First World War, but was to prove a more difficult proposition altogether. Experience had shown that combining neutrality with being one of the world's major merchant shipping nations was difficult, but it had worked. In union with neighbouring Sweden until 1905, Norway had become almost completely demilitarised after the First World War. Rearmament did not really begin until 1937, so that by 1939 Norway had a poorly-trained conscript army, an air force with few modern aircraft and a small navy with few modern ships. Conscription had been introduced, but at first this was just forty-four days and even as war approached was only increased to eighty-four days.

The Royal Norwegian Navy had two battleships, although very small with a ship's company of 270 men each and an armament no larger than 8.2-inch guns, effectively the nominal armament of a heavy cruiser, and both dated from 1901, while another two ships granted the same outdated classification dated from 1898. Not surprisingly all four had been reclassified as coast defence ships. Six destroyers, of which three dated from 1936-7, and the other three from 1910-13, were of First World War size, displacing just 550 tons each. There were also twenty-two small torpedo boats and nine small submarines.

Despite the official policy of neutrality, much reliance was placed on automatic protection by British sea power. Despite this, there were Norwegian protests when a British destroyer, HMS *Cossack*, intercepted and boarded the German supply ship *Altmark* to release British merchant seamen taken prisoner after the German *Panzerschiff*[3] *Graf Spee* had sunk their ships.

Earlier, the United Kingdom and France had considered invading Norway during the Russo-Finnish War, also known as the 'Winter War', of 1939-40, largely to make it easier to support Finland.

Germany invaded Norway on 9 April 1940. There were two reasons for the invasion. Clearly, control of both Denmark and Norway ensured that the approaches to the Baltic remained under German control, but there was also the need to protect the vital supplies of iron ore from Sweden. As the Gulf of Bothnia froze in winter, the only all-year route for the ore from Sweden to Germany was via a Norwegian port, after a railway journey from Sweden. The fact that Norwegian airfields and ports provided the ideal bases with which to harass the Arctic convoys from Scotland and Iceland to Murmansk and Archangel was only to become a factor after the invasion of the Soviet Union in 1941. The Anglo-French plan to invade Norway would have centred on the port of Narvik, which might have aided Finland, but more probably would have denied Germany easy access to Swedish iron ore, and no doubt this strategic material would have been of value to the two allied nations.

The day before the German invasion, the Anglo-French Supreme War Council had ordered British warships to start laying mines in Norwegian waters to force German iron ore convoys into the open sea where they would be attacked by British and French naval forces. Minor British warships were also deployed in case of any German action against Norway. It was around this time that the British Admiralty realised that the Germans had plans to invade Norway.

The Norwegian Campaign

Norway was a more difficult proposition for the Germans than Denmark, or even Poland. There was no land border, while the terrain was very difficult, with high mountains and the coastline heavily indented by numerous fjords. In April, much of the country was still covered by snow. Another factor was that the Norwegians had time to mobilise, with the king and the government escaping from Oslo, and there was time to ask the United Kingdom and France for assistance.

The problems of geography had been taken into account by the German military planners. With typical German thoroughness, troops were landed from the sea more or less simultaneously at Oslo, Kristiansand, Bergen, Trondheim and Narvik, and air-landed at Oslo and Stavanger.

As with most military operations, all did not go according to the plan. The main initial setback was the sinking by shore-based artillery of the troop transport *Blücher*, which was carrying the main headquarters staff.

The two allies were supportive of Norway's request for help, and despite their armies sitting in France expecting a German attack at any time, the decision was made to send an expeditionary force to Norway. It was estimated that at least 50,000 troops would be needed to liberate the country, but little over half that number, an initial 13,000 British and Free Polish troops and 12,500 French troops, were despatched quickly, with air and naval forces.

For the allies, further problems arose. Good airfields were scarce in Norway because of the terrain, while the country was out of range of aircraft operating from bases in most of the United Kingdom, and nowhere within France was within range. Aircraft carriers initially had to be used as aircraft transports rather than as the mobile airfields which they were supposed to be, with RAF aircraft then flying from frozen lakes. In any case, neither the Royal Navy nor the *Marine Nationale* had high performance aircraft that could match a Luftwaffe Messerschmitt Bf109.

Despite these shortcomings, at first all went well at sea. On 10 April, shore-based naval aircraft from HMS *Sparrowhawk*, the Royal Naval Air Station at Hatston, on the mainland of Orkney, sank the light cruiser *Königsberg*, anchored at Bergen. This was the first sinking of a substantial operational warship by aircraft. That same day, what became known as the first Battle of Narvik saw two German destroyers and several merchantmen sunk, at the cost of two British destroyers, but on 13 April, in the second Battle of Narvik, nine destroyers and the battleship HMS *Warspite* sank the remaining eight German destroyers, a type of warship of which the Kriegsmarine did not have sufficient numbers.

The initial British and Free Polish landings were near Narvik on 12 April. Narvik was chosen as it was seen as being easier to take and to hold than Trondheim, but it was recognised that Trondheim's capture was essential if Norway was to be liberated. Even so, Narvik was not captured and the army commander of the force delayed taking the town, initially because he wanted to wait for the snow to melt, and then because he wanted the support of a half brigade of French *Chasseurs Alpins*, not realising that these were assigned to another operation. His last excuse was that he did not want to wound civilians by using naval gunfire to suppress the German defences, which were, of course, being strengthened during the delay.

Further British troops were landed at Namsos, a hundred miles north of Trondheim, and at Andalsnes, south of Trondheim. The northern force was expected to move south and capture Trondheim, but had to contend with four feet of snow and lacked air cover. Those at Andalsnes had to face repeated German attacks from the south while being expected to cut railway lines and then move north.

Having returned to his First World War post as First Lord of the Admiralty, the Royal Navy's political head, Winston Churchill, favoured an amphibious assault on Trondheim, but was dissuaded by the chiefs of staff on the grounds that this would risk too many troops and also place major units of the Royal Navy at risk. Plans for a land-based pincer movement were examined and found to pose as many risks as the amphibious assault.

This left British and French troops fighting their way towards Trondheim. One British brigade managed to get halfway to Trondheim before being forced back north to Namsos, and only survived by being evacuated by the Royal Navy during the night of 3/4 May. There was a similar outcome for a combined British and Norwegian force as they advanced from Andalsnes towards Lillehammer, before being forced back.

In short, the entire Norwegian campaign was cursed by complacency and one senior officer maintained that if the allies found withdrawal difficult, the Germans would also be unable to advance… but they did! Fate also played a part. When a new commander was appointed for the southern British forces, he fell ill and had to be replaced. His successor was flown in by the RAF but when the aircraft landed en route at Kirkwall in Orkney, it crashed, killing two crew members and seriously injuring the other occupants.

Within days of the invasion, the Luftwaffe had gained aerial superiority. Namsos and Andalsnes were both subjected to heavy bombing. Having transported aircraft to Norway, two aircraft carriers attempted to provide air cover, but as mentioned already, at this stage of the war the Fleet Air Arm lacked high performance fighters. The RAF was little better, and although Hawker Hurricanes later arrived, for most of the duration of the campaign, obsolescent Gloster Gladiator biplanes provided the mainstay of the fighter defences, operating from a frozen lake at Lesjeshogen, forty miles from Andalsnes. The Hurricanes, when they arrived, were better, but still outclassed by the Messerschmitt Bf109s.

Eventually, on 24 April, Narvik was shelled continuously by the battleship HMS *Warspite* and three cruisers, but the British troops surrounding the town still failed to press home an attack, even though by this time there were 20,000 of them and the German garrison consisted of just 6,000 men.

Although the *Marine Nationale* did not have the same successes as the Royal Navy, Admiral Derrien, aboard the light cruiser *Montcalm*, commanded a small force that included the light cruiser *Émile Bertin*, and three auxiliary cruisers converted from merchantmen. Under heavy Luftwaffe attack, these ships provided a valuable convoy escort service. The two allied navies worked well together, prompting the French naval historians Auphin and Mordal to write,

> Never in history had there been more cordial relations than those established in the battle area off Norway. Not merely was this collaboration in the technical field, but the far more important field of human relations – the spirit of *camaraderie* between the French officers and their brethren of the Royal Navy. Whether they sailed with the Home Fleet or on escort duty off the fjords of Norway, French and British ships, side by side, learned to sustain and to parry the fierce attacks of Germany's formidable air force.[4]

Losses by the French included the *contre-pilleur*, or super destroyer *Bison*, 2,400 tons, while another super destroyer, *Maillé-Brézé*, was lost when one of her torpedoes blew up while she was alongside at Greenock, on the Clyde in Scotland.

The lack of leadership for the land forces and the absence of effective air cover ashore meant that the campaign was ill-fated. There was no chance of the allied forces gaining their objectives. Worse was to come on 10 May, when the Germans smashed their way into the Netherlands and Belgium and headed towards France, completely bypassing the Maginot Line. As the situation in France went from bad to worse, on 24 May the decision was taken to evacuate the allied forces from Norway and use them to reinforce the defences in France. The paradox was that in order to move the troops quickly, Narvik had to be taken, and this was finally achieved on 27 and 28 May by two battalions of the French Foreign Legion and a battalion of Norwegian troops. By 8 June, more than 24,000 British, French, Norwegian and Polish troops were taken off, but by then Paris had been cut off from the sea.

The withdrawal was costly. On 8 June, the aircraft carrier HMS *Glorious* was steaming towards Scapa Flow in Orkney, carrying not only her own aircraft but also the surviving aircraft of a squadron of Hawker Hurricane fighters. The Hurricane pilots had landed aboard with great difficulty and daring as their aircraft did not have arrester hooks, so that their aircraft could get back to the UK rather than leaving them to be destroyed in Norway, as ordered. Despite the difficult situation, no reconnaissance flights were in the air, and there was not even a lookout in the crow's nest – the ship did not have radar. That afternoon, *Glorious* was spotted by the two German battlecruisers, the sisterships *Scharnhorst* and *Gneisenau*, shelled and sunk. This was despite a valiant attempt to attack the German ships by the two destroyers *Acasta* and *Ardent*, both of which were also sunk as they tried to attack the Germans using torpedoes.

Many of those aboard the *Glorious* were believed to have survived the sinking, but most were drowned or died from exposure, leaving just thirty-nine survivors of the 1,500 men aboard.

The Allies And The Germans In 1940

As the prospect of another war with Germany grew, British and French thinking had assumed that it would follow the same pattern as the First World War. They were not alone in this. The Netherlands, Norway and Denmark all assumed that once again their security would lie in neutrality. German troops were expected to enter Belgium and be held along a line running from Belgium to the Swiss border. The French invested heavily in the fortified Maginot Line, which ran from the border with Belgium, close to the Ardennes, to the Swiss border. An extension of the Maginot Line to the coast would have left Belgium unprotected and would have soured relations between France and Belgium, but without it France was left exposed to a German invasion through Belgium.

There were differences between the first and second wars that should have been obvious to the two allies. Japan and Italy would not be allies this time round, and this was important even if Japan and Italy had remained neutral, but this seemed unlikely as both were engaged in territorial expansion of their own. The Soviet Union was unlikely to be an ally, even though up until August 1939, relations between the USSR and Germany were hostile.

Any question that this would be a different war was soon resolved when Germany invaded Denmark and Norway, both of which had remained neutral during the First World War and had hoped to remain so in the Second.

It was clear that air power would be far more significant than in the earlier conflict. Not only was the threat of the bomber recognised, but many believed that the 'bomber would always get through'. Fortunately, as war approached, the British managed to establish their Chain Home anti-aircraft radar network which was, by providing advance warning of attack and the location of enemy aircraft, a force multiplier, in modern terms, that enabled the Royal Air Force to make the most effective deployment of the available fighters.

The Belgians assumed that Germany would invade, and that there was a danger that, as in the First World War, very little of the country would remain unoccupied, and even that would need British and French help. Yet there was no attempt by Belgium to ally itself with the British and French, and even these two allies did not exercise together. In fact, both sat waiting for the Germans to take the initiative. Once fighting began, the French objected to any attempt at strategic bombing of German forces for fear of retaliatory attacks against French towns and cities.

Like the Danish and the Norwegians, the Netherlands had been neutral during the First World War and like them expected to remain so in the Second. Unlike the other two countries, Dutch neutrality was underpinned by a strong pacifist movement that had developed between the two wars. The Dutch armed forces were poorly equipped, and the best equipment was assigned to the Netherlands East Indies, although even there the navy had nothing more powerful than light cruisers.

Both the UK and France had acted promptly once war was declared. On the day after, the British Expeditionary Force was despatched to France with an initial 152,000 men supported by an air component of twelve RAF squadrons and 9,393 personnel. In addition, the RAF sent the 'Advanced Air Striking Force' (AASF), drawn from No1 Group, Bomber Command, with ten squadrons of Fairey Battle day bombers, to which were added two squadrons of Bristol Blenheims and, later, two squadrons of Gloster Gladiators. In due course, the BEF's air component was to have four squadrons of Hawker Hurricane fighters, four squadrons of Blenheims and five squadrons of Westland Lysander army cooperation aircraft. On 10 May, as the German advance started, ten squadrons of Hurricanes were quickly moved across the Channel to bases in France.

The aircraft deployed by the RAF were inferior to those of the Luftwaffe. The Fairey Battle had been conceived as a light bomber with the performance of a fighter, but hadn't the speed of a contemporary fighter. It was also a poor bomber with limited performance. The Hurricane was far better than the biplane Gladiator and highly manoeuvrable, but it was not a match for the Bf109, and the sole British high-performance fighter at the time, the Spitfire, had only started to enter service with Fighter Command in early 1939.

Apart from the shortcomings of the available aircraft and the numbers deployed, there were other issues as well. Tactics were still evolving and would continue to evolve throughout much of the war. One important point that was not appreciated at the beginning of the fighting was that bomber operations were best conducted by as many aircraft as possible, forcing the enemy's defences to divide their fire and even to be overwhelmed by the bomber formations. This not only brought the maximum force to bear and inflicted the most damage on the target area, but it also minimised losses amongst the bomber force. This rule applied regardless of whether the bombers were light, medium or heavy. It was also important to maintain the element of surprise when attacking, although this was difficult over a war zone where attacks were always expected.

The absence of collaboration and training exercises was another factor. There had been some initial discussions with the Belgians during the winter of 1939-40, but no action. Of course the Belgians also suffered from a shortage of both manpower, especially trained and experienced manpower, and equipment. Possibly the need to address these problems inhibited British and French senior officers who were having difficulties of their own getting enough men trained and sufficient modern equipment and were scared of spreading their available resources too thinly.

It is impossible to judge, despite the benefit of hindsight, whether the British and French forces would have made a greater impact if they had struck at the Germans before the invasion started. At this stage of the war, with many in the United Kingdom still hoping for peace, such operations might have been politically impossible. The French certainly feared that attacks on Germany would bring attacks on French towns and cities in retribution. On the other hand, they would have made the German invasion of the Low Countries and France more difficult and could even have forced Germany to divert forces from operations in Norway. As it was, the British and French just sat waiting. For them, this was the period of the 'Phoney War', a war without fighting on land until the invasion of Norway, while for the Germans it was the 'Sitting War' or *Sitzkrieg*, which seems to have been the more accurate description.

As in Poland and Norway, when the Germans attacked the odds were in their favour. The Luftwaffe was able to deploy 3,834 aircraft, of which 1,482 were bombers and dive-bombers, 42 were ground attack aircraft, 248 *Zerstörer* or fighter-bombers, and 1,016 fighters. By contrast, the total of all RAF aircraft amounted to 456, of which 261 were fighters, 135 bombers and 60 reconnaissance aircraft. While the bulk of the French *Armée de l'Air* was in France, this still only provided a further 1,604 aircraft, of which many were either obsolete or obsolescent. The French had 260 bombers, 764 fighters, 180 reconnaissance aircraft, and another 400 or so aircraft in army support duties. Belgium had just 250 aircraft, of which 90 were fighters, 12 bombers and no less than 120 reconnaissance aircraft. The Netherlands had 132 aircraft, of which 35 were fighters and 23 fighter-destroyers, or fighter-bombers.

Not only were the Germans numerically superior in the air, they had a strong advantage in the quality of their aircraft, a modern air force. Many of the aircrew had taken part in the Spanish Civil War even before the Polish and Norwegian campaigns, meaning that they were already experienced and combat-hardened veterans. On the ground, the Germans had their famous and highly effective *Panzer* or armoured units, and ground-air coordination was good as the Luftwaffe was primarily a tactical air force and the strategy of *Blitzkrieg* was based on rapid advances by armoured forces with close air support.

Yet, as mentioned earlier, the Germans had weaknesses: they suffered from a reliance on horse-drawn transport, and they had no dedicated air transport squadrons.

The French army also lacked mechanisation. Two out of the three cavalry divisions were still using horses, while the British had by this time largely confined horses to ceremonial duties. Most French troops were conscripts, and mobilisation was needed to bring its army up to fighting strength, while the relatively small cadre of professional soldiers was heavily involved in the colonies, their strength augmented by locally recruited troops. There were tanks, but with eight different types, maintaining them was difficult. Much of the artillery dated from the First World War and the new 47mm anti-tank gun was in short supply. Command was heavily centralised and bureaucratic, with generals in the field having limited authority and few chances of showing initiative. In the air, while excellent new aircraft types had been introduced, the pace of manufacture had been slowed by nationalisation of the aircraft industry and the disorganisation that followed.

The interwar British army had been relatively small and completely professional, with conscription not introduced until war seemed to be inevitable, and like the French a large proportion of its personnel was deployed to the colonies supporting locally-raised armies. The reserve force was known as the Territorial Army, whose members were often referred to as 'Saturday night soldiers'. The British army was generally regarded as being unable to expand sufficiently in a crisis and, while they went on a summer training camp, the capabilities of the 'terriers' was regarded as limited, in part due to their having trained on obsolete weapons.

Apart from the lack of conscripts, the other difference between the British and French armies was that British generals were granted substantial autonomy with which to plan and carry out their assignments. This was a major strength when the officers concerned were competent and determined, but, as the debacle in Norway had shown, it was a major weakness if generalship was weak or indifferent.

While the French made extensive use of colonial troops, the United Kingdom was dependent on the governments of the dominions, meaning Australia, Canada, New Zealand and South Africa, authorising the use of their armed forces.

The Belgian army had expanded rapidly as war approached and continued to do so, so that by May 1940 it had 600,000 men, a substantial number for a country with a population of 8.2 million. This provided a field army of 18 infantry divisions, 2 divisions of *Chasseurs Ardennais* (mountain troops that were partially mechanised), and two mechanised cavalry divisions, but with just ten tanks. There were no anti-aircraft guns, but the Belgians did have four anti-tank guns!

Like the French, the Belgians had put their faith in fortifications, with modern forts covering the bridges at Eben-Emael, which overlooked the junction of the Albert Canal and the River Meuse. Possibly collaboration between France and Belgium allowing the extension of the Maginot Line along the frontier between Belgium and Germany would have been more effective, but the Germans could still have invaded Belgium and then France through the Netherlands.

Neutrality had saved the Netherlands during the First World War, and the plan was to hinder any invader by flooding vast areas of land. As with the Belgians, the Dutch had not learnt the lessons of the Spanish Civil War and were not prepared for the rapid pace of a *Blitzkrieg* advance and airborne assault.

In home waters, the Dutch had just one cruiser and a destroyer, as well as some small craft and fifty or so obsolete naval aircraft. They could field an army of 400,000 men in wartime, organised as four army corps each with two divisions. This was less impressive than it seems, having no tanks and just twenty-six armoured cars. There were 656 guns in the artillery, none of which was up-to-date. These were consequences of having a strong pacifist movement in the Netherlands between the wars. On 10 May, the Dutch had just 175 combat aircraft, of which only 132 were airworthy, and just half modern.

The German army was also based on conscription, but with a strong core of professional officers and senior non-commissioned officers. In 1939, it had two million men in 106 divisions, but following the invasion of Poland, it had expanded by fifty per cent, with another million men in 44 new divisions. The ruling Nazi Party had its own troops, the Waffen SS, with another three divisions, while the German paratroops were part of the Luftwaffe, which initially had a division of these highly-trained troops, while a second division was added later.

The Low Countries

Having learnt the lessons of the First World War, the Germans believed in fighting a war on just one front, but this was not followed slavishly as fighting continued in Norway on 10 May when the assault on the Low Countries started.

When a German aircraft force-landed in Belgium on 7 January, a plan for the invasion of the country fell into Belgian hands, but conveniently for the Germans, the warning was ignored. The Germans took no chances and revised their plans. This seems incredible, and one can only assume that the Belgians felt that the plans were fake and intended to create a crisis that could be exploited by the Germans. On the other hand, a sense of hopelessness and inevitability may already have taken hold.

At 0430 hours on 10 May, a force of ten DFS 230 gliders was towed into the air by Junkers Ju52/3 transports. Aboard the gliders were seventy-eight specially trained engineers from the Seventh Airborne Division. Despite the leader being left behind when his glider's tow broke, landing prematurely while still inside Germany, the remaining nine gliders landed on the roof of Fort Eben-Emael and the area immediately surrounding it. Scrambling out of the gliders, specially shaped charges were used to blow holes in the roof and keep the 1,200 troops inside imprisoned for twenty-four hours while the Fourth Panzer Division swept across the river and canals into Belgium. The engineers had completed their work when their leader caught up with them at 0830 hours. This audacious assault on the fort cost just six German dead and another twenty wounded.

Another twenty-one gliders were used to seize other important crossings into Belgium, including the bridges at Veldwezelt and Vroenhoven which were taken completely intact after an officer at headquarters refused permission to blow the bridge at Veldwezelt. The bridge at Kanne was blown after permission was given by the officer commanding Fort Eben-Emael.

Meanwhile, paratroops were overwhelming the Dutch defences, landing from 0500 hours in a long carpet to take the bridges at Dordrecht and Moerdijk, over the Nieuw Maas at Rotterdam, and the airfield at Waalhaven, where despite continued heavy fighting, no less than 250 troop-carrying aircraft landed during the day. A 30-mile stretch of Dutch territory was taken in advance of the arrival of the Panzer armies. Other paratroops took the airfields at Delft and The Hague in an attempt to capture members of the Dutch Royal Family and the leaders of the main political parties. The Dutch put up a stiff resistance, but unwisely decided not to destroy the bridges in the hope that they could be retaken, despite the overwhelming strength of the invaders. At Moerdijk, lightly-armed German paratroops fought off strong Dutch counter-attacks for two days until they were relieved by a Panzer division.

Several of the thirteen Junkers Ju52/3m transports sent to carry troops to seize Ypenburg were shot down. The infantry division sent to take The Hague suffered heavy losses after only 2,000 of the 7,000 men had been landed or dropped, so the attempt to take the city had to be postponed and the troops diverted to take the port of Rotterdam. After fierce fighting, Rotterdam was declared an open city, but even so it was bombed by the Luftwaffe. The Dutch air force lost half of its aircraft on this first day, and had been wiped out by the time the country surrendered on 14 May.

Distracted by the invasion of the Netherlands, British and French troops were hastily sent north to help the defenders, but this spread the available forces too thinly and despite Allied forces moving into Belgium to strengthen its defences, no preparations were made to stop the German assault through the Ardennes, which the British and French had regarded as impassable, so that the Germans advanced rapidly through the Ardennes and onto the plains of northern France, nearly cutting the British and French armies in two.

The Belgians continued fighting until surrender on 28 May. The tiny state of Luxembourg, with no standing army, was occupied on 10 May, and eventually its territory was incorporated into the Third Reich, despite 97 per cent of the population later voting against this in a referendum in 1941.

The Fall Of France

The Germans were through to France on 14 May 1940. The commanders of both the Allied armies and the consensus of opinion amongst the political elite in London and Paris was that it would be five or six days before the Germans crossed the River Meuse, but within twenty-four hours they were over. The Battle of France had started. To the Germans this was *Fall Gelb*.

The British and French forces had been weakened by their move north into the Netherlands and Belgium, an unwise move as it should have been clear that there would be little they could do to stop the German advance. It was fortunate that these forces were not cut off by the speed of the German advance, but unfortunate that no less than thirty French divisions were sitting on the Maginot Line waiting for a German attack that never came.

Worse, the vital front line between Namur in Belgium and Sedan on the French border was held by the French Second and Ninth Armies, frequently rated as being comprised of poor quality troops whose morale had deteriorated during the eight months of phoney war. While the French Second Army did not suffer substantial casualties during the aerial attack, the poorly trained troops were unnerved by the Junkers Ju87 Stuka dive-bombers with their 'trumpets of Jericho' sirens that screamed as the aircraft dived steeply towards the target. One French general recalled that anti-aircraft gunners stopped firing and 'went to ground' while the infantry cowered in the trenches.

The British had ten divisions in France, but it was in the air that they were weak. Wisely, the best of the RAF's fighters, the new Supermarine Spitfires, were held in reserve in England and Scotland waiting for when they would be needed to defend the United Kingdom. The RAF's heaviest bomber at this time was the Vickers Wellington, later to be redesignated as a medium bomber, but this useful aircraft was also held back. Also held back was another bomber, the Handley Page Hampden, a thin aeroplane with no room for another seat beside the pilot, but with a deep forward fuselage for the bomb bay, and which was known within the RAF as the 'flying pan handle'. It was clear that there were those in the United Kingdom who did not believe that the Anglo-French force on the other side of the English Channel could hold back the Germans.

In fact, British armoured units in France were poorly deployed. Rather than being in massed formations, they were in small numbers ready to plug any breaches of the front line. In the air, the same problem could be found, again poorly deployed, but worse, slow to react, and any operations were mounted in small numbers that were easy prey for the Luftwaffe's fighters and German anti-aircraft defences.

As already mentioned, the French themselves did not want to attack Germany from the air for fear of reprisals on French towns and cities, but many in the British government did not want attacks on ammunition factories as these were 'private property'. British fighters were allowed to strafe German airfields with their machine guns (as they didn't have the more effective cannon at this time), but not to bomb them. It was not until May 1940 that the British cabinet decided that it would not consider any German peace offers.

Hitler had wanted to strike west in 1939, but was discouraged by his generals who wanted to consolidate their hold on Poland, and by the argument that armies traditionally did not like to advance in the depths of winter. As it happened, the winter of 1939-40 was noted at the time as being the worst on record. There was also the argument that a winter of inactivity would bring about a change of heart in London and Paris so that the Allies would realise that helping Poland was out of the question.

Yet, as the Germans advanced through the Ardennes, the poor roads meant that progress at first was slow, and tailbacks as much as fifty miles long developed. Had the British and French not considered such an advance impossible and mounted reconnaissance operations, they would soon have realised that the Germans were easy targets for the RAF and the Armée de l'Air. This was an opportunity lost.

Within two days, the RAF's bomber strength in France fell dramatically from 135 aircraft to 72, and another 40 were shot down the next day. As the situation became increasingly desperate, bomber squadrons operating from England joined in, but to little effect and at great cost. On 12 May, six Fairey Battles of the AASF, with an escort of two Hawker Hurricane fighters, were sent to attack the Vroenhoven and Veldwezelt bridges over which German forces were streaming. Four of the Battles were shot down as they approached the bridges, which were left undamaged. Despite his aircraft 'burning like a torch', Flying Officer McIntosh managed to land it safely behind enemy lines, where he was taken prisoner and with his crew spent the rest of the war imprisoned. One German officer pointed out to McIntosh that they had taken the bridges early on Friday morning, but the RAF had not attacked until Sunday, giving the Germans two whole days to establish strong anti-aircraft defences. This instance was typical of much that was happening as the Germans spread across northern France.

On 21 May, the air component of the BEF was down to a handful of Lysanders, while what was left of the Battles were confined to night operations to keep losses to a sustainable level, even though the aircraft was really only suitable for day operations. Two additional Hurricane squadrons were sent to France because of desperate pleas for more air cover by the army, but the Air Officer-in-Command of Fighter Command, Air Chief Marshal Sir Hugh 'Stuffy' Dowding, argued successfully against sending more on the grounds that this would 'bleed white' the air defences of the United Kingdom.

As British and French forces pulled back towards the coast, with the largest grouping being at the French Channel port of Dunkirk, the Luftwaffe persuaded Hitler that it could finish off the troops. Hitler agreed and held back his armoured ground formations. The RAF's Fighter Command tried hard to provide air cover for the evacuation, and even gained local air superiority for short periods, despite the difficulty of providing constant air cover given the short range of British fighter aircraft at this stage of the war, while the Fleet Air Arm and RAF Coastal Command kept the evacuation area free from attacks by U-boats and E-boats.

Ironically, in the period leading to the evacuation of the BEF, the Germans were beginning to question just how long their luck would hold. Strong counter-attacks were expected, and on at least two occasions the advance was halted to allow the Germans to consolidate their forces and bring forward supplies. On 21 May, the sole counter-attack came, when British armour moved south from Arras, but without support from French forces this soon ran out of steam and the British moved back towards the Channel ports.

Between 26 May and 3 June, 338,000 British, French and Free Polish troops were evacuated from Dunkirk in Operation Dynamo, mainly by the Royal Navy and by merchant vessels, including cross-Channel ferries 'taken up from trade' (to use a traditional naval term), as well as many smaller vessels including fishing boats and motor yachts, many of which carried men off the beaches to larger ships for the Channel crossing, while the French navy also helped in the evacuation. Often overlooked was the role of French forces, and especially the army, in holding back the Germans during the evacuation from Dunkirk. Some British units were also detailed for this unwelcome duty, with its clear implication that those involved would be killed or become prisoners of war.

The Battle of France had cost the RAF 931 aircraft and 1,526 casualties. The BEF's air component lost 279 of these aircraft, and the AASF 229, with another 160 from Bomber Command and 60 from Coastal Command.

The Germans had estimated that occupation of Luxembourg, Belgium, the Netherlands and France would cost 90,000 dead, 200,000 wounded and perhaps 1.9 million prisoners, but in the six weeks that the operation had taken, they had lost only 29,640 dead and 133,573 wounded. On 22 June, French leaders were forced to sign an armistice in the very same railway carriage where Marshal Foch had accepted the German surrender in 1918.

Chapter Two

After Dunkirk

Such was the widespread public relief that the bulk of the expeditionary force had been rescued from the beaches at Dunkirk, and elsewhere in France including Cherbourg, that the newly-appointed wartime prime minister, Winston Churchill, had to remind everyone that wars were not won by evacuations. Churchill was right, especially since the BEF had lost most of its equipment, including many lorries which were to prove to be a bonus for the Germans.

In fact the fall of France was nothing short of a disaster. It was clear now that the Second World War was not following the pattern of the First World War as had been so widely expected. The British Empire really did stand alone. The difference between the two wars was reinforced as Italy, a First World War ally, entered the war on Germany's side on 10 June 1940.

On 17 June, Marshal Pétain sued for peace with Germany. Winston Churchill broadcast on the radio to the British people,

> *The news from France is very bad, and I grieve for the gallant French people who have fallen into this terrible misfortune. Nothing will alter our feeling towards them or our faith that the genius of France will rise again. What has happened in France makes no difference to our actions and purpose. We have become the sole champions now in arms to defend the world cause. We shall do our best to be worthy of this high honour. We shall defend our island home and with the British Empire we shall fight on unconquerable until the curse of Hitler is lifted from the brows of mankind. We are sure that in the end all will come right.*

It is hard now to appreciate just how big a blow was the loss of France as ally. The impact was especially severe in the Mediterranean, where the two navies had collaborated and even shared the base at Alexandria. With Italy, a strong power, also in the war, the risk that the Mediterranean could be cut in two and Malta invaded seemed very real.

The whole Atlantic coast of Europe from the North Cape to the Bay of Biscay was in enemy hands. The Luftwaffe had the airfields of France and Belgium from which to strike at the British Isles, while the Kriegsmarine had French bases so that their warships, and especially their submarines, the infamous U-boats, were closer to the main shipping lanes and could stay on station longer without the hazardous choice of sailing around the north of Scotland or through the Straits of Dover. Germany also had French food production and an enlarged pool of manpower for German industry, as well as French factories.

The Germans acted quickly to seize the Channel Islands, which had been demilitarised, and with as many residents as possible evacuated. This did not stop the Germans from bombing Jersey and Guernsey, the two largest islands, killing forty-four people.

Hitler expected Italy to move equally quickly to invade Malta, but although the Italian bombing started early on 11 June and eventually Italy with German help besieged the islands until August 1942, invasion did not happen.

The fear of being hemmed in had already resulted in British forces invading Iceland in May 1940 after the country had declared independence following the German occupation of Denmark, which was responsible for Iceland's foreign affairs and defence. Iceland had refused British protection for fear of provoking Germany, but the British realised that Iceland, with no defences, was vulnerable and that if Germany invaded, the United Kingdom would have been partially encircled. This decision was to pay dividends after the German invasion of the Soviet Union required both the United States and the UK to send convoys with armaments to the USSR, when Iceland was one of the convoy assembly points and a base for maritime-reconnaissance aircraft, but it was deeply resented by the local population and once the USA entered the war, British forces withdrew from Iceland and handed over to the Americans.

While France had surrendered, the Germans did not occupy a substantial part of the south and south-west of the country, which became known as Vichy France after the spa town in which its government was based. Vichy was allowed to keep an army of 100,000 personnel and no attempt was made at first to seize French warships. Given the weakness of the Kriegsmarine, the decision not to seize the French warships may seem surprising, but there were manpower shortages for the Germans, and the calibre of weapons on the French ships differed from those on the Germans' own ships. At first, the British were uncertain about the leanings of Vichy France and its leader, effectively a military dictator, Marshal Pétain, but any doubts were not to linger for long. On 5 July, Pétain broke off diplomatic relations with the United Kingdom. Factories based in Vichy started producing equipment for the Germans, while a number of senior officers proposed an alliance with Germany, which was rejected. With the position clarified, targets in Vichy France became legitimate for the RAF. There was still concern for French civilians, and when bombing a lorry factory one night at Nantes, a bomb was dropped in the river to warn the workers that a raid was imminent and to give them time to seek shelter.

What Next?

Post-Dunkirk, British attitudes ranged from the wildly over-optimistic to the excessively pessimistic. The former included the idea that France could be rescued with landings at a suitable opportunity, while the latter, which was much more widespread, expected an invasion. At the extreme, some even thought that the invasion of the United Kingdom could come via Ireland, with landings in the south and an advance northwards, with shorter crossings of the Irish Sea to Anglesey off the coast of North Wales and across the North Channel from Northern Ireland to south-west Scotland.

The idea of a German invasion was solely based on the fact that the Germans would want complete domination of Western Europe, but in fact the idea had not occurred to Hitler in planning the war. He always claimed that an accommodation could have been reached with the United Kingdom, but when the British refused to surrender, it seemed that an invasion was the only solution.

Excessively pessimistic or not, the fear of an invasion through Ireland was so strong that the British started to provide the Irish with the means of improving their defences, despite severe shortages of modern equipment for the UK's own armed forces. Fighter aircraft and small ships were supplied. The Irish Free State had not had combat aircraft up to this point, and from independence to the outbreak of the Second World War, its navy was equipped with converted fishing vessels. The fact that an invasion force would have to sail past the south coast of England or the north coast of Scotland and then down the west coast, and all the time vulnerable to attack from the sea and the air by the Royal Navy and Royal Air Force seems to have been overlooked.

Before the war, the UK had cancelled its treaty rights to use certain ports in southern Ireland, which would in any case have been resisted by neutral Ireland. Many in the UK, the USA and Canada felt that using bases in Ireland would have reduced losses on the North Atlantic convoys, and there is no question that these would have been invaluable, but a heavy British military presence would have been needed to secure these bases against the Irish Republican Army which would have been bound to attack them. As it was, Ireland proved an invaluable additional source of food and manpower, with many Irish volunteering to join the British armed forces. Volunteers also came in large numbers from Northern Ireland, which despite being part of the United Kingdom was not included in conscription, largely because of its internal self-government and the recognition that not everyone was in favour of it being part of the UK rather than what was eventually to become the Irish Republic.

At first, there was an air of disbelief. Some even considered landings in France at the earliest opportunity, despite the lack of equipment and the Germans moving quickly to consolidate their position, using slave labour to create defences, and especially what was to become known as the 'Atlantic Wall', the strong coastal defences on the French side of the English Channel.[1]

Fortunately, realism prevailed, and aerial reconnaissance soon showed that the Germans were gathering barges in French and Belgian ports, which could only mean one thing, that an invasion of the British Isles was being planned.

The immediate reaction to this possibility took two forms: bombing of the invasion barges and an emergency strengthening of the home defences.

The importance of bombing in any future war had been recognised long before the Second World War broke out. There had been bombing of London and east coast towns by both Zeppelin airships and large Gotha bombers during the First World War, killing 1,413 people, and the Spanish Civil War had served as a further reminder of the growing effectiveness of air power. Between the wars, an observer corps (later to become the Royal Observer Corps) had been formed using civilian volunteers, and by 1944 these were manning 1,500 observation posts, with personnel working in pairs and reporting to group centres which controlled up to thirty-six observation posts.

Duties of the Observer Corps included warning of attacking enemy aircraft which had managed to sneak under the radar net. Much later when the V-weapons were fired towards British targets, the observation posts were rearranged and placed at half-mile intervals along the coast of south-eastern England. As the V-1 rockets flew over, rockets were fired by the nearest post to help direct fighters to the course of the missile.

Well before the war, as early as September 1935, the British government sent a circular to local authorities stressing the need for air raid precautions, ARP, but it was not until April 1937 that the Air Raid Wardens' Service was established. In just over a year, this had attracted some 200,000 personnel, but later that year, prompted by the Munich Crisis, another 500,000 joined. At this time, trench shelters were dug in public parks and by September 1939 there were sufficient trench shelters for 500,000 people. Also 1.5 million Anderson shelters had been issued, free of charge, to homes with gardens. The Anderson shelter was a corrugated structure, dug into the ground and surrounded by soil or sandbags, which would not have given protection against a direct hit but was intended to prevent injuries from shrapnel as bombs exploded. Gas masks had been issued to the entire population, and civilians given guidance on blackout precautions and how to create a gas-proof room in their home.

While present day broadcasts and newspaper features on the German bombing campaign against London inevitably seem to feature London underground stations of the deep level tube lines being used as air raid shelters, the authorities refused to allow the tube station platforms to be used as air-raid shelters, even when the bombing started in late summer 1940. The decision was only reversed after Londoners took the law into their own hands and started to invade the stations. Unfortunately, before long the authorities were proved right, and on a number of occasions bombs penetrated to platform level with considerable loss of life, especially at Bank Station in the City of London and at Balham.

It had been expected that as soon as war was declared the Germans would immediately start a bombing campaign, and maintain this for sixty days, with each ton of bombs reckoned to kill or wound fifty people, giving two million casualties. This was pessimism on a grand scale, prompted by the widely-held belief mentioned earlier that 'the bomber will always get through'. The British Chain Home radar network was completed just in time, but the pessimists ignored the vital fact that until the invasion of the Low Countries and France, the Germans had few aircraft capable of ranging over the British Isles. There was a weakness in intelligence assessments as well since in the late 1930s the Luftwaffe had decided against developing heavy bombers in favour of dive-bombers and medium/light bombers. The reason for this was that the Luftwaffe modelled itself as a tactical air force operating in close support of fast-moving armoured ground forces. It was not until later that a heavy bomber, the Dornier Do217, entered service, and by then it was too late and there were insufficient numbers to make a difference.

The preparation of improved home defences preceded the fall of France and even the evacuation of Dunkirk, as this was announced on 14 May 1940, prompted by the German invasion of the Low Countries. First came the Local Defence Volunteers and within twenty-four hours of its announcement more than 250,000 men had come forward. Membership of the new force included those who were too old or too young for military service, and it was the former that gave rise to the popular title of 'Dad's Army'. At first, the Local Defence Volunteers had no uniforms and few weapons, with most having to provide their own, which in rural areas meant farmers and gamekeepers with shot guns, with the less fortunate having to use farming implements. The supply of weapons did not improve with the evacuation from Dunkirk as so much had been left behind and the British army took precedence in the supply of new equipment.

The initial intake of men consisted of volunteers, but compulsory service was introduced early in 1940.

While many of the volunteers had some military experience, much of this was far in the past. Those who had left the armed forces in the late 1930s were soon recalled as war threatened and only the oldest were available for the LDV.

Training was a priority, but at first was haphazard. The more fortunate and successful units were taken in hand by military veterans, but much training was down to private initiative. One of the most successful units was established by wealthy backers at Osterley Park, in the London suburbs. This was run by Tom Wintringham, a former communist who had fought with the International Brigade during the Spanish Civil War, which no doubt was the ideal background for the type of tactics that would be necessary if the Germans invaded. In just two months, July and August, this trained 5,000 men before it was taken over by the government as 'War Office No.1 School' for training in what became known as the Home Guard.

Uniforms soon started to be provided, cheap khaki overalls, while army ranks were adopted from February 1941. To improve standards, from August 1940 Home Guard units were affiliated to the army's county regiments. There was a temporary ban on recruitment in October 1942, after which the government started to actively use the Home Guard as a training ground for boys aged 17 or 18 prior to conscription, and by the summer of the following year there were 1,750,000 Home Guard personnel in 1,100 battalions whose members had an average age of 30, largely due to the number of youths who had joined.

Many units were formed by larger businesses, with, for example, the bus company Southern Vectis on the Isle of Wight forming its own company from amongst its employees. Many British Broadcasting Corporation locations also had their local units, with former soldiers who had been employed by the BBC as commissionaires, drilling senior personnel.

Duties varied widely. Many were expecting to be fighting, in Churchill's words, 'on the beaches and in the hills', but throughout the period immediately after

Dunkirk while the British army was busy training new recruits and re-equipping, the Home Guard kept watch on the coastline, manned road blocks and guarded airfields and factories, with the only excitement for many being the occasional rounding up of downed Luftwaffe aircrew. Later, specialised units were formed, with 140,000 personnel manning anti-aircraft batteries from September 1944, which many seemed to have resented, partly because they had no choice in the matter. Yet by manning anti-aircraft guns, the Home Guard spared soldiers for front-line duties.

The threat of invasion was taken seriously and a warning system of an invasion called the Beetle network was established and operational by 25 August 1940. Operation Banquet was also prepared, a plan to convert all training aircraft other than fighters to light bombers able to attack German troop formations as they came ashore and advanced inland.

In December 1944, the Home Guard was stood down, with the threat of invasion long past. But while the Home Guard was no longer to be seen on guard duty or on parade, other features remained to remind the population that the threat of invasion had been taken seriously. The most enduring of these were tank traps, usually large cubes of concrete positioned to hinder the advance of German Panzers across the country. Less obvious were underground headquarters units with secret wireless stations, of which thirty-two were built. These would be manned by members of the specially selected 'stay behind teams', intended to act as resistance units. The wireless stations all had a number of outstations to feed details of the positions of German units. Most were in the south and south-east of England, but there were others in East Anglia and the Midlands, with one as far north as Northumberland.

After occupation, the war was expected to continue, and even the United States, although not in the war at this stage, started to design bombers with sufficient range to be able to attack Germany while flying from bases in the United States.

The British government intended to evacuate the Royal Family to Canada if the invasion happened. This would seem to be logical, although King George VI and Queen Elizabeth had refused offers to be evacuated from London to save them from enemy air attack, and their two daughters, Princess Elizabeth, the heir apparent, and her younger sister, Princess Margaret, also stayed in London.

Chapter Three

Lessons of Invasions Past

Many Britons like to think that their islands are secure, safe from invasion, because of the sea, conveniently forgetting about the Norman conquest, or for that matter, the much earlier Roman conquest, and in between these major events the many raids and landings by the Vikings. The Vikings did in fact settle in the north-east of England. King Harold's failure to stop the Normans was due in no small part to the fact that his troops had to be force-marched from Stamford Bridge in Yorkshire after battling with invading Danes, emerging victorious only to face defeat near Hastings. The force that reached Hastings was incomplete, as not all of Harold's troops managed to assemble there.

Naturally, these earlier invasions had lacked the variety of landing craft and landing ships that became available during the Second World War, but in 1940 the Germans also lacked these things.

By the end of June 1940, the Germans had already managed to occupy British territory, taking the Channel Islands. As the Channel Islands were part of Normandy in 1066, the islanders sometimes joke that they had invaded England in 1066. Nevertheless, in 1940 they were impossible to defend, and making the best of a difficult situation, the British government decided to demilitarise the islands, pulling out troops, warships and aircraft, and offering the islanders the chance of evacuation, although it proved impossible to evacuate everyone from the two main islands, Jersey and Guernsey. Only the third largest island, Alderney, was completely evacuated.

The Germans took the Channel Islands landing from the sea and also arriving by air. They did not use paratroops but landed transport aircraft at the airports on Jersey and Guernsey.

The Romans

Earlier invaders of the British Isles did not have the option of arriving by air, yet they managed to come ashore in sufficient numbers to overwhelm the native population. The Roman conquest had been planned for some years. The first landings were in 55 and 54 BC, with what might be described today as probing expeditions under Julius Caesar. At the time, he was the commander of the Roman armies in Gaul, present-day France. Opinions are divided over whether the aim was to improve his reputation in Rome, or to discourage the English tribes from supporting their counterparts in Gaul, who had been troublesome. Teaching the English a lesson would have helped secure Gaul for Rome.

Julius landed in Kent in 55 BC, and was successful in several battles with the local tribes. He repeated the exercise in 54 BC, and left after exacting promises of tribute from the tribes in the south-east of England.

What followed was not occupation but diplomatic and trading links, which the Romans also enjoyed with other territories on the edge of their empire. The Romans moved to demand tribute and hostages to ensure that these client states did not provoke any incident and were effectively under the sway of Rome. At around this time, leadership of the tribes became a matter of succession, and this led the disappointed would-be leaders of some of the tribes to travel to Rome to plead for help in instances of disputed succession.

Caesar Augustus prepared to invade England three times, in 34 BC, 27 BC and 25 BC. They did not go ahead, with those of 34 BC and 25 BC cancelled because of uprisings elsewhere in the Roman Empire, while that in 27 BC was cancelled because the English seemed prepared to collaborate. Two English kings, although in reality tribal leaders (the country was not united at this time) fled to Rome. According to contemporary accounts, Augustus realised that he was earning more in customs dues from the English than could be earned through taxation after conquest.

Caesar Caligula had planned an invasion in AD 40, but this was hopeless in its execution, with his troops lined up in battle formation facing the English Channel and ordered to attack the water. They were then ordered to gather seashells, which he referred to as 'plunder from the ocean due the Capitol and the Palace'. This seems like further evidence of Caligula's insanity, but some historians believe that it may have been a punishment for an earlier mutiny by the troops.

It was not until almost a hundred years had passed that conquest actually began, in AD 43 under the Emperor Claudius. What had changed was that the political situation in England was unstable. One tribe, the Catuvellauni, had displaced another, the Trinivantes, as the most powerful in the south-east, taking over the former capital of the Catuvellauni, Camulodunum, present day Colchester, and were intimidating the neighbouring tribe, the Atrebates, who were led by a former ally of Julius Caesar, Commius.

Some believe that many of the same troops humiliated by Caligula were amongst those used by Claudius for the invasion. Four legions with a total of around 20,000 soldiers, and about the same number of support troops, were assembled under the leadership of Aulus Plautius. This force is believed to have departed from a point near Boulogne and landed near Richborough in Kent, but there is no strong evidence to support this, as some accounts say that the force sailed eastwards, while from Boulogne Richborough would have meant sailing northwards. On the other hand, there is archaeological evidence of a Roman presence at Richborough dating from the time. Others suggest that the Romans sailed as far west as Chichester, or even the Solent, which would have been a long and exposed crossing. The Romans had in fact come late to seafaring, and in the early days of the Roman empire had used the Phoenicians as mercenary sailors.

Landings to the west seem highly unlikely as the invading Romans were checked by a substantial English force at a river crossing believed to have been close to Rochester in Kent, and the resulting battle continued for two days. One of the legion leaders, Hosidius Geta, was almost captured, but escaped, after which the battle turned in the Romans' favour. The English tribes were forced back to the River Thames, which they were forced to cross to escape the pursuing Romans, who suffered some losses in the salt marshes of Essex. Some of the Roman troops crossed the Thames by swimming; the river was far wider and shallower than today. Shortly afterwards, Claudius himself joined the advancing Roman troops, but he was not renowned for his military skills and was clearly there simply to accept the surrender of English territory, with eleven tribes supposed to have surrendered. Some accounts suggest that the Romans were accompanied by war elephants which helped cow the English into submission.

The remaining English tribesmen fled to the north and the west. A Roman force advanced west subduing further tribes and advancing at least as far as Exeter in Devon, which became an advanced base, and may even have reached Bodmin on the north coast of Cornwall. Another Roman force advanced north to Lincoln. By AD 47, Roman control extended south of a line drawn from the Humber to the Severn estuary, and late that year the Romans advanced into Wales. To the north, the Pennine mountains were occupied by an English tribe that had allied itself with the Romans.

By AD 60 the Romans had reached Anglesey, overcoming stiff resistance in the so-called 'Menai massacre', but were prevented from completing the conquest of Wales when the troops were forced to return to the south-east of England to counter the rebellion led by Boudica. The new emperor, Nero, had earlier, in

AD 54, appointed Quintus Veranius as governor for Rome's new territory. He was chosen because he had successfully dealt with the troublesome hill tribes of Anatolia, the larger part of modern Turkey. It was not until AD 76 that Wales was finally subdued, by which time Roman rule had extended at least as far north as York.

Despite the growing area under Roman control, elsewhere resistance to the Romans had resumed. Although the total population of Britain, England and Wales, was far lower than today, the Romans only had a force of between 40,000 and 50,000 men, and communications were difficult with a vast area to cover, with troops marching with the assistance of pack animals. One of the worst outbreaks of anti-Roman action was in north Wales, where a Roman cavalry base was overrun. A new governor, Agricola, arrived in AD 76 to face several cases of insurrection. The Welsh uprising was put down without mercy, the tribe concerned being exterminated. Anglesey was invaded once more and the inhabitants forced to surrender on Roman terms.

The area under Roman control was suppressed as far north as the border with Scotland in AD 77 using overwhelming military force, and then Roman occupation was extended along the Solway Coast of Scotland. It seems that the Romans had reached the north of England in AD 71, or shortly after, and by AD 79 had moved into Scotland with a number of military camps, especially in the Lowlands, and seem also to have ventured along the coastal strip north of the River Tay by AD 80 under the leadership of Agricola. Before he was recalled to Rome in AD 84, Agricola had built forts along the Highland Line,[1] and controlled the entrances to many of the glens leading into the Highlands. On the other side of the country, he had secured much of Argyll, and may even have ventured into Kintyre.

Agricola's successors have left little in the way of written accounts and have not been mentioned in those of other writers, but it seems that they did not share his enthusiasm for conquering Scotland. The forts he built were gradually abandoned. Clearly the cost of incorporating 'Caledonia' into the Roman Empire outweighed the benefits. A strong defensive line running across northern England just south of the present Anglo-Scottish border was built, completed in 122 and is now known as Hadrian's Wall. An attempt to push the area under Roman control north to the Forth-Clyde line was made with the construction of the Antonine Wall in 142, but this was abandoned after another twenty years and the Romans withdrew behind Hadrian's Wall. In the years that followed, there were at least four major attempts to conquer Scotland, which has a greater number of Roman marching camps than anywhere else in Europe.

Meanwhile, the Romans had been using Colchester as their capital for the new province of 'Britannia', but the greater strategic importance of London was obvious and a small settlement became the new capital, known to the Romans as 'Londinium'.

Roman rule was broadly tolerant, the Romans seeing themselves as civilising and educating the people in their empire to make them emulate themselves. Even neighbouring Celtic tribes who allied themselves with the Romans were treated well, and within the Roman Empire there was a large degree of religious tolerance. In the British Isles, the main exceptions to this were the Druids, who were not just a religious hierarchy but had significant political authority over the Celtic tribes and were administrative rivals to the Romans. The Romans showed that when their authority was contested, their rivals would be eliminated, and this was the fate of the Druids.

The Vikings

Despite Rome having ruled England and Wales as 'Britannia', implying a unified state, after the Romans withdrew the two countries were as divided as ever, with tribes rather than kingdoms as we would understand them, and many linguistic and cultural differences between them. During the eighth century this began to change and by the mid-ninth century England was divided into four independent kingdoms: East Anglia, Wessex, Mercia and Northumbria, with a total population of between 500,000 and one million people. Mercia, covering the present-day Midlands and extending down to Kent, was by far the strongest military power. While most of the population lived in the country, there were already a number of towns, largely a legacy of Roman rule, of which the most important were London and York. There were also a number of ports, including Dover, Harwich and Ipswich, enabling England to trade with her continental neighbours.

Scandinavia generally had lagged behind England and the continent, still living in the iron age, but during the eighth century this area also began to change and the iron age gave way to the Viking Age. The inhabitants did not see themselves as Danes, Norwegians or Swedes at this time, but rather as belonging to specific locations, such as Jutland. Christianity, which had reached Britain and Ireland some centuries earlier, had still to penetrate Scandinavia. The term 'Viking' applied to all of the Scandinavian seafaring peoples regardless of the individual territory they came from.

While Scandinavians farmed, they were more heavily involved with fishing for herring, and if herring stocks were not good enough, they took to sailing to other countries including the British Isles, and had developed many trading links. The start of the Viking raids came in the closing years of the eighth century, initially attacking and ransacking Christian monasteries, many of which were located on small islands, which offered the seclusion sought by the monks but which were difficult to defend.

One of the first recorded raids was in 789, when ships from Hordland, in present-day Norway, landed on Portland, in present day Dorset but then officially off the south coast of Wessex. They were met by a royal reeve from Dorchester, whose duty it was to identify foreign merchants, but he was killed on the spot. Further raids must have followed, as in 792 King Offa of Mercia made arrangements for the defence of Kent. In 793, a Viking raiding party sacked the monastery at Lindisfarne, off the coast of Northumberland on the north-east coast of England. The following year an abbey near Jarrow was sacked. In the years that followed, attacks spread to the west coast of Scotland and to Ireland.

It was not until after the middle of the ninth century that the Vikings began to see the potential for settlement in the British Isles. Planned landings with larger groups of men replaced the earlier raiding parties. In 866, Vikings captured York, the second largest city in England. Many Anglo-Saxon kings tried to reach an accommodation with the Vikings, often handing over large areas of land, with the King of Northumbria handing over his lands in 876. The main defender of England was the King of Wessex, Alfred the Great, who had come to the throne in 871 after the death of his brother. Initially, Alfred the Great had little success, and was driven back to present-day Somerset, in the south-west of Wessex, in 878.

Alfred gathered fresh forces and the tide started to turn, and in 886 the Treaty of Wedmore was signed between Norse East Anglia and Anglo-Saxon Wessex, with a border established between the two regions. The area to the north and east of the boundary became known as the Danelaw as it was under Viking control. Alfred next started building defended towns or 'burns', as well as founding a navy and organising a peasant militia with half of his troops on active service. These measures were important as Viking attacks continued, and it was not until 896 that the Vikings gave up and dispersed, settling across East Anglia and Northumbria while some moved to France, settling in what became Normandy. Alfred's strategy continued after his death, and in 920 the governments of Northumbria and Scotland placed themselves under the control of Wessex. After the Battle of

Brunanburh in 937, Viking power in the north of England collapsed, and in 954 the Vikings were expelled from York.

Further unification of England followed, and Edgar the Peaceful was recognised as King of England by the Anglo-Saxon and remaining Viking populations. Nevertheless, this was a high point, and in 980 Viking raids resumed. Instead of regrouping and fighting as Alfred had done, under Ethelred the Unready it was decided that the best means of coping with the Vikings was to pay protection money, the *Danegeld*. In 991, the Vikings were given £10,000, and over the next ten years the English were forced to pay ever larger sums. This soon proved unpopular with the English population, and stronger measures were called for, so on St Brice's Day 1002, King Ethelred proclaimed that all Vikings living in England would be executed, and what followed became known as the St Brice's Day massacre.

The Vikings were not finished with England. In 1013, King Sweyn Forkbeard of Denmark invaded England, and when Ethelred fled to Normandy, Sweyn took the throne. He died within a year and Ethelred returned, only to face another invasion in 1016 by the Danish King Cnut, or Canute, who became King of England after the Battle of Assandun. He was also King of Denmark, but the two kingdoms separated on his death in 1035, when Edward the Confessor became king.

A further Viking invasion, this time from Norway, followed in 1066. King Harold took a strong force northwards to face the Norwegian invaders, commanded by King Harald of Norway. A first battle on 20 September at Fulford was won by the Norwegians, but on 25 September, the Battle of Stamford Bridge, in the East Riding of Yorkshire, saw English victory, with Harald killed. But Harold then had to force march his army south to face another invasion by William, Duke of Normandy.

The Norman Conquest

Another group of people who sought an excuse to invade England were the Normans, the descendants of the Viking settlers forced out of England who had chosen to go to northern France, with the region becoming known as 'Normandy'. William, Duke of Normandy, had a claim on the English throne due to his family links with King Edward the Confessor, who had died without an heir. When Edward died in January 1066, he was succeeded by his brother, Harold.

William's landings in England came days after the English victory at Stamford Bridge. The invading army consisted not only of Normans, but also French and Breton troops. Harold marched south to face the invaders, leaving a substantial part of his army in the north in case of any further invasion attempts. On 14 October, near Hastings, the two armies met, and in the Battle of Hastings, Harold was killed, allegedly by an arrow in the eye, and his forces beaten.

William assembled a large invasion fleet, which contemporary writers put at 726 ships, but this is disputed today, and contemporary accounts of the number of men were no better, varying between 14,000 and 150,000 men, the latter being highly unlikely given population numbers at the time. Modern historians have also only been able to provide a range for the numbers of William's troops, of 7,000 to 12,000 men, of which 1,000 to 3,000 were cavalry, with about an equal number of archers, and the remainder being infantry. Pope Alexander II gave his support after the invasion succeeded, but some sources maintain that he gave his support for the actual invasion, with the right to fly a papal banner. What is known is that William's forces were ready in August, but adverse winds kept the invasion fleet in port until late September. William is also supposed to have believed that Harold's forces were deployed along the coast rather than fighting in the north of England.

William's fleet did not have to battle with Harold's navy, and landed at Pevensey in Sussex on 28 September. Their first move was to build a wooden castle at Hastings, from which they raided the surrounding area to obtain supplies.

Harold probably did not learn about William's landings until he was marching south. He stopped in London before resuming the march, having forced his troops to march twenty-seven miles a day for the 200 miles from Stamford Bridge to London. On the second part of the march, from London to the Sussex coast, William's scouts kept a watch and reported on Harold's progress. Eventually Harold took up a defensive position on Senlac Hill, present-day Battle, some six miles from William's castle at Hastings. Harold is reckoned to have had between 7,000 and 8,000 troops, with relatively few archers and cavalry.

The battle took place on 14 October, starting at around 9 am and taking all day. Harold's army stood as a shield wall along a ridge and this proved so effective that William's troops were thrown back with heavy casualties. William's Breton troops panicked and flew, tempting Harold's troops to pursue them, but they were attacked by Norman cavalry. This encouraged the Normans to make two feigned withdrawals, again with the cavalry exacting a heavy toll amongst the English troops. The decisive event was the death of Harold, who was in the midst of his troops. Even the story about Harold being killed by an arrow in an eye may be a post-battle embellishment, although some suggest that the archer was one of his own men, an accident, and an early case of what today might be described as 'blue on blue'.

Harold's corpse was not recognised until the following day. The bodies of his troops, including some of his brothers, were left on the battlefield. Harold's mother, Gytha, offered William her son's weight in gold for the return of the body, but the offer was refused. Some accounts maintain that Harold's body was thrown into the sea, others maintain that he was buried at the top of a cliff.

William had expected the submission of the remaining English leaders, but Edgar the Atheling was proclaimed king by the Witenagemot, a council of nobles, with the blessing of the archbishops of Canterbury and York. William marched to London by a circuitous route and defeated an English army that attacked him at Southwark. Unable to storm London Bridge, he crossed the River Thames at Wallingford, in Berkshire, some miles to the west of London, and eventually approached London from the north-west. Unable to assemble a fresh army to confront William, Edgar's supporters surrendered at Berkhamsted. William was crowned at Westminster Abbey on Christmas Day 1066. In an attempt to placate the remaining English nobility, they were confirmed in their lands and a grant of land was made to Edgar. Nevertheless, when he returned to Normandy in March 1067, William took English hostages, including Edgar, while leaving control of England with his half-brother Odo, and a close friend, William Fitzosbern.

That was not the end of the matter, and William the Conqueror, as he became known, faced successive uprisings over the next few years and was not secure on the throne until 1072. The English aristocracy who resisted had their lands confiscated and many went into exile, some to Ireland or Scotland, but others went as far as the Byzantine empire, which was desperate for mercenaries. William rewarded his followers with lands and built large castles at strategic positions throughout the land. Norman French was introduced as the language of the administration. Slavery was abolished, although the feudal duties of serfdom remained. Anglo-Saxon government structures survived.

In the meantime, the conquest was still far from assured. Resistance continued. There were outbreaks of resistance in Kent and in Mercia, forcing William to return to England in late 1067. The following year, there was further violence in Exeter, and a fresh rebellion in Wales. There was a rising in Northumbria, still to be conquered by the Normans, while Harold's sons, who had escaped to Ireland, raided the south-west of England.

In 1069, in late summer a large fleet was sent by Sweyn II of Denmark and this encouraged a new wave of rebellions, many of which were in the south, but culminated in a fresh rebellion in Northumbria. Resistance also followed in Mercia. William defeated the Danes, who promised to leave in spring 1070, while his forces suppressed the uprisings in Northumbria in what has become known as the 'Harrying of the North'.

Early in 1070, having crushed resistance in Mercia, William was re-crowned by papal legates, symbolically reasserting his right to be king. A purge of senior clergy followed, deposing the Archbishop of Canterbury while the death of the Archbishop of York meant that both provinces could be headed by men loyal to William. Similar changes were made elsewhere, while monasteries that had safeguarded some of the wealth of their local nobility saw these treasures confiscated.

All was not over. Although Sweyn II had announced his decision to withdraw to Denmark once spring arrived in 1070, he instead sent troops to the Fens to join rebels led by Hereward the Wake. On this occasion, William made a payment of *Danegeld* to Sweyn and the Danes returned home. A Norman attack on the Isle of Ely effectively ended all resistance.

Unrest on the Continent in 1071 kept William away but he returned in 1072 and marched north to deal with King Malcolm III of Scotland, with a fleet providing support for his troops. What followed was the Treaty of Abernethy, which forced Malcolm to expel Edgar the Atheling, who had fled to Scotland. Malcolm was to be William's man, but there's some confusion over whether this applied to the whole of Scotland, or simply Cumbria and the Lothians.

The Normans were few and outnumbered by the English and Welsh. It is believed that some 8,000 Normans were settled throughout William's new realm to provide stability, being given grants of land taken from rebellious English nobility. The confiscation of this land led to more revolts, which in return led to more confiscations. Land was held directly from the king and in return for military service. Many English and Welsh women were forcibly married to Norman supporters of William. In the end, few of the English nobility survived and those that did lost their land which was conferred on William's followers, so that by 1086, according to the *Domesday Book*, only about five per cent of the land south of the River Tees was still in English ownership.

Conclusion

It is clear that while all three invasions of England left their mark, none was as far reaching as that of the Normans. More than the Romans or the Vikings, this influenced British history and culture, as well as changing the landscape and influenced architecture as well. The legacy of the Romans was largely lost in the unrest and change that followed their departure, a period which has been described as the 'dark ages', while that of the Vikings was fleeting as these were still basically primitive people, less sophisticated than the Romans, although they did make a mark to some extent on language. The Normans changed the language of the country, injecting words that were French in origin.

From 1066 onwards there was progress, and while the pace of change may have varied, there was no reversal, no going back to the old pre-Norman days. England was a truly united nation, with an increasingly strong concept of nationhood. It would take around 200 years before Wales and England united to make Britain, and longer still to add Scotland to create Great Britain, and then Ireland to make the United Kingdom of Great Britain and Ireland. London was clearly the nation's capital, and in due course would be the centre of an empire far larger than anything the Romans could have imagined.

Invasions were considered several times, but the only one to have had any success was that of William of Orange in 1689, and this was more of an unopposed landing to get rid of the unpopular James II. James II did not stand and fight, but instead fled to France, losing the Great Seal of his kingdom in the Thames as he did so.

Earlier, Spain had attempted to invade during the reign of Queen Elizabeth I in 1588, but the Spanish Armada was destroyed by Britain's navy (although the term 'Royal Navy' was some time away) and by the weather.

A French invasion of England was a possibility on many occasions, especially during the Napoleonic era, and the possibility resurfaced yet again in the late nineteenth century, with a series of 'London Defence Positions' created during the 1880s, before common interest took hold and led to the *Entente Cordiale* at the turn of the century. The Germans were expected to invade during the First World War, but it soon became clear that they lacked the means, with fighting already on two fronts and then at Gallipoli. The point was that the Royal Navy never lost control of the seas. This was helped in the First World War when a pre-war First Sea Lord, Lord Fisher, had scrapped ships that were 'too old to fight or to run away', and also ensured that the bulk of the Royal Navy was stationed in home waters, or within reach in the Mediterranean. At the start of the First World War, Fisher returned briefly as First Sea Lord, but that is another story.

Of course, one reason for the success of the Norman conquest and its continued shaping of the nation was that it was the last invasion. In this sense, it also gives a strong pointer to what a German invasion might have been like.

Chapter Four

The Germans Prepare Their Plans

It seems unlikely that Hitler thought of invading England until after the fall of France. He had earlier considered that if the United Kingdom did not go to war with Germany, he would have allowed the British to keep their empire on condition that the former German colonies were returned. Hitler wanted much of Europe, and needed it, both for *Lebensraum* and for food and raw materials. On its own, Germany was short of all three, and the country's only natural resource was coal. Food production required the import of massive quantities of fertilizer, and the shortage of this during the First World War had raised the spectre of starvation.

General Franz Halder, chief of the army general staff, recalled in his diary a meeting with the Führer early in July 1940, after French surrender:

> Hitler was in very good humour, he admitted that the course of the campaign had been 'a decided miracle', and gave us his opinion that the war would be finished in six weeks. After that he wished to conclude a reasonable peace with France, and then the way would be free for an agreement with Britain.
>
> He then astonished us by speaking with admiration of the British Empire, of the necessity for its existence, and of the civilization that Britain had brought into the world. He remarked, with a shrug of the shoulders, that the creation of its Empire had been achieved by means that were often harsh, but 'where there is planeing, there are shavings flying'. He compared the British Empire with the Catholic Church – saying they were both essential elements of stability in the world. He said that all he wanted from Britain was that she should acknowledge Germany's position on the Continent. The return of Germany's lost colonies would be desirable but not essential, and he would even offer to support Britain with troops if she should be involved in any difficulties anywhere. He remarked that the colonies were primarily a matter of prestige, since they could not be held in war, and few Germans could settle in the tropics.

> He concluded by saying that his aim was to make peace with Britain on a basis that she would regard as compatible with her honour to accept.

It was, of course, unrealistic to believe that the United Kingdom could surrender and still retain its position as a major colonial power. The French managed to retain their colonies, ruled from Vichy, but these were relatively weak countries. Iceland had declared independence from Denmark when that country was occupied by the Germans. Australia, Canada, South Africa and New Zealand would undoubtedly have done the same had the United Kingdom surrendered, and India, where nationalist fervour had been steadily growing, would have become unmanageable. Would German troops helping the British retain control of a reluctant colony have been acceptable? It would have simply highlighted British weakness.

Halder had more to say on the matter on 13 July, and the following day as well:

> The Führer is greatly puzzled by Britain's persisting unwillingness to make peace. He sees the answer (as we do) in Britain's hope on Russia, and therefore counts on having to compel her by main force to agree to peace. Actually that is much against his grain. The reason is that a military defeat of Britain will bring about the disintegration of the British Empire. This would not be of any benefit to Germany. German blood would be shed to accomplish something that would benefit only Japan, the United States, and others.
>
> The Führer [writing on 14 July] confirms my impressions of yesterday. He would like an understanding with Great Britain. He knows that war with the British will be hard and bloody, and knows also that people everywhere today are averse to bloodshed.

Once the French surrendered, Hitler expected the British to sue for peace. Why they did not was something he could not understand. He eventually decided that the British were placing their faith in the Russians coming to their aid. This was an interesting conclusion as at the time Germany and the Soviet Union were not only allies on paper, having signed a non-aggression pact, but the USSR was also an important trading partner, and would remain so until the following summer. There was in any case little warmth between the United Kingdom and the Soviet Union, and the former supported Finland in her 'Winter War' with the Soviet Union.

It was clear that the British would have to be knocked out of the war. The chances of their being able to return to the Continent were slim, but they could still attack German forces in the occupied territories, bomb targets within Germany itself, and maintain a close blockade of German ports and those in the occupied territories. In short, Germany could not win the war and consolidate its gains with the United Kingdom still fighting. Hitler would also have known that there was a substantial and influential peace lobby in the UK, led by Lord Halifax, pre-war foreign secretary and both Chamberlain's and King George VI's first choice of prime minister to succeed Chamberlain. Halifax had nevertheless turned against Hitler after the Munich Agreement in late 1938. He had also turned down the chance to be prime minister, not only believing that Churchill had the better strategic sense, but that he could do much better serving under Churchill when he could curb his impetuosity.

There was, in short, only one way to force the UK to make peace: invasion.

Invasion in this context is usually regarded as being the invasion of England. This is not to forget the rest of the United Kingdom. England was home to the majority of the population of the United Kingdom, and the location of most of its industry, as well as having the main naval, army and air force bases, and the major ports. Scotland and Wales had coal mining and steel-making, with the Clyde still being one of the world's major shipbuilding centres, but the most modern strategic industries such as aircraft manufacture and warship building were mainly in England. In any case, Germany did not occupy the whole of France until late 1942, so perhaps a similar arrangement would have spared Wales, Scotland and Northern Ireland, and even the north of England, from a German invasion. Even without occupation, Vichy France had shown itself to be malleable to German wishes, and some senior military figures had offered to join the German war effort – offers that were rejected, largely to drive home to the French that they had been defeated.

Hitler had ideas of his own about the invasion, and at one briefing with his army commanders, including General Gerd von Rundstedt, he crossed the room to a map of Great Britain and drew a large circle around Taunton and the Blackdown Hills in Devon, saying, 'Your airborne troops could be used here as flank protection. This is a strong sector and, besides, this important defile must be opened.' He continued by stressing the importance to the Royal Navy of their base at Plymouth. Von Rundstedt later explained that he could no longer follow Hitler's thoughts, and so asked at what points on the south coast the landing was to take place. But Hitler kept strictly to his order that operations were to be kept secret and said, 'I cannot tell you yet.'

The German military had considered the prospect of invading England early in the war, indeed before the heavy fighting began in the north and the west. As early as November 1939, the Kriegsmarine had produced a report on the invasion of England, but the report was not optimistic about the prospects of success. While not concluding that an invasion would be unsuccessful, the authors were cautious. Both short crossings and longer crossings, further west as the English Channel broadened, were considered.

The following month, the combined armed forces, the Wehrmacht, or defence ministry, produced its own report, advocating a surprise attack on East Anglia with sixteen or seventeen divisions. This meant a longer crossing, but attacking across the low-lying coastline and flat fields and fens of East Anglia would have its advantages. The Kriegsmarine could not support this plan as its staff officers believed it was too ambitious and would leave the navy having to defend the invasion fleet while also facing battle with the Royal Navy. The Luftwaffe felt that the plan could only go ahead in good weather, and was not optimistic that good weather could be guaranteed over the North Sea. The Luftwaffe also recognised that in its attack on Poland, it had not faced an adversary as strong and well-equipped as the Royal Air Force. Even after the fall of France, the Luftwaffe realised that the RAF had not used its full capabilities during the Battle of France and had in fact suffered less than the British army in the withdrawal.

The commander-in-chief of the Kriegsmarine, Grand Admiral Erich Raeder, explained on 11 July 1940 that a landing on the English coast would be very much a 'last resort'. Instead, he proposed heavy aerial attacks on major cities and ports so that the population would feel the full effect of modern all-out warfare. This, of course, ignored the fact that while the Luftwaffe was a strong and experienced air force with good equipment, it had developed as a tactical air force, without heavy bombers or long-range aircraft. Raeder also stressed the need for a substantial transport fleet, and for minesweeping operations. Meanwhile the Germans started a propaganda battle, applying psychological pressure to the British. Both sides had dropped leaflets on the other, hoping to persuade the civilian population to apply pressure on their government. The leaflets were of doubtful value, with the head of the RAF's Bomber Command, Air Chief Marshal Sir Arthur Harris, maintaining that all they were doing was giving the Germans enough toilet paper to last the war. The Germans went one step further, with broadcasts by William Joyce, an Irishman later hung by the British for treason. He had retained a British passport despite being born in the United States before his family moved to Ireland in 1909 when he was 3 years old, and then to the UK in 1922. On 6 August 1940 his broadcast 'Germany Calling' included this message:

> I make no apology for saying again that invasion is certainly coming soon, but what I want to impress upon you is that while you must feverishly take every conceivable precaution, nothing that you or the government can do is really of the slightest use. Don't be deceived by this lull before the storm, because, although there is still the chance of peace, Hitler is aware of the political and economic confusion in England, and is only waiting for the right moment. Then, when his moment comes, he will strike, and strike hard.

Preparing For Invasion

On land the Germans had indeed proved unstoppable, but at sea it was a different matter. Before the First World War, the Kaiser had given the navy equal status with the army and there had been a massive shipbuilding programme, but during the 1930s the navy had been, if not exactly neglected, at least left at the back of the queue for funding and materials. Plan Z, the plan for a future German navy able to hold its own with the Royal Navy, was only just being implemented. Many believed that it was unaffordable, that there would not be sufficient raw materials to build so many ships, that there wasn't sufficient manpower to man the ships, and that there would not be enough fuel to send so many ships to sea.

Hitler, by contrast, took a continental view, even though he wanted Germany's colonies back. He did not even see the sea until he was 45 years of age. He was, of course, born in a landlocked country, Austria.

More important than all of this, however, was the simple fact that Plan Z was not intended to be ready until the mid-1940s, with senior officers in the Kriegsmarine having been assured by Hitler that war with the United Kingdom would not come until 1943 or 1944. The outbreak of war in 1939 was not expected by most Germans, and especially not by the naval staff.

So, Plan Z was basically stillborn. Worse, the Kriegsmarine had suffered badly during the Norwegian campaign, losing ten of its scarce destroyers and two light cruisers, the ships that would be the most useful operating in the confined waters of the English Channel. Germany had very few ocean-going U-boats at the outbreak of war, but in any case, submarines were meant to destroy enemy ships, not support an invasion.

The Royal Navy was, as in the earlier conflict, widely stretched, but even the Home Fleet was superior to the entire Kriegsmarine in numbers. It had battleships, which the Germans did not have in summer and autumn 1940, aircraft carriers and destroyers. Its forward base in wartime was at Scapa Flow on the south coast of the Orkney mainland, well situated to maintain a blockade of Germany, but its main bases were all in the south of England, equally well placed to tackle an invasion force. The only problem was that with the fall of France and Belgium, Chatham, Portsmouth and even Devonport, part of Plymouth, were all within easy reach of German bombers.

The Luftwaffe could certainly destroy naval bases and the homes of the dockyard workers situated close by, but it was less effective at destroying ships at this stage in the war. It did not have the torpedo bombers that were the most effective way of sinking or disabling a warship, for as one American admiral had put it, 'it was far easier to get water into a ship from the bottom than from the top!'

We shall see later the measures taken by the Allies for the Normandy landings, and the equipment developed for amphibious warfare. This was not available in 1940.

Equipment

The planned German invasion of England was to be the first amphibious assault since the invasion of Norway, a country with a small population and armed forces. It really needed to be compared with the ill-fated Allied landings at Gallipoli during the First World War. It was to be the first fully mechanised invasion, with tanks and artillery. Yet the timescale for preparing the equipment was short. Even worse, Germany's resources were finite and the economy was in difficulty even before the invasion of Poland that had started the war. As can be seen in the appendices at the back of this book, a whole range of equipment was considered necessary. Barges for transport; armoured vehicles to support the initial assault; bridging equipment or temporary jetties until a significant port could be captured and made operational again after the expected sabotage of major ports by the British as they retreated.

While the Germans knew that the British had left much of their equipment behind when evacuated from France, British industry was still intact and functioning. The British might have been forced out of Belgium and France, but the Germans knew that they were a far stronger nation than any they had encountered so far in the war.

Although the Germans were to develop a landing craft later in the war, this was really intended for river crossings and might not have been suitable for a seaborne assault. This was known as the *Pionierlandungsboot 39*, Engineer Landing Boat 39, a self-propelled craft capable of carrying 2 vehicles, 45 troops or 20 tons of cargo, with clamshell doors and a landing ramp at the bow; but in autumn 1940, just two prototypes had been delivered. The Kriegsmarine also set about developing a larger craft, known as the *Marinefährprahm*, which displaced 220 tons, but even the prototype was not available until spring 1941. They needed shallow draft craft, ideally with flat bottoms for beaching, and needed them quickly, almost immediately if the invasion was to go ahead before the start of the winter storms.

The only solution was to gather as many river and canal craft as possible and gather them in the Channel ports where they could be loaded ready for the invasion. Rivers and canals on the Continent were broader than those in Great Britain. Some of the barges were self-propelled, as were the coasting vessels also 'taken up from trade' for the invasion. In total some 2,400 barges were assembled, of which most, 1,200, were from the Netherlands and Belgium, while 860 were from Germany and 360 from France. Around a third of the barges were self-propelled, although not necessarily powerful enough for the open sea, while the rest were to be towed by tugs. Even so, while the barges were available in quantity, they lacked the qualities needed for an invasion over the open sea. They would have been slow and, even worse, unstable. There were not enough barges for the first wave, and the chances of these returning promptly to bring a second wave into what would be a battle with the defenders, were low. The British also had torpedo-carrying aircraft in both the Royal Air Force and the Fleet Air Arm, and these forces would have been combined under RAF Coastal Command, something which happened regularly when Fleet Air Arm torpedo-bombers were based ashore.

The barges were classified according to size but in reality were of many types with not enough standardisation. Appendix A gives the main types, but in essence two types of inland river barge were generally available in Europe which were the *Peniche*, which was 38.5 metres long and carried 360 tons of cargo, and the *Kampine*, which was 50 metres long and carried 620 tons of cargo. Of the barges collected for the invasion, 1,336 were classified as *Peniches* and 982 as *Kampinen*. For simplicity's sake, the Germans designated any barge up to the size of a standard *Peniche* as Type A1 and anything larger as Type A2.

Renowned for their ingenuity and inventiveness, despite the short timescale the Germans were up to many of the challenges presented by an amphibious invasion, with many specialised items prepared, as covered in detail in Appendix B. One of the obvious needs, especially given the German army emphasis on fast-moving armoured warfare that had served it so well in Poland and in the invasion of the Low Countries and France, were tanks, and it was essential that the vulnerable first wave had the benefit of armoured support. The Type A barges could disembark several medium tanks onto an open beach, but only once the barges were sitting on the beaches at low tide. The clumsy system of lowering the ramps also meant that the tanks, their crews and those of the barges would be exposed to enemy fire for some time. The solution was to develop tanks that were amphibious, as the Allies discovered in 1944.

There were also, as shown in Appendix B, structures that could be assembled to make landing easier, but despite all of this, there was no doubting that what the Germans really needed was to capture a port quickly, something easier said than done as the Allies were to discover in 1944.

Hitler Decides

On 16 July 1940, Hitler issued his Directive No.16, 'on preparations for a landing operation against England'. This was a mixture of the over-ambitious and the realistic. He recognised that it was essential that the Royal Air Force should be destroyed, or at least crippled to the extent that it could not mount operations against the landing fleet. He was also realistic about the weather, telling a conference of the Wehrmacht commanders-in-chief on 21 July that he retained some doubts about the landing operation, saying that 'if it is not certain that preparations can be concluded by the beginning of September, other plans will have to be considered'. The other plans included an attack on the Soviet Union.

The timescale was in itself unrealistic, as Germany had no great history of amphibious operations and the Royal Air Force was not the only threat to an invasion force. The Royal Navy was still in good shape, despite some significant losses in the first year of war. It was not surprising that amongst those present it was the navy that again raised the first doubts about the possibility of a landing.

On 31 July, Raeder advised Hitler that the navy's preparations could not be completed before 15 September, leading Hitler to order that this would be the cut-off date for all preparations. Even so, his final decision on whether or not to mount the operation would depend on the Royal Air Force being destroyed. Operations against the Royal Air Force, what would be known by the British as the Battle of Britain, would start after 5 August, and would be allowed between eight and fourteen days if the invasion was to go ahead in 1940.

The Plan

Surprisingly, the Luftwaffe did not have any strategic plan to support the invasion. It knew that it had to destroy the Royal Air Force or at least gain, and maintain, local aerial superiority over the landing areas. There was no list of targets as such, other than attacking RAF bases and the Chain Home radar network. Attacks on communications targets, aircraft factories and their suppliers, ports and naval bases, were not finalised. When the Battle of Britain started on 13 August, designated by Goering as *Adlertag*, 'Eagle Day', the RAF had had seven weeks since the fall of France to prepare and reorganise, while it had not committed its full strength to the closing stages of the Battle of France for fear that it needed to conserve its strength in case France fell.[1] In short, for the RAF this was the culmination of four years of building a modern air force capable of defending the country. The RAF had defence in depth.

Originally the *Oberkommando des Heeres*, OKH, German Army High Command, had wanted to land on a 200-mile front that would have stretched as far west as Lyme Regis in Dorset, to Ramsgate on the north coast of Kent in the east. This was opposed by the navy, which knew it could not protect or supply and resupply such a wide front, especially with the major naval base of Portsmouth in the middle of it. A compromise was agreed with landings between Brighton in the west to Hythe in the east. Another army scheme, to land in East Anglia, had been opposed by the air force because of the changeable weather conditions over the North Sea, while again the navy was concerned about intervention from the Royal Navy. Under the revised plan, a first wave of 67,000 men would seize and hold the beaches, while an airborne division would land inland. These advance forces would be joined by a second wave consisting largely of armoured units that would break out from the beachheads. Overall, 160,000 men were to be landed and a force of 2,000 barges assembled for the operation.

The numbers did not look realistic. The Normandy landings were to take 7,000 ships of all kinds to land 75,215 British and Canadian troops and 57,500 US troops, a total of 132,715 men, plus armoured vehicles, artillery and motor vehicles. The German first wave would have been vulnerable until reinforced, and remember that the plan was for the first wave landing craft to have to return to France to collect the second wave, meaning a delay of more than twelve hours given the slow speed of the landing craft or barges.

Landings between Brighton and Hythe were a marked contraction of what the army had wanted originally, but the Kriegsmarine wanted it to be even more concentrated and confined, between Dover and Eastbourne. The naval general staff maintained that the area between Le Havre or Cherbourg and the Dorset coast would be highly exposed to ships operating from the Royal Navy's bases at Portsmouth and Devonport. It was not just that the strength of the Royal Navy and its control of the seas was a problem, covering too wide a front also meant that the various ports and landing beaches had high tides at different times. This would be less of a problem with purpose-designed landing craft, but even so, it ruined any chance of a surprise attack.

Chief of the army's general staff, General Halder, rejected the naval advice, saying, 'From the army's point of view I regard it as complete suicide, I might just as well put the troops that have landed through the sausage machine.'

The army's plan called for troops to be launched from Cherbourg to Lyme Regis; Le Havre to Ventnor on the southern coast of the Isle of Wight and to Brighton; Boulogne to Eastbourne; Calais to Folkestone, and from Dunkirk and Ostend to Ramsgate. Paratroops, or *Fallschirmjäger*, be dropped near Dover and Brighton. Once the coast and the landing beaches were held, the first wave, by now supported by armour, would push north, taking Gloucester and encircling London, which would be besieged until the occupants and defenders surrendered. Pushing north as far as Northampton, the Germans believed that this would be enough to secure a British surrender.

The army's plans were for the invasion to be carried out by six divisions drawn from Army Group A's Ninth and Sixteenth Armies. German units involved in the invasion would include the *SS Leibstandarte Adolf Hitler* regiment, the *Großdeutschland* regiment, 2 mountain, 2 *Jäger*, 2 *Fallschirmjäger*, 4 Panzer, and 2 motorised divisions. In addition, the 7th Infantry division was considered one of the best in the *Heer*, and the 35th almost as good.

The choice of some of the landing sites was interesting and suggested that intelligence was not as up-to-date or thorough as it might have been. Apart from shoals just off the beach at Ventnor, itself not very long, getting vehicles and especially armour up the two steep, narrow and winding roads from the beach to the town, itself with fairly narrow streets, would have been difficult, leaving troops and vehicles as easy targets and congestion building up. Getting out of Ventnor over and around St Boniface Down would have been almost as difficult. Landings near Bembridge or St Helens would have been easier, and although the landing fleet would have been vulnerable on the approach, they would soon be covering the main approach to Portsmouth and once at Ryde would have the Royal Navy's major port, as well as the main submarine base at Haslar, part of Gosport, less than three miles away as the artillery shell flies.

All available canal, river and sea-going ships from Germany and the occupied territories were to be recorded and intensive embarkation and disembarkation exercises were to be conducted. Occupation forces were to be prepared and briefed, while a 'Black Book' was assembled so that prominent citizens could be arrested. The 'Black Book' was the idea of an SS officer, Walter Schellenberg, a member of Himmler's staff.

The Landing Craft

Eventually, the agreed plan was to mount amphibious landings along the south coast between Hythe in Kent and Rottingdean to the east of Brighton in East Sussex. High cliffs to the east of Hythe, and especially between Folkestone and Dover, ruled out landings in this area, although the early capture of one of these ports was important, but Newhaven in East Sussex, a minor cross-Channel port, would also be useful. The 7th Parachute Division would land inland from Hythe and Lympne. A rapid advance across the South Downs and then the North Downs was necessary to ensure that the defending forces did not command the heights. The first operational objective was to secure a line running from Gravesend on the River Thames to Fareham on the River Wallington in Hampshire and on down to the coast west around Warsash at the seaward end of Southampton Water.

The plan was thorough, and the landing position of the paratroops, who, unusually, were not part of the army but of the Luftwaffe, was sufficiently close to give a good chance of an early meeting with ground troops. One problem with paratroops was that they would have been lightly armed and they needed to combine as soon as possible with troops equipped with tanks and artillery. The other weakness was that the transport aircraft were piloted by instructors from the bomber training schools, which meant a break in the supply of pilots to the bomber units which were recovering from their losses in the Battle of Britain. The transport aircraft, the venerable Junkers Ju52/3M was just that, venerable. It lacked the speed and carrying capacity of contemporary American transports. Originally designed as a 'bomber-transport', when aircraft were expected to fulfil both roles, it lost the bomber role during the Spanish Civil War as more capable bomber aircraft entered service.

Further west, Army Group A was to land four divisions in West Sussex and Hampshire, and possibly also the Isle of Wight, and advance north to meet up with the other six divisions and then move round to the west of London to encircle the capital. Some of the units would then advance westwards to meet Army Group B, whose three divisions would have landed in Dorset in the area around Lyme Bay, and would then advance towards Bristol and Gloucester.

The Invasion Fleet

At sea, the Germans are usually referred to as having 'invasion barges' and it is true that the bulk of the invasion fleet was to have consisted of canal and river barges. Continental canal barges were, and still are, much larger than those used on the narrow canals of Great Britain. Even Irish canals were wider. Choosing such craft for the crossing of the English Channel had several advantages, one of which was that they were shallow-draft, flat-bottomed craft that could get close to the landing beaches and once stranded at low-tide would be both accessible and able to remain upright. Another big advantage was their ready availability as time was very short, and not only did the Germans lack the time to produce a large purpose-built invasion fleet, but they also lacked the manpower, materials and industrial resources. Even before the outbreak of war in 1939, which took many Germans by surprise, the country lacked the resources to adequately equip its armed forces for warfare on land, in the air and on the seas. The Kriegsmarine was last in the queue for expansion and modernisation, but as already mentioned, the German army lacked mechanised transport and was heavily dependent on horses, even for pulling its artillery, while the Luftwaffe lacked long-range heavy bombers and an adequate air transport force.

Many of the barges would have been self-propelled, but the state of the tides and the weather conditions would have been important, and so too would the level of moonlight.

In the short time available, the Germans did manage to produce a number of items that would have helped the invasion if it could be delayed to the following year. More details are given in Appendices A-C at the back of this book. Tanks were fitted with flexible hoses that would enable them to draw in air while they operated below the surface, although these, and landing craft capable of carrying vehicles, were really only suitable for use on rivers and for the invasion of the Soviet Union, which started in June 1941. Heavy artillery, much of it rail-mounted, could fire from northern France across the English Channel. This was so successful that most of Dover's civilian population was evacuated as the town and port came under heavy and continuous artillery fire.

On the other hand, the Germans lacked the battleships and coastal monitors[2] that would be able to provide close covering fire for landings along the south coast, especially for those invasion beaches that were beyond the range of German coastal artillery. The Germans had two battleships unfinished at the start of the war, and two battlecruisers. They also had their *Panzerschiffe*, but these were just two in number after the loss of the *Graf Spee* in December 1939 and were intended for commerce raiding.

The weakness of the Kriegsmarine that had been third in the queue for expansion and modernisation was by this time becoming a fatal weakness preventing the execution of the German war plans. Heavy gunfire from the sea did not simply compensate for the lack of artillery ashore, it was also of heavier calibre than most land-based artillery, and because of the mechanised loading arrangements, a single naval gun was worth an army battery in the number of shells it could fire in any given period.

It was entirely up to the Luftwaffe not only to destroy the Royal Air Force but also wrest control of the seas around the British Isles from the Royal Navy. Warships operating at speed were also harder to hit than ground based artillery positions. In an invasion, it would also have to break up British troop concentrations and destroy the lines of communication, especially those south of London leading to the south coast and the landing areas. This would be difficult as the somewhat haphazard and entrepreneurial way in which Britain's railways had developed had one advantage, which was that there were still many different, and at one time before the country's railways were grouped in 1923, competing, lines, between London and the coast. If one route was blocked, not one but often many diversionary routes existed. In the period immediately before the war, with financial help from the state, the railway companies had assembled large stocks of supplies ready to repair the damage expected from bombing raids.

Closing the Straits Of Dover

Invasion or not, the Germans wanted to close the Straits of Dover, which during the First World War had been the hunting ground for the Royal Navy's Channel Patrol, usually known as the 'Dover Patrol', which kept the sea routes from Dover and Folkestone to Calais and Boulogne open for ships supplying the British forces in France. With Belgium and northern France occupied, there was little point in recreating the Dover Patrol, but preventing the British from using the Straits made much sense to the Germans as it would disrupt vital coastal convoys, and could also offer German warships, including U-boats, the chance of using the Straits, the most direct route from the North Sea end of the Kiel Canal to France and the open seas. Germany's newly won naval bases on the French Atlantic coast made this much less important, but nevertheless control of the Straits opened up the options for German naval commanders.

Closing the Straits to British warships would also enhance the prospects of an invasion of the south coast of England.

This was a time when there was extensive coastal shipping around the coasts of the British Isles. Some of the coastal shipping, or 'coasters', even carried passengers, although much of this traffic had been lost over the previous eighty years to the railways. The heavy reliance on coal for heating homes and offices, schools and other public buildings, as well as for electricity generation and town gas supplies, helped to sustain these ships as they were cheaper at carrying bulk cargo than the railways, and not much slower than the coal trains that trundled along often at less than 10 mph with frequent stops to let passenger trains and even express goods trains pass.

It was clear to the Wehrmacht that the use of shore-based heavy artillery could close the Straits of Dover to shipping, given that the distance between the French and English coasts was just 21 miles, 34 kilometres. The order was given that every heavy artillery piece held by the army and the navy (coastal artillery) be deployed along the French coast, with the largest pieces to be placed at the Pas-de-Calais. The emplacements were to be built by the *Organization Todt*, which used slave labour, and work started on 22 July 1940.

Within a couple of weeks there were four 11-inch, 28cm, traversing turrets operational plus seven army railway guns mounted on heavy bogied goods wagons. Six of the army guns were also 11-inch K5 heavy artillery, while one was an 8.3-inch, 21-cm, K12, which had a range of 71 miles, 115 km. Such weapons were impressive, but were only really viable against static land targets.

These artillery pieces were bolstered by smaller weapons. The largest of these were thirteen 11-inch and five 9.4-inch pieces while there were also motorised batteries with a total of twelve 9.4-inch and ten 8-inch guns, which could in theory be fired at shipping. The problems included, as with most land-based artillery, the long loading times, the lack of suitable armour-piercing shells, and slow traverse speeds.

The range of the larger guns was impressive, especially as a 15-inch gun on a battleship or battlecruiser normally had a range of around twenty-five miles and carried almost a ton of high explosive. In the case of the German shore-based artillery, punch may well have been sacrificed for range. Naval guns, with powered turrets and loading, reacted more quickly to rapidly changing events.

These batteries were strengthened in September by the addition of four heavy naval batteries, named *Friedrich August*, *Prinz Heinrich*, *Oldenburg* and *Siegfried*, which was later renamed *Batterie Todt*. The first of these, *Friedrich August*, had three 12-inch guns, while *Prinz Heinrich* had two 11-inch, *Oldenburg* two 8-inch, and *Batterie Todt* two 15-inch guns. Better still for the efficiency of these weapons was the fact that they were directed by observer aircraft backed up by *DeTeGerät* radar based at Blanc Nez and Cap d'Alprech, which had a range of 25 miles and could detect even small patrol craft just off the British coast. By mid-September, two more radar sets were installed, with a further *DeTeGerät* at Cap de la Haque and a *FernDeTeGerät* with longer range at Cap d'Antifer, near Le Havre at a point where the Channel started to widen.

The army also planned to improve its artillery covering the Channel, but only after the invasion. Mobile artillery batteries were to be included in the second wave once the beachhead was in place. The basis of this would be the 16th Army's *Artillerie Kommand 106*, which would provide covering fire for reinforcements as they approached the English coast, and also for the resupply operation. This was a substantial unit, with twenty-four 5.9-inch guns and seventy-two 3.9-inch, 10-cm, guns. These weapons would be mainly deployed near Dover and Hastings.

For the British, there was the added concern that the Germans might manage to seize Dover with the coastal artillery and radar around the castle. Once that happened, even the Royal Navy would be hard pressed to interrupt the flow of supplies and reinforcements coming across the Channel.

Even before the German naval guns arrived, those of the army started firing across the Channel in early August and continued to do so until 1944, by which time the Allies had landed in Normandy and were advancing along the coast. There is no record of any ship being hit by German coastal artillery, although a seaman was killed by shrapnel and others wounded by shell splinters. Those ashore in Dover were less fortunate: during more than three thousand alerts, there were 216 civilians killed in the area and damage to more than ten thousand premises.

'German Invasion Plans for the British Isles 1940'

With typical German thoroughness, the Wehrmacht Department for Maps and Communications produced *German Invasion Plans for the British Isles 1940*, a small book which provided a military and geographical assessment of England and Wales. This was produced on 15 August and several thousand copies were produced, but not distributed.

The book was based on studies conducted earlier and which had resulted in the production of three portfolios. Portfolio A was a description of the country as a whole and included a booklet with photographs and a sheaf of maps. Portfolio B concentrated on London. Portfolio C largely consisted of photographs of the coast to assist in the selection of invasion beaches. In addition, military objects were added, a combination of targets and key points, depending on which side held them.

In the book, the country is covered region by region and there are descriptions of the major industries, density of population, transport networks, and a look at what may be described as the lie of the land, drawing attention to the features that might affect an advance and those that might provide a commanding view of the surrounding area. Information was given on distances, tidal conditions and borders, as well as weather and climate. England was stated as having more roads than Germany and that the roads were generally good. The railway network was quoted as having good coverage, although not always matching military needs, and the canals were effective when first built. It says nothing about the fact that the canals were narrow compared to those in Europe, or that there were many locks and, worse still, time consuming and labour-intensive flights of locks.

The English weather was noted as having modest warmth in summer and mild winters, but with heavy precipitation and low levels of sunlight.

Social matters were not ignored, and the appraisal was not always flattering. There was a not inconsiderable upper class and a large and prosperous middle class, noting that they had a far more comfortable lifestyle than in Germany, but a lower level of education. The working class is noted as being on poor to average pay, while the long term unemployed had a low material and intellectual standard of living. The state of the slum dwellers was put down not to undeserved poverty but to 'insufficient competence in domestic matters'.

One problem with the German assessment of the 'longer-term unemployed' was that it did not take into account British mobilisation. No country mobilised as completely as Great Britain. There was no mobilisation in Northern Ireland, but volunteers for the armed forces came forward from both sides of the border, even though those from the south risked being treated as traitors by their own government. It was not just mobilisation for the armed forces, but for industry as well, and it was not just mobilisation of men, but women without small children were also called up. Some civilian occupations were so important that they were protected from conscription, but others were almost eliminated. While the Germans were able to keep domestic servants well into the war, the British could only do so if their servants were too young for conscription or too old.

Racial differences were not ignored, with the Welsh being described as smaller and darker than the English and having ancient Celtic roots. The make-up of the English was shown to have considerable Nordic influence.

There was little on Scotland or Northern Ireland. This adds to the belief that the occupation would be centred on England, especially the south and the Midlands, but while Ireland was to be reunified under overall German control, there would be no doubt that Germany would interfere in the running of these countries.

The book included maps and photographs, and even a glossary of military terms with translations, and, almost as if the Germans saw themselves as tourists, a selection of phrases.

The Battle of the Barges

The Battle of Britain was not the only priority for the Royal Air Force. Even while the Battle of Britain continued, before the end of August RAF reconnaissance had spotted considerable activity on the canals and rivers of Germany and the occupied territories; barges were being moved *en masse* to the ports along the Channel coast. Guy Gibson recalled in his book, *Enemy Coast Ahead*:

> Everything was ready. Every port from Antwerp to Dieppe was packed like lumber floating in a river with thousands of these invasion barges. The Huns knew, of course, that our meagre bomber force would attack them. Light flak guns were brought from far and wide to put up a cordon of steel which would ensure that no bombs could be dropped within a mile; flak towers were erected, balloon barrages were put up.

At the beginning of September, the battle of the barges began. It went on day and night, Blenheims, Hampdens, Wellingtons all taking part in low-level attacks which not only destroyed many barges on the spot, but also killed many troops whose billets were in the warehouses nearby. Each squadron was given a port which was to be considered its own particular port and the pet baby of all concerned; each crew was given a basin; in each basin there were so many barges, sometimes 200, sometimes even 400. Bomb loads were organised so that the maximum amount of damage could be done per aircraft. Many small bombs were carried, even hand grenades which would, at least, do some damage if they hit the right spot.

After each raid a reconnaissance was made, and the CO would call all crews together.

'I have got some pictures of C Basin at Antwerp. Yesterday there were 400 barges there; today's reconnaissance shows 350. Who is on C Basin?'

Some pilot would shuffle to his feet.

'Well, you sank sixty, you and the rest, but that is not enough. You have to put all your bombs in that basin, not a stick starting on the edge and then doing its job, but every single bomb. Otherwise those bastards over there are going to come and invade us and then you will have to fight with your bare hands.'[3]

One problem was that the RAF did not have the really heavy bombs that were available later. Had a 12,000lb 'Tallboy' or a 22,000lb 'Grand Slam' been dropped into the middle of a basin, the damage would have been considerable, with barges not simply damaged, but capsized and rammed together. Of course, the bombers of 1940 could not have carried such weapons even if they had been available. It was also true that many smaller bombs were, in these circumstances, better than a few larger ones, which at the time would have been no heavier than 4,000lbs, known as 'cookies'.

The 'fog of war' didn't help – the lack of reliable information. Rumours abounded. Guy Gibson again:

> In my particular basin, a thing shaped like a heart in the middle of Antwerp dockyards, I once gained 100 barges and neither the CO or anyone else around could tell me I was responsible for them. Taking things all round, we were sinking them fast despite all the anti-aircraft fire they would put up against us. But our losses were heavy and we all knew we would have to win the Battle of the Barges before they started to move out. There were rumours that they actually had moved out and that we had sunk them. There were rumours that thousands of German soldiers were buried on the east coast of England; soldiers who had been hit by Bomber Command, who had been drowned and washed ashore. These rumours were untrue, and no one in this country will ever know anyone who saw a dead German soldier, although many a man will claim to know someone who knows someone else who buried one... We made our biggest raid on Antwerp [on 15 September 1940]. It was the night of the full moon; many barges were sunk, many blew up destroying others around them. They were full of stuff and we could see, there and then, there was no doubt about it, the Germans were ready.
>
> Flying low around these docks we could easily see the tanks on board, the guns on mountings at the stern of each invasion craft, the tarpaulins over sinister objects at the docks. 'Der Tag' was drawing near for the

Hun, and September 15th was, perhaps, the day when they realised that it would be no use.[4]

The pace of bombing was stepped up still further. On 17 September, Winston Churchill's speech in the House of Commons was reported on the radio, or as it was known then, the wireless. Churchill had told the assembled members of Parliament that Italian troops had started to advance eastwards in Libya, although they had still to reach the British front line. He continued to warn that an invasion of England could come at any moment.

A few days later an invasion scare did sweep across Britain. It is claimed that an RAF Coastal Command pilot on a night patrol noticed some dark shadows on the sea beneath his aircraft. He failed to notice the small clouds in the sky above his aircraft and so didn't make the connection between the clouds and the shadows, but instead radioed that the invasion was on!

It was far from being on. The American journalist William Shirer in his *Berlin Diary* reports wrote also of the bombing of the Channel ports and concluded that he thought it 'highly improbable that the German army would ever be able to assemble in the ports of Boulogne, Calais, Dunkirk, Ostend or on the beaches, enough barges or ships to launch an invasion in the force that would be necessary.'

'Cromwell'

The threat of invasion was so real that the code-word 'Cromwell' was introduced to warn the armed forces and civil authorities that an invasion was imminent. The trouble was that many of those involved assumed that receiving the code-word 'Cromwell' meant that an invasion was actually underway. This was to have unfortunate consequences, and in one case the consequences were fatal.

During the first week of September, aerial reconnaissance of the Dutch, Belgian and French Channel ports showed that at Flushing, Ostend, Dunkirk, Calais and Le Havre, there was a substantial gathering of barges. Ostend had had 280 arrive during the week, while these were accompanied by motorboats and small coasting vessels. No less significant, large numbers of bombers had moved into airfields in the Netherlands and Belgium, while there were large numbers of dive-bombers on the French coast along the Straits of Dover. In planning an amphibious operation, the state of the tides was an important factor, while the state of the moon was helpful for amphibious operations, and vital for those involving paratroops. Tide and moon would be at the best for an invader over the three days of 8-10 September.

As well as the moon and tide, there was another factor, the weekend. Even in wartime, the armed forces were not at their most ready at weekends. This was a factor in the timing of the Japanese attack on the US Pacific Fleet at Pearl Harbor more than a year later, when the United States Navy and the United States Army Air Force were simply not prepared, and the two most senior officers for each service were actually playing golf on the Sunday morning.

At 17.20 on Saturday, 7 September, the British chiefs-of-staff met, and by 2007 they had decided to bring the forces under their command to a state of 'immediate readiness' and issued the code-word 'Cromwell' – to warn that an invasion was imminent.

In the UK, most duty officers were relatively junior and many of them had not been fully briefed, largely on security grounds. On receiving the code-word 'Cromwell', many thought that the signal meant that an invasion had actually begun. Coastal artillery units sprang into action, Home Guard units were mobilised and manned their defensive positions. There was a plan to use all available training aircraft other than fighters as bombers, Operation Banquet, and as the police rounded up trainee pilots from places of entertainment, those who arrived back at their units were shocked to see bombs being loaded onto their aircraft. More than half of RAF Bomber Command's bombers were assigned to support ground forces.

As these preparations got underway, many local initiatives were taken. Home Guard platoon commanders were only supposed to ring church bells – silenced for the war as these were only to be rung to warn of an invasion – if they saw at least twenty-five Germany troops, but several took matters into their own hands and rang the bells, so that everyone, including the regular army units, thought that the invasion had begun. In East Anglia, the Royal Engineers destroyed several bridges. Three Guards officers, racing back to their base in Lincolnshire, were killed when their car ran over a mine, just laid to stop German forces advancing.

It was not until dawn on the Sunday morning, 8 September, that everyone realised that the invasion had not happened.

Delay

Almost a week later, on 14 September, the day before the planned invasion, Hitler briefed the commanders-in-chief of his armed forces. He told them that while the Kriegsmarine had completed its preparations for Sea Lion, the preconditions for the operation had still to be met, despite the 'enormous' successes of the Luftwaffe. He did not want to cancel the operation as it would boost British morale. It seems that while the air attacks had originally been intended to prepare for an invasion, Hitler had come to see the invasion preparations as an end in themselves, supporting the air war which he had come to believe might of itself provide victory.

While the next suitable invasion dates were 24-27 September, Raeder, head of the navy, realised that the air campaign would not achieve its aims by that time and proposed 8 October as the next date. Hitler insisted on 27 September with 17 September as the date for the final decision. Only if on 17 September all was not ready would 8 October be considered. Meanwhile the air campaign had to continue without interruption.

Despite this, Goering was already planning an intensive air campaign covering all of Great Britain and had decided that his strategy should not be driven by the demands of the invasion. It seems that both the heads of the air force and the navy had decided that Sea Lion would not go ahead. The Wehrmacht had also decided to disperse the invasion ships and barges to avoid further losses to RAF bombing.

Eventually Hitler also came to see that the preparations were futile. The losses due to the RAF's bombing campaign were such that on 2 October he ordered all preparations in support of the invasion to be 'largely dismantled'. His Directive No.18 of 21 November stated that it might be possible to resurrect the plans in the spring of 1941, but in early December his attitude had changed and one of his senior officers noted that Sea Lion was finished.

By this time another senior staff officer, General Alfred Jodl, the German army's chief of operations, took a considerable share in killing off Operation Sea Lion when he summarised his views in a memorandum to Hitler. 'The plan for an invasion of England would mean from the start a great risk – which had been further increased by the unsatisfactory results of the air offensive, due to the bad weather. If the landing did not succeed, this failure would endanger the whole of the achievements of the war thus far obtained. The invasion should therefore be executed only if there were no other way of forcing England to her knees.' He continued by stressing that such a way could be found by attacking and usurping the British positions in the Mediterranean – of which Jodl enumerated Gibraltar, Malta and the Suez Canal. The loss of these positions, he concluded, would bring the war to an end. Jodl's proposal of using strategic positions in the Mediterranean to put greater pressure on the British made much sense, and were in fact a mirror image of later Allied plans pending the landings in Normandy. They were also less risky than an invasion of England, or even of an invasion of the Soviet Union. Fortunately, they were ignored by Hitler.

Hitler had far more ambitious plans in mind. On 18 December, his Directive No.21 ordered the Wehrmacht to prepare to 'crush Soviet Russia in a rapid campaign', which was to be code-named 'Barbarossa'.

The invasion of the Soviet Union was to mean that the Germans were to fight the war on two fronts, three if North Africa was taken into account, something that had proved difficult during the First World War and was to contain the seeds of Germany's defeat in the Second World War.

One point that emerges clearly from the plans for Operation Sea Lion was the lack of coordination and cooperation between the German army, navy and air force. This was inherent in the so-called 'Führer system' in which individual chiefs of staff were encouraged to seek the Führer's ear and his support. There was no attempt to balance the arguments, no oversight other than that of Hitler himself. There was no equivalent of the British Chiefs of Staff meetings or a War Cabinet. Hitler was convinced from the start that he alone really knew how to win the war. Partly this was the result of so much early success, with Hitler convincing himself that this was down to his genius. His chiefs of staff had gone along with his plans.

In the case of Sea Lion, despite Jodl's appraisal, many of the generals opposed Raeder, feeling that he had failed to provide the support needed, while Raeder in turn was extremely critical of the army's plans. The Luftwaffe view was that it alone could bring success, destroying the RAF and Britain's air defences. This is the one thing that British and German air force leaders had in common – they both believed that the air war could deliver success much more quickly than the forces on the ground or at sea.

Chapter Five

The Battle of Britain

Today, the Battle of Britain has attained an iconic status, and has entered British folklore as a struggle between David and Goliath. Unlike the bombing campaign, there is little controversy over the battle, no question of whether it was 'right' or 'wrong', although strong disagreements remain over strategic matters and tactics. The significance of the battle cannot be underestimated as it was the first major battle in the air, and the first between air forces rather than between armies or navies as hitherto. So it was very much a British 'first', and a German one as well.

The term 'Battle of Britain' was coined by the country's wartime leader, Winston Churchill in a speech to the House of Commons on 18 June 1940, in which he explained that the Battle of France had ended and the Battle of Britain was about to begin. This, of course, suggests a battle on land and in the air, but Churchill recognised that the German Kriegsmarine lacked the ability to put a large number of troops ashore or to confront the Royal Navy, not least because of its heavy losses in the Norwegian campaign. If they were to have any chance of invading, the Germans would first have to destroy the Royal Air Force, and seaborne landings would have to be accompanied by airborne landings.

The Germans also had names for the operation: *Luftschlacht um England* or *Luftschlact um Grossbritannien*, meaning 'air battle against England' or 'air battle against Great Britain'. In other words, both sides were using much the same name.

One myth that persists to this day is that the Battle of Britain was won by the Supermarine Spitfire fighter, but the Spitfire was very much in the minority of RAF fighter aircraft in 1940 as deliveries had only started early in 1939. The mainstay of Fighter Command was the Hawker Hurricane, a slower aircraft, albeit easier to repair and with a tighter turning radius. Both aircraft used the Rolls-Royce Merlin liquid-cooled engine. Even the Hurricane excelled when compared with many other aircraft of the day, such as the Gloster Gladiator, a biplane that had suffered so badly in both Norway and France, and the Boulton Paul Defiant, which was hampered by its rear turret and the weight of the air gunner. In a way, the Defiant, a monoplane, was a throwback to the First World War when many fighter aircraft had had rear-gunners, and many, including Churchill, believed that all fighter aircraft should have this configuration. The weight of the rear-gunner was crucial, limiting performance while of little practical benefit once enemy fighter pilots realised that there was a rear-gunner and adjusted their tactics accordingly.

Some strategists, such as the Minister for Aircraft Production, Lord Beaverbrook, believed that all fighter aircraft should have two engines, as did the Bristol Beaufighter, ignoring, or ignorant, of the fact that in piston days, a single engined aircraft was far more manoeuvrable than a twin-engined aircraft. One manufacturer, Westland, had indeed produced a single-seat twin-engined fighter, the Wyvern, but only two squadrons were formed, largely because the aircraft had been conceived for a strategic situation that never happened – a rerun of the First World War.

Britain's top-scoring surviving fighter pilot of the war years was Group Captain J.E. 'Johnnie' Johnson. In his memoirs, *Wing Leader*, he recalled the state of Britain's fighter defences during the Battle of Britain. Despite many recognising that war was inevitable, and the ten months of time bought by the Munich Agreement, as well as more than seven months of the 'phoney war', all was not well.

Even the Spitfire did not match the Messerschmitt Bf109 in speed or armament. The Bf109 had the novel feature of a cannon that fired through the propeller boss, and cannon fire was far more effective than machine gun fire (and it also had eight wing-mounted machine guns). The only other aircraft to have a gun mounted in the propeller hub was the American Bell Airacobra, generally regarded as unsuccessful. The early Spitfires had eight wing-mounted machine guns, and while Spitfires with a cannon in each wing did appear in 1940, the cannon often jammed leading the pilots to demand the return of the machine guns, which at least worked!

The Luftwaffe also had the more experienced pilots, with many of them having fought with the Condor Legion in the Spanish Civil War and many more having had air combat experience over Poland. At this time, conversion trainers were unknown, although later twin-seat Spitfires appeared for the Irish Air Corps and twin-seat Hurricanes were built for what was then the Imperial Iranian Air Force. British pilots did not even have lectures on tactics at this early stage of the war. Newly-fledged pilots, sometimes with less than twenty hours on Spitfires or Hurricanes, arrived at their first squadron not knowing whether they could outturn a Bf109, but knowing that they couldn't outrun one, especially if they were flying a Hurricane. They did not have the comfort of knowing that their aircraft were better armoured than the Bf109 and provided better protection for the pilot, or that the Bf109 had a fatal weakness in its tailplane, which was not as strong as it could have been.

> What went on when flights of Spitfires and Messerschmitts met? When squadron met squadron and wing encountered wing? Could the 109s turn inside us?... What was the most important asset of a fighter pilot – to shoot straight, to keep a good lookout or to be able to stay with his leader at all times?[1]

The other enduring myth of the Battle of Britain was that the conflict was won by 'The Few'. This term is relative. Overall, there were less than 3,000 RAF and Fleet Air Arm fighter pilots, which today would be regarded as a very large number. Nevertheless, they were initially outnumbered by their German opponents. Had the Air Officer Commanding RAF Fighter Command, Air Chief Marshall Hugh 'Stuffy' Dowding, not resisted strong political pressure to send substantial reinforcements across the Channel as the Battle of France was being lost, there would indeed have been even fewer and the Battle of Britain could have been lost. As it was, the total included a number of Fleet Air Arm pilots as the Royal Navy had more pilots than aircraft, and no high-performance aircraft at all. One thing in Britain's favour was that the first of the airmen from the nations overrun by the Germans had fled to the UK to continue the fight, and some of these had had air combat experience over Poland and then France before crossing the Channel.

The Outset

Most conflicts have clearly defined starts and finishes. The Battle of Britain is one of the few exceptions. It did not start immediately after the fall of France on 22 June 1940, although there were the occasional isolated Luftwaffe sorties against Britain. Some German sources put the start date as 4 July while others put it as late as 13 August, which Goering classed as *Adler Tag*, 'Eagle Day'. The British put the start date as 10 July, but also put the first phase as running until 12 August, with the second phase running from 13 August.

The first phase saw British shipping and ports as the target, described by the Luftwaffe as the *Kanalkampf*, 'Channel Struggle'.

On 10 July, the RAF lost its first pilot of the Battle of Britain, but in an accident rather than in conflict. Sergeant Pilot Ian Clenshaw of No.253 Squadron from Kirton-in-Lindsey was patrolling over the Humber Estuary in poor visibility when he lost control of his aircraft and it crashed. He was 22 years old, a bank clerk who had joined the Royal Air Force Volunteer Reserve in spring 1939.

Later that morning, a coastal convoy was attacked by a solitary Dornier Do17Z bomber escorted by ten Messerschmitt Bf109s while off the North Foreland in Kent. Such a hit-and-run raid was not unusual and damage was slight.

At around 13.25 on the same day, the Chain Home stations near Dover noticed large numbers of aircraft massing beyond the Pas-de-Calais, and these were promptly reported to the operations room for 11 Group at RAF Uxbridge. Six Hurricanes of No.32 Squadron from RAF Biggin Hill were on patrol and immediately vectored to the area as another six of No.56 Squadron on standby at RAF Manston were scrambled. They arrived over the Channel to find a convoy under attack by *Luftflotte* 2. The Luftwaffe aircraft were on three levels, with the lowest level of some twenty Dornier Do17Z bombers attacking the ships. Above was a middle level of thirty Messerschmitt Me110s providing close support for the bombers while above flew twenty Messerschmitt Bf109s providing top cover.

This was the standard Luftwaffe formation at this stage of the war and was based on experience gained in Spain, Poland, the Low Countries and France. The Me110s were to provide a defensive circle around the bombers, leaving the Bf109s to swoop down for the kill. The British fighters were both outnumbered and outclassed. Nevertheless, while some swept down to tackle the bombers, the rest tackled the Me110s. Climbing to attack the Bf109s would have been pointless as it would have taken too long, and in any case the Bf109s were swooping on the Hurricanes, anticipating an easy victory. Despite the odds being stacked against them, all of the Hurricanes survived this first encounter and set off to return to their bases, where one from No.56 crash-landed at Manston, and two from No.32 also crash-landed, one at Hawkinge and one at Lympne. Other fighters had also reached the battle area and the attack was repelled, although one ship was sunk.

This was not the only aerial combat of the day, as throughout the long summer afternoon and evening there were further battles from as far south as Beachy Head on the Sussex coast to as far north as the Firth of Tay, north of St Andrews, in Scotland. As darkness fell, the RAF had flown 641 sorties and lost six aircraft, against the Luftwaffe losses of eight fighters and four bombers.

At RAF Bentley Priory, from where the fighter defences were coordinated, it was possible to develop a complete picture of what had become known as the Air Defence of Great Britain as events unfolded. At Bentley Priory each group had its own controller and plotting room. The controllers were assisted by members of the Women's Auxiliary Air Force, each with teams working four shifts, twenty-four hours on and twenty-four hours off. The system was designed to ensure that the groups reinforced each other if any one came under heavy pressure, usually with either Nos.10 or 12 Groups being needed to assist No.11 Group.

This system of overlapping groups seemed to work well, especially between Nos.10 and 11 Groups. Keith Lawrence was a young pilot officer from New Zealand flying Spitfires with No.234 Squadron, which moved to Middle Wallop during the battle:

> The majority of fighting was, of course, over Kent and the south-east. No.11 Group was well supported by Air Vice-Marshal Brand at 10 Group. He co-operated well with AVM Park, and whenever Park needed reinforcements from 10 Group he would call on some of the squadrons at Middle Wallop, Warmwell or other airfields that were close to 11 Group. A good two-thirds of our flying was in support of 11 Group as there were fewer enemy raids along the south coast, partly because such raids were at the extreme range of fighter escort.
>
> When we were scrambled to reinforce 11 Group, with the order 'Scramble 234 Squadron', we were off the ground within 5-6 minutes. Once airborne, the CO would report 'Crecy Squadron airborne' and then we would get our orders from Middle Wallop sector controller: 'Crecy Squadron patrol Guildford [or patrol Brooklands] angels 20'.[2] That was an easy 15 minutes' climb up to Guildford or Brooklands. Brooklands was quite a landmark and when we got there the CO would report 'Crecy Squadron Brooklands angels 20'.
>
> The controller at Wallop could see on his table the whole of the raid, the numbers of German bombers and where they were coming in. We continued to be controlled from our sector station even when we were over Kent. The Wallop controller was co-operating with the controller of 11 Group, who would know from his ops room table that 11 Group squadrons had been scrambled and which formations they were intercepting. Likewise, the 10 Group controller would have been told which formations he was to tackle and so on.
>
> With our wonderful system of radar, the controller could track the incoming bombers once they had reached more than 15,000 feet. The difficulty was that, by the time they got to 18,000 feet and set course for England, it was only a matter of 10 to 15 minutes before they crossed the coast. The controllers were pilots who had either been on ops themselves,

or had been experienced fighter pilots. For the most part the VHF radio was good and we could hear them quite well. The controller could position us at a reasonable height to intercept and make an attack.

At the time we didn't know much about what was going on in 12 Group. We didn't know anything about the co-operation (or lack of it) between 11 and 12 Groups, and only learnt about that afterwards. All we had to do was go on readiness every morning at first light and remain on readiness until 'scrambled' or relieved by the pilots on the duty roster.[3]

The outstanding success of the Battle of Britain was the Chain Home radar network. This minimised the relative disadvantage in numbers of the RAF compared to the Luftwaffe by ensuring that aircraft were only in the air when they needed to be, saving the waste of fuel and manpower in standing patrols, and also ensured that aircraft were directed to where they were needed. It also avoided the problem with standing patrols that the aircraft in the air could be running low on fuel and forced to return to base just when they were needed. It was what today would be described as a 'force multiplier'.

It was important that RAF aircraft were not mistaken for those of the Luftwaffe, which was a problem at first, but before long an early form of identification friend or foe, IFF, system was deployed aboard the RAF's fighters.

The brunt of the Battle of Britain was borne by the less glamorous Hawker Hurricane, first flown by No.111 Squadron. Closest to the 'front line' of this air war were those squadrons stationed along the south coast of England, with one of the busiest bases, and most vulnerable, being RAF Tangmere in West Sussex. One of the Tangmere Hurricane squadrons was No.501, one of whose pilots was Pilot Officer Peter Hairs. He was very appreciative of the value of radar, and able to explain how the IFF worked:

> ...The very effective system of radar, which, although in its infancy, was remarkably accurate, and enabled the ground control to use the limited aircraft at their disposal to the fullest extent and minimised standing patrols, which are not only wasteful but tiring for those slogging around. Radar was able to pick up the enemy aircraft before they left the French coast while still forming up, and so ample warning was received and the defending squadrons could be deployed and sent off in time to meet the attack at the most convenient point.

> Often we would get a phone call through from control to say that things were building up over the Channel some time before the order to scramble came through. To ensure that our own fighters were not plotted as enemy aircraft, our aircraft were fitted with an instrument that gave out a regular signal for 15 seconds each minute – this was synchronised with the controller by a small instrument like a clock in the cockpit. On one occasion we were scrambled from Hawkinge as evening was drawing and climbed through a thin layer of cloud near Dungeness and control came through to say some enemy aircraft were in the vicinity. Nothing could be seen and so a section of us broke away and came down below the cloud once again. We broke cloud only to find ourselves in the middle of some twelve Bf109s which were on their way home. I don't know who was the more surprised! What I recall mostly about the mix-up was the patterns weaved by the tracer bullets, which showed up brightly in the gathering dusk and I was intrigued by the way the tracers seem to travel through the air so lazily. I was, however, brought back to earth (not literally) by a thump behind and looking in my rear-view mirror saw my tailplane in tatters.[4]

The deep fascination showed by Hairs in tracer was something shared by many pilots, especially those in bombers, over the war years.

While the first phase of the battle was inconclusive, the losses to British merchant shipping and the strain on the Royal Navy, which also had to escort convoys across the North Atlantic and the Bay of Biscay, was such that the Admiralty soon decided not to run convoys through the English Channel. To this extent, the *Kanalkampf* was a success for the Germans. This was not so surprising as attacks on shipping off the coast always meant that the RAF had further to go to defend the convoys, while the Luftwaffe fighter pilots were still well within their radius of action. The small size of many coasting merchant ships at that time was also a factor, with many displacing less than a thousand tons, and so vulnerable to even a single bomb hit.

The RAF Under Attack

During the opening phase of the Battle of Britain, both sides had learnt much about tactics. For the RAF, this was conclusive proof that the Boulton Paul Defiant, with its heavy rear-facing turret and second man, was no match for an agile German fighter. The Luftwaffe in turn soon realised that the twin-engined Messerschmitt Me110 was at a disadvantage when pitched against a Spitfire in a dogfight.

Perhaps even more important, the Germans had come to realise that the big advantage possessed by the British was radar, the Chain Home network. This was nothing less than the 'brain' behind the RAF's fighter defences, and also behind anti-aircraft defences, always giving timely warning and ensuring that defences were well directed and coordinated. The inevitable conclusion was that if an invasion was to go ahead, the RAF would have to be destroyed. An operation was planned for this, *Adlerangriff*, Eagle Attack, and the date for the start of the offensive was known as *Adlertag*, but this was delayed by the weather until 13 August.

This time the targets were not shipping and ports, but RAF stations and the Chain Home radar stations.

As usual, the Luftwaffe's planning was impeccable. The day before the start date, 12 August, a determined assault was made on four of the Chain Home stations by a specialised fighter-bomber unit, *Erprobungsgruppe* 210, which attacked all four stations. Three of them were knocked out but all were operational again within six hours. One reason for this was that the radar stations were difficult targets, with the masts difficult to hit, and of a lattice construction that meant that only a direct hit was likely to cause serious damage.

On 13 August, *Adlertag*, *Erprobungsgruppe* 210, sometimes referred to as *Erpro* 210, opened the attacks on RAF airfields and forward landing grounds, giving priority to those close to the Channel coast, including RAF Manston and Hawkinge. There were further attacks on the Chain Home network in the days that followed, while attention then turned to RAF stations further inland, such as Biggin Hill and Croydon. A climax was reached on 15 August when the Luftwaffe effort peaked with the greatest number of sorties during the Battle of Britain. Surprisingly, the Luftwaffe assumed that the RAF had concentrated its fighter units in the south of England, so, expecting little opposition, *Luftflotte* 5 attacked the north of England, outside the range of the Messerschmitt Bf109, with aircraft based in Denmark and Norway, and the attackers relied instead on the longer-range twin-engined Messerschmitt Me110, and suffered heavy losses as a result. The lesson did not need repeating and *Luftflotte* 5 did not return in strength during the battle.

Despite the all-out effort on 15 August, casualties did not peak until 18 August, often described as 'The Hardest Day'. Both sides suffered their heaviest losses, but for the Luftwaffe the big lesson was that the Junkers Ju87 Stuka dive-bomber, which had served it so well in Spain, Poland, Norway, the Low Countries and

France, was easy prey for British fighters. The trouble for the Germans was that this was the Luftwaffe's precision bomber.

Both sides were in need of the respite granted by more bad weather which limited operations for a week, during which the RAF took the opportunity to move more squadrons forward. One of these was No.234, moved to RAF Middle Wallop, whose pilots included a New Zealander, Pilot Officer Keith Lawrence. He recalls the way in which operations were conducted:

> When we got to Middle Wallop it was straight into action. On the very first day, one of the chaps I came over with on the boat from New Zealand was killed, Cecil Hight. At the end of the first week of September the squadron returned to St Eval [in Cornwall] to 'rest' and train new pilots. During four weeks' fighting we lost eighteen Spitfires in action.
>
> At that time, the end of August, whenever we lost an aircraft, a replacement was soon flown in as there was, by now, a steady flow of new Spitfires from the factories at Castle Bromwich. The ATA [Air Transport Auxiliary] pilots would usually fly them in, but also pilots from Ferry Command. I can remember them being flown in and going to the hangar for inspection. They were supposed to be ready for immediate action, but not before our ground crews were satisfied. Twenty-four pilots and twenty aircraft was roughly the disposition of the squadron which was aimed for. We flew as a squadron in twelves and rotated the on and off-duty times so that the twenty-four pilots shared the flying.
>
> We had quite a few actions over the south coast. On one particular scramble (which I missed) there was a big raid over Sussex during which No.234 Squadron probably destroyed or damaged ten Me110s.[5]

The inspection of newly arrived aircraft by the squadron's own mechanics was probably very reassuring as aircraft produced by hastily trained factory workers during wartime were known to have left the factory and the pre-delivery test flight with some faults. One of the worst on record was an Avro Lancaster bomber delivered to No.617 Squadron, the famous 'Dam Busters' later in the war, with the control wires fitted so that every control movement resulted in the aircraft doing the opposite to that intended.

At the time, RAF fighter squadrons would fly in close formation with only the formation leader (normally the CO) searching the sky for other aircraft. The twelve aircraft would fly in four tight 'vics' of three, although some squadrons would have an 'arse-end Charlie' or 'tail-arse Charlie' to weave on the watch for enemy fighters attempting to attack from behind. The squadron did not break formation until the CO had spotted an incoming German formation, called out its position on the radio, and then shouted 'tally ho'. As they headed for the bombers, they often found themselves engaged in a dogfight with the escorting Bf109s.

While there was an attempt to ensure that the initial attack was guided and coordinated, in the melee that followed it was every man for himself, so the squadron formation was lost and the aircraft were widely scattered. Aircraft were either attacking German aircraft or being attacked, but in just two or three minutes it would be over and the sky deserted. The pilots, many of them still very young and inexperienced, would then have to make their way back to base. It was usual for a newcomer to a squadron to be taken up with his aircraft accompanied by that of a more experienced pilot so that he could see the local landmarks and so, if visibility was good, be able to find his own way home after action.

If there was cloud obscuring the view of the ground, the fighter pilots could call their base for a homing beacon, transmitting for four seconds or so. Most air stations had three homing stations, and by triangulation would identify the location of the fighter, and provide a course for the homeward flight. It was not usual to re-formate. Indeed, if returned in formation, those on the ground could safely assume that they had not found the enemy. After an encounter, aircraft returned to base in ones and twos, usually over a period of around twenty minutes. After this time, any that had not arrived were feared to have either force-landed or baled out, or worse. Usually news of those who had survived a mishap came fairly quickly, but after thirty or forty minutes, often the worst was assumed. This was not unreasonable as downed pilots could be back with their units within hours.

By contrast, with the experience of the Spanish Civil War behind them, Luftwaffe fighter pilots had evolved different tactics from the RAF. Instead of tight formations, fighters were sent in loose sections of two aircraft, known as a *Rotte*, with the leader followed by a wingman about 600 feet behind him, flying slightly higher. The leader searched for enemy aircraft and both covered the other's blind spots. Anyone attacking the leader risked being caught between the two aircraft. Some credit this formation to that evolved by Oswald Boelke in 1916, or to the Finnish Air Force, which decided on a similar tactic in 1934. Nevertheless, it was the Luftwaffe that used this tactic with modern aircraft and the RAF did not use it at first.

The two-fighter patrol evolved into a four-fighter *Schwarm* with each pilot flying at a different height and all four keeping a lookout. It also had the advantage of making the formation more difficult to spot at a distance, while a tight crossover turn enabled the *Schwarm* to change direction quickly. This was far better than RAF's dependence on the formation leader, and possibly also the 'tail-arse Charlie', to spot enemy aircraft.

Naturally the more experienced RAF fighter pilots soon realised that their formations were far from ideal. Some units introduced more weavers flying slightly above the main formation to keep an additional lookout, but these tended to be the less experienced pilots and were often the first to be shot down, sometimes without the other pilots realising what had happened. As the battle continued, the South African Squadron Leader Adolph 'Sailor' Malan, in command of No.74 Squadron, decided on a variant of the Luftwaffe tactics that became known as the 'fours in line astern', which soon proved to be more efficient and was later adopted throughout Fighter Command.

The air stations that had been completed before the war usually had decent accommodation for personnel and aircraft, although few fighter stations of the day had hard runways. The newer airfields, prepared rather than constructed in haste, often had bell tents for accommodation, with marquees for the messes. Many of these airfields would have two or three squadrons, with the only communication being a shared field telephone that would ring once for one squadron, twice for another and three times for the third. This left everyone on edge until the ringing stopped!

Soon the airfields closest to the air battles became untenable, including Manston, Ford, Tangmere, and the Fleet Air Arm's main station at RNAS Lee-on-the-Solent, more usually known as 'Lee' and home to HMS *Daedalus*. Naturally, not all airfields were convenient for the Battle of Britain, and often squadrons were accommodated at airfields other than that from which they flew their sorties.

Even airfields such as North Weald, less exposed, were often bombed. Aircrew could return to find that their accommodation had been destroyed, along with their possessions. Many had just the clothes they stood up in, and one pilot remembers going to the pub in order to have a bath! At one time, with his fellow pilots, he had to sleep on mattresses laid in rows in a shed.

Life for the pilots was demanding – either waiting for action or actually being in action, none of them knowing at breakfast whether they would survive the day, or even the morning. Pilot Officer Irving 'Black' Smith served with No.151 Squadron, a Hurricane unit at North Weald. He recalls daily life:

> Throughout August 1940…the squadron would be released at nautical twilight (2200-2230 hours), go to bed, and be up again at 0230 to 0300, having a cup of tea and probably an egg for breakfast, to be airborne from

North Weald at nautical twilight at around 0400 hours, in a formation of twelve aircraft, no lights, dimly in sight of each other and flying at low level about 50 feet above the ground, to land at first light at Rochford to be on readiness at dawn.

If nothing was happening, No.151 would be relieved by No.56 Squadron at midday, but if things were happening, there was no relief. If No.151 was on afternoon readiness at Rochford, they would go back to North Weald at dusk, the aircraft being serviced overnight. This was an efficient but tiring routine, and getting enough sleep was a problem.

Food was also a problem. All food at Rochford had to be sent in boxes to the tents. One often missed it and on occasions we did not get anything to eat until we were back at North Weald. But North Weald was not organised to serve the needs of pilots, and I remember often pleading with the mess staff to boil an egg or two out of hours. This is not a criticism, as the RAF was just starting to learn what it was all about, and it takes quite a long time to change entrenched attitudes and procedures in wartime, especially administrative ones.[6]

This clearly shows that the RAF, supposedly *the* service for airmen, had no idea and had given no thought to what life would be like under actual combat conditions. One pilot had no change of clothes at all and the uniform he was wearing was frayed and a 'greenish-colour' in his own words. His superiors at RAF Digby were unimpressed as they had not seen action and had no idea how bad the situation was in the forward stations. He was lucky to escape punishment.

The Final Phases

Soon the Luftwaffe extended its campaign into a third phase, attacking RAF airfields and aircraft factories, as well as other industries such as tyre and engine factories that supplied the aircraft industry. The aircraft factories were attacked from 19 August and on 23 August the campaign was extended to the RAF's airfields, although some had been attacked earlier. On the night of 24/25 August, several parts of the East End of London were attacked, setting a large area ablaze. This, the first big raid, is believed by some to have been a mistake as a formation of Heinkel He111 bombers failed to find a target and ditched their bombs, but others feel the attack was deliberate and an attempt to undermine the will of the civilian population. It is almost inevitable that any attack on industrial targets can lead to bombs drifting off-target and onto surrounding housing or other civilian areas, such as shopping areas, hospitals or schools. The following night saw a further escalation of the air war as the RAF mounted a retaliatory raid on Berlin, much to the chagrin of Goering, who had boasted that Berlin would never be bombed. In his fury, Hitler demanded attacks on London.

Starting on 24 August, the crux of the battle became a contest between Air Vice-Marshal Keith Park's 11 Group and Kesselring's *Luftflotte* 2. In the fortnight that followed, there were no less than thirty-three heavy attacks, of which twenty-four were against airfields. RAF Eastchurch on the Isle of Sheppey, an RAF Coastal Command station, was attacked seven times because it was thought to be a fighter station by the Germans. Biggin Hill and Hornchurch were struck four times each; Debden and North Weald twice; Croydon, Gravesend, Hawkinge, Manston and Rochford were each attacked once.

Spitfires continued to arrive at RAF stations to replace losses, but it took longer to train new pilots than build aircraft, and new pilots were also those most likely to be lost once they joined an operational squadron. The typical replacement had nine hours' flying time in an operational training unit, OTU, but no weapons or air-to-air combat training. Some sixty Fairey Battle bomber pilots were transferred to Fighter Command, where at least they could fly a useful aircraft! Around fifty-eight Fleet Air Arm fighter pilots also volunteered for secondment to the RAF, which had high performance fighters, which they had not. By this time, the RAF had many aircrew from the British Empire, and especially the dominions of Australia, Canada, New Zealand and South Africa, while French and Belgian pilots had escaped to continue the war, although the Free French forces had still to be organised. They were soon joined by Czechoslovak and Polish pilots, usually flying in their own squadrons such as No.303 (Polish) Squadron, but who had been held back by Dowding until late in the Battle of Britain as he was concerned about their lack of English. His fears were unjustified as one Czech, Josef Frantisek, who had the distinction of having flown first in his own country, then with the Polish Air Force and then the French Armée de l'Air before finally joining the RAF, became the battle's top-scoring ace.

What today would be described as 'mission creep' meant that the third phase led inexorably to the fourth phase, which was really the start of the blitz against British cities.

The Big Wing

Despite its earlier success and experience gained during the Spanish Civil War and the start of the Second World War, the Luftwaffe had much to learn as this was the first time that it had encountered determined and successful resistance, but of course there was so much more for the RAF to learn. This could only be done as the war progressed.

At RAF Duxford, Wing Commander Douglas Bader's 12 Group had been organised to operate as a 'Big Wing' of Nos.242, 302 and 310 Hurricane squadrons, and Nos.19 and 611 Spitfire squadrons. The idea was that of AVM Trafford Leigh Mallory, who saw it as a means of meeting the enemy in overpowering strength and have the Hurricanes deal with the bombers while the faster Spitfires tackled the fighters. This would break up the enemy formation.

This was the theory, but Bader knew that if the idea was to work, his wing would have to be scrambled early, but 12 Group was only called into action by the controllers of 11 Group if their aircraft were having difficulty in containing the enemy attack, which meant that inevitably the Duxford wing was scrambled late. Forming up so many aircraft into a 'Big Wing' meant that their arrival was delayed further. AVM Keith Park criticised the Big Wing for arriving late, and his frustration was shared by the pilots of the wing. Often the wing would consist of just three squadrons other than the planned five.

In an attempt to simplify the creation of the formation, with the Hurricanes of Nos.242 and 310 taking off from Duxford and the Spitfires of No.19 taking off from Fowlmere, and instead of forming up, all the aircraft would head for the rendezvous climbing as quickly as possible. The Spitfires were intended to arrive at the rendezvous slightly to one side of the Hurricanes and between 3,000 and 4,000 feet above them, so that the Spitfires would be at the level of the enemy fighters and the Hurricanes at the bomber level.

Part of the problem was that Duxford reinforced 11 Group and no doubt the 'Big Wing' would have had more chance of proving itself had it been comprised of 11 Group instead of 12 Group. On the other hand, arriving late had one advantage as 12 Group were able to patrol over 11 Group's airfields while aircraft landed, keeping the Luftwaffe away as any aircraft is at its most vulnerable to enemy attack while landing.

Outcome

Could the Luftwaffe have destroyed the RAF? Goering was prone to bombast. He had promised to finish off the British and French armies at Dunkirk, but had failed; he had promised that Berlin would not suffer an air raid, but again he was wrong. He had also promised to finish the RAF, but again, he had failed. More sober and contemplative minds such as the head of the German Navy knew that they were not strong enough to rule the waves and that the Luftwaffe could not guarantee air superiority over the English Channel and North Sea, let alone the mainland of Great Britain. In short, they realised that an invasion was impossible.

Dowding, in a report to the Chief of the Air Staff, Sir Hugh Trenchard, maintained that the Luftwaffe had achieved 'very little' at the end of August and beginning of September. Of the sector stations, only Biggin Hill was shut down, and that just for two hours.

It was also the case, as records show, that not only was aircraft production keeping pace with losses, aided by the Civilian Repair Organisation (CRO) and Air Servicing Unit (ASU) airfields, which between them repaired almost 5,000 aircraft, but the supply of new pilots was holding up better than many believed at the time. Statistics show that on 1 July 1940, RAF Fighter Command had 1,200 pilots, and a month later there were 1,400, and the numbers continued to increase to 1,600 in October and 1,800 by November. In addition to the repaired aircraft, 496 new aircraft were supplied in July, although this dropped slightly to 467 in August and again in September. On 3 August, RAF Fighter Command had 1,061 fighters, of which 708 were serviceable, while on 7 September there were 1,161, of which 746 were serviceable. By contrast, the Luftwaffe did not at any time during the Battle of Britain have more than 1,200 pilots.

If British pilots were 'The Few', the Germans were even fewer.

Chapter Six

The State of the Navies in 1940

Despite early encounters at sea between the Royal Navy and the Kriegsmarine, and despite the Norwegian Campaign, until the fall of France in June 1940 the Second World War had been a land war, albeit with close tactical air support. This was partly because of German weakness at sea early in the war, and it was something that would not be rectified, except for the creation of a strong submarine arm. Germany had given priority to the Luftwaffe, the air force, followed by the army, which despite its strategy being based on fast advances by armoured vehicles, lacked mechanised transport in sufficient quantity. The Luftwaffe was also deficient in air transport.

The Kriegsmarine had not fared well in the Norwegian campaign. With the fall of France, the two remaining combatants could no longer face each other on land, and had to continue fighting at sea, and in the air.

The Royal Navy

In 1939, the Royal Navy was one of the world's largest, but it was also the most thinly spread. The largest element was the Home Fleet, which as the name suggests was stationed in home waters, and the second largest was the Mediterranean Fleet. In addition there were five 'stations' at Hong Kong, Singapore, Bermuda, Simonstown (in South Africa, near Cape Town), and the West Indies. The Home Fleet was the descendant of the Grand Fleet of the First World War, but for most of the interwar period had been known as the Atlantic Fleet.

Despite the severe economic depression that in reality had dominated most of the interwar years, in 1939 the Royal Navy and Royal Marines totalled 129,000 men, and on mobilisation this figure rose to 202,000 as members of the Royal Naval Reserve (RNR) and Royal Naval Volunteer Reserve (RNVR) were called up. Many of the RNR members were serving in the Merchant Navy and brought good navigational and engineering skills to the expanded wartime navy, while the RNVR consisted of many whose experience extended no further than yachting, and perhaps not even that.

Despite the difficult economic situation worldwide, each year between the two world wars had seen a flotilla of new destroyers introduced, often replacing older ships with seven, eight or even nine new ships. On the debit side, the British government had tried to set an example and encourage if not outright disarmament, then a steady reduction in armaments. The Washington Naval Treaty of 1922 had set upper limits on the size of the major types of warships as well as the total tonnage allowed the major navies, and also set upper limits on armament. Yet, while Germany and Japan showed increasing disregard for these limits as the 1930s passed, the British government tried to reduce them further. The King George V-class of battleships had 14-inch guns instead of the planned 15-inch, even though two post-First World War battleships, HMS *Rodney* and *Nelson* had been completed with 16-inch guns. The heavier calibre not only meant that these weapons were more potent, but they also had a longer range. The aircraft carrier, *Ark Royal*, only the second British aircraft carrier to be designed and built as such from the keel up, had to conform to new lower maximum limits on individual carrier tonnage, so her flight deck lacked any armour plating at all. Senior officers knew that she was extremely vulnerable to aerial attack, and it was a surprise when she was sunk by a submarine-fired torpedo.

Efforts to rebuild the Royal Navy during the late 1930s by the then First Sea Lord, Admiral Sir Ernle Chatfield, had been hampered by a lack of slipway capacity in Britain's shipyards. Shipbuilding had been seriously affected during the depression years and yards had closed or reduced their capacity. The Royal Navy had received between seven and nine new destroyers each year, but larger ships came along more slowly and it was not until war loomed that orders were placed. At this period of its history, the Royal Navy did not have frigates, which had gradually faded away during the middle and later years of the nineteenth century. Wartime needs were to see the frigate reinvented, and the appearance of another smaller escort vessel, the corvette, but these developments were still some time away in 1940.

The service had been weakened from its high point of 1914. Lieutenant Commander E.C. Talbot-Booth reminded the readers of his book, *All the World's Fighting Fleets*, published almost on the eve of war, that by 1940 the Royal Navy would have just 21 capital ships, meaning battleships and battlecruisers, as against 68 in 1914, 69 cruisers as against 103, and 190 torpedo craft as against 319. The fact that there were also seven aircraft carriers with six of advanced design following, did not really close the gap, especially as two of the carriers were the oldest of their type in the world, while another, HMS *Hermes*, was very small and the two light battlecruiser conversions, *Courageous* and *Glorious*, had flight decks that were too short for high performance aircraft. There was also the problem that the Fleet Air Arm had no high-performance aircraft, with the Admiralty believing that it was not possible to operate such aircraft from carriers, despite what was happening in the United States Navy and the Imperial Japanese Navy. One point Talbot-Booth did not make was that the 1939 cruiser was much larger and more capable than its counterpart in 1914, and the same could be said for the destroyers, some of which in 1939 were almost as large as the 1914 light cruiser.

In 1939, under its commander-in-chief, Admiral Sir Charles Forbes, the Home Fleet consisted of 5 battleships, 2 battlecruisers, 2 aircraft carriers, 3 squadrons with a total of 15 cruisers, 2 flotillas, each with 8 or 9 destroyers, and around 20 submarines. While the main bases were at Portsmouth, Devonport (next to Plymouth) and the Nore, at Chatham, all convenient to protect the English Channel and the Straits of Dover, as well as the Western Approaches, the main forward base in wartime was at Scapa Flow in Orkney. This showed that the Admiralty, as with the other services, expected the war to follow the same course as in the First World War, although it was realised that the much smaller German Navy would not be able to engage in a fleet operation along the lines of the Battle of Jutland in 1916.

There were other bases in Scotland. There was Rosyth, but it was not adequate as a major naval base, it was far from the open sea, and there were always fears that an attack on the Forth Bridge would leave the approaches blocked. Invergordon on the Cromarty Firth was also small, and access to the Firth was through a narrow channel that could easily be blocked or mined. Despite its importance in the earlier conflict, Scapa was neglected between the wars and it was not until 1938 that the Admiralty started to prepare it. Nevertheless, it was also recognised that making Scapa secure would not be easy, and this was proved early in the war when on 14 October 1939, *U-47* penetrated the anchorage to torpedo the battleship HMS *Royal Oak* which sank with the loss of 833 lives.

The *Royal Oak* was far from being the first major British naval casualty of the war. The first had been the aircraft carrier *Courageous*, two weeks after the start of the war on 17 September 1939. She was engaged in a submarine sweep, but with just two destroyers as escorts. This was a hazardous undertaking, often described as being akin to searching for a needle in a haystack. She sank in twenty minutes taking 500 men with her, many of whom would have been trapped below decks in the dark as the lighting failed when the torpedoes struck. It was small consolation that the first German aircraft to be shot down, on 26 September, was accounted for by fighters from Britain's newest aircraft carrier, HMS *Ark Royal*.

The first merchant ship to be sunk had been on the day war broke out, the liner *Athena*, 13,500 tons, torpedoed off the Hebrides, without the warning required by the Hague Convention. Out of the 128 who lost their lives, 28 were Americans, giving Hitler the opportunity to claim that they were victims of a British attack intended to try and drag the United States into the war against Germany. Despite this claim, the U-boat commander was later to claim that he thought the ship was either an armed merchant cruiser or a Q-ship, essentially a decoy, posing as a merchant vessel but with a hidden armament.

Armed merchant cruisers were already operating as convoy escorts by this time. These ships were 'taken up from trade', hastily equipped with obsolete 6-inch guns, and usually their merchant crews would be conscripted into the Royal Naval Reserve. One such was the *Rawalpindi*, a P&O liner, which was on escort duty on 23 November 1939 when the convoy was threatened by the German battlecruisers *Gneisenau* and *Scharnhorst* while off Iceland. The *Rawalpindi* turned to face the German ships and after an unequal battle, lacking their speed, firepower, gunnery direction and armour protection, she was sunk.

Better news came before the end of the year, but far from home waters, on 13 December. The heavy cruiser *Exeter*, with the light cruisers *Ajax* and *Achilles*, encountered the German pocket battleship (or *Panzerschiff*, 'armoured ship') *Graf Spee*, which had been engaged in commerce raiding off the mouth of the River Plate. Despite being outgunned, the superior tactics of the three cruisers managed to damage the German ship so much that she sought shelter in Montevideo, in neutral Uruguay, where she was allowed three days for temporary repairs. She took a skeleton crew when she sailed on 17 December, and once out to sea she was scuttled.

On 14 February, the *Graf Spee*'s supply ship, the *Altmark*, carrying British merchant seamen made prisoners after their ships were sunk, was boarded by men from the destroyer *Cossack* in the Jossingfjord, and 303 men set free. The destroyer had challenged the *Altmark* at sea but the supply ship had run into the shelter of Norwegian territorial waters. HMS *Cossack* had sought permission to enter Norwegian waters but her way had been barred by Norwegian warships, but *Cossack* eventually managed to catch her prey. The Norwegian government sent a strong message of protest to the British government, but allowed the *Altmark* to continue back to Germany. Many believe that the '*Altmark* incident' gave Hitler the excuse he needed to invade Norway. His real reason was the need to secure Norwegian ports to allow supplies of iron ore from Sweden to be shipped to Germany even in winter, when the more direct route from Sweden, through the Gulf of Bothnia, froze.

The Germans had believed that a *Panzerschiff* could only be countered by a battleship, but clearly this was not the case. It showed that realism was not entirely absent when one of *Graf Spee*'s two sister ships, *Deutschland*, was renamed *Lutzow* because someone worried about the impact on the nation's morale if *Deutschland* was sunk.

In 1940, the *Panzerschiffe* were redesignated as heavy cruisers.

On the Offensive

Often criticised for its failure to institute a convoy escort programme for the most crucial years of the First World War, the Royal Navy did not make the same mistake again, and a convoy system was introduced on the outbreak of hostilities. As in the earlier conflict, a close blockade of German ports was introduced. This was hampered during the first months of war by Belgian, Dutch, Danish and Norwegian neutrality until these nations were invaded in 1940.

Between September 1939 and June 1940, half a million men and 89,000 vehicles were shipped across the Channel, protected by the Royal Navy, without loss.

So successful were the defensive minefields laid by the Royal Navy that by the time the last of 3,600 mines had been laid to create a barrier in October 1939, three U-boats were lost.

For the Germans, the first year of the war at sea was beset with difficulties, the most important of which was the relative weakness of the Kriegsmarine compared to the Royal Navy, with few ocean-going submarines. To get to their hunting grounds, not only U-boats but also surface raiders had to sail around the north of Scotland, and even through the Denmark Strait between Iceland and Greenland, to reach their operational area. The fall of France presented the Kriegsmarine with a windfall of well-located and well-equipped naval ports from which to operate. Despite British concerns that the Germans might take French warships to strengthen their fleet, this never happened, and when the Germans eventually did attempt to try after the invasion of the South of France in late 1942, the French resisted, scuttling some ships while others escaped to Spain and North Africa.

As mentioned earlier, the Royal Navy was called into action alongside the French *Marine Nationale* to counter the German invasion of Norway, but despite winning two actions at Narvik, in the withdrawal suffered the loss of the aircraft carrier *Glorious* and her two escorting destroyers.

The Royal Navy organised Operation Dynamo, the evacuation from Dunkirk, protecting the ships from enemy U-boats and E-boats, the fast motor gunboats and motor torpedo boats that could have wreaked havoc, and this included shore-based Fairey Swordfish of the Fleet Air Arm operating alongside Royal Air Force Coastal Command aircraft.

There had been no such thing as a 'phoney war' at sea, as indicated earlier in this chapter. What there was as the war developed was a need to maintain supplies. Apart from large coal reserves, the United Kingdom had few fuel resources of its own with very limited oil production and relatively little hydro-electric power. British iron ore for the most part had too high a sulphur content for steelmaking. The country had to import more than half of its food, and under wartime pressures, with an enlarged population, and land taken out of agriculture for military bases, this became even more difficult. Attempts were made to bring additional farmland into production, sometimes forcing farmers to use land that was unsuitable due to frequent flooding, and also by using country estates and parks for food production. Much prime farmland was taken over to provide land for airfields, especially in the major agricultural areas of Lincolnshire and East Anglia, which were closest to enemy territory for bomber bases, army barracks and training grounds, and the demand for these facilities increased after the United States entered the war.

Food, raw materials and fuel, as well as military equipment, had to be convoyed across the North Atlantic. Much food and fuel came from even further afield, so there were convoys from South America, the Far East, Malaya, as it was then known, and Australia and New Zealand. Pressure on merchant shipping and on the Royal Navy's ability to protect shipping grew after June 1940 and Italy's entry into the war, which made the Mediterranean all but impassable and forced convoys from east of Suez to sail via the Cape of Good Hope. This situation was so bad that even supplies for the British forces in Greece and North Africa had to use this extended routeing. When finally the Mediterranean reopened for shipping after Allied troops landed in Italy in 1943, the Allied war effort gained the equivalent of almost a million tons of shipping through being able once again to use the shortest possible routes to the Indian Ocean and Australia and New Zealand.

The Kriegsmarine in 1940

Raeder believed that there was a danger of war between Germany and both the United Kingdom and France even before the Munich crisis of 1938. This possibility was not discussed officially. Nevertheless, the belief amongst senior German naval officers at the time was that any war would see the Kriegsmarine operating against British and French merchant shipping rather than seeking a major fleet action as at Jutland and which had so concerned their predecessors during the First World War.

The German naval staff appreciated that the location of the British Isles hindered German access to the open sea, but the First World War had also shown that the UK's strategic weakness was the country's heavy dependence on overseas trade. The German position could be improved if Norway, Denmark, the Netherlands, Belgium and northern France as far south as Brest were to be occupied, giving Germany unrestricted access to the North Atlantic. The Luftwaffe would also benefit, being able to attack British convoys in the Atlantic, including the Bay of Biscay and the Western Approaches, while British ports on the south coast from Dover to Plymouth, including the major naval base of Portsmouth and the major merchant port of Southampton, would also be exposed to attack from the air and from the sea.

Admiral Heye prepared a paper, *Seekriegsführung gegen England*, 'Sea Warfare Against England', on 25 October 1938. The paper was more interesting for what it did not say, indeed it gave little idea of how the war would be conducted at sea, and it was very dismissive of the potential for the U-boat. Like Raeder, Heye believed that British anti-submarine measures were so sophisticated that there would be little scope for submarine warfare. The one concession that he did make in giving the U-boat a role was the use of the 'cruiser U-boat'. He envisaged a small fleet of large cruiser U-boats that would each have four 12.7-cm, 5-inch, guns, and a high surface speed of 25 knots, which could engage British merchant shipping on the surface. Even so, the paper felt that once forced to dive, the slow speed of the submarine would mean that these large U-boats would be at the mercy of the Royal Navy's anti-submarine measures.

Heye's idea was similar to the concept of the cruiser submarine that had been the British M-class and the French *Surcouf*, but with lower calibre weapons for the German boats. The cruiser U-boats would be positioned along the main convoy routes and close to major ports, but it was also felt that they would end up playing a sacrificial role because of the concentration of counter-measures at such locations.

The main thrust of the paper was that the Kriegsmarine should engage in commerce raiding using the *Panzershiff*. Each *Panzershiff* would be escorted by light cruisers while a squadron of powerful battleships would be necessary to enable the *Panzershiff* to break out into the open seas. Heye also considered it necessary that the Kriegsmarine should have its own aircraft, with aircraft carriers as an integral part of the service. These plans were delayed by the continuing insistence by Goering that all German service aviation should be controlled by the Luftwaffe.

Plan Z

Raeder appointed the commander of the fleet, Admiral Carls, to head a planning committee. Carls was enthusiastic about the paper and was amongst the first to urge that the Kriegsmarine should begin planning for war. The naval staff had already drawn up a series of plans for the expansion of the service, starting with Plan X, which was superseded by Plan Y, which in turn was superseded by Plan Z.

Plan Z was very much Raeder's baby. It envisaged big battleships and aircraft carriers, armoured cruisers and many smaller vessels, and was later developed by Raeder's U-boat commander, Karl Dönitz, to include 249 U-boats. Finalised in late 1938, it was given Hitler's approval in January 1939. Most of Plan Z was intended to be completed by 1945, but the full plan would not be completed until 1947. This assumed that war would not break out as early as 1939.

The initial plan called for no less than four aircraft carriers, although this was intended to rise to eight later with the addition of some smaller ships; six large battleships, known as the H-class; three battlecruisers, known as the O-class, later to be increased to twelve; twelve P-class *Panzershiffe*; two heavy cruisers; light cruisers and large destroyers; and 249 U-boats. Given the size of the projected fleet, and especially the number of major surface units including capital ships, it is surprising that there were only intended to be fifty-eight destroyers.

This was an ambitious plan, but Germany did not have the shipbuilding capacity to fulfil it, and also lacked the necessary materials. The fuel that this vast fleet would consume exceeded the total fuel consumption of Germany in 1938. Germany was effectively rebuilding its new navy from scratch, as there had been no sustained construction of major warships since the end of the First World War, so the slipways were not available.

The first German aircraft carrier, the *Graf Zeppelin*, had been started in 1936 and she was launched in 1938, after which plans were made to begin work on a second ship, the *Peter Strasser*, although she was never started. Orders were placed in 1939 for carrier versions of the Messerschmitt Bf109 fighter and the Junkers Ju87 Stuka dive-bomber, designated as the Bf109T and the Ju87C. In the middle of that year, the two battleships *Bismarck* and *Tirpitz* were both launched and the keels laid for the first three of the H-class battleships.

Despite Hitler's approval for Plan Z, the Minister for Air, Hermann Goering, refused to allow the navy to have its own aviation, despite the British having recognised belatedly that combining all service aviation in the Royal Air Force had been a mistake. German inexperience in carrier aviation also meant that the *Graf*

Zeppelin was obsolete even before she was launched, with a design on a par with the British *Courageous*-class and France's sole aircraft carrier, the *Bearn*.

Dönitz meanwhile was lobbying for a stronger U-boat arm, which did not please his superior, Raeder, but eventually Plan Z was amended further to allow the construction of 300 U-boats. Early in 1939, Dönitz had a book published, *Die U-Bootswaffe*, 'The U-boat Arm', and while it did not mention the wolf pack or group tactics, it made the case that the U-boat was to be the major offensive weapon and that merchant shipping would be a primary target. It took British Naval Intelligence until 1942 to obtain a copy. While Dönitz may have seemed to be stretching the already ambitious Plan Z beyond reason, his ideas were far more realistic than those of Raeder, as the U-boats were cheaper to build, required fewer raw materials than the big ships, and also made better use of increasingly scarce manpower.

The pessimism of both Raeder and Dönitz at Germany's 'early' entry into the war was, surprising enough, shared by senior officers in the Luftwaffe. These men knew that the Luftwaffe had been created as a tactical air force, highly effective in supporting ground troops in Blitzkrieg warfare. This policy had left the Luftwaffe with a fundamental weakness, the absence of a longer-range heavy bomber, as this programme had been scrapped during the late 1930s in favour of building large numbers of twin-engined medium bombers and single-engined dive-bombers. But dive-bombers were of limited use against hardened targets or those with substantial anti-aircraft defences and well-trained gunners.

War meant that RAF bombers could reach Germany but that the Luftwaffe could not reach the UK unless bases were secured in northern France.

This was a direct parallel with the Kriegsmarine, as bases in France would ensure that U-boats and surface raiders did not have to take the long passage around the British Isles, which used scarce fuel and also exposed the naval vessels to interception by the British, as well as reducing the amount of time that could be spent on the open seas.

Germany went to war with its air force and navy ill-prepared, and everything depending on the army. Even the Germany Army, the *Heer*, at this stage, was far from impressive. It had faced no resistance in the Sudetenland or Austria, or indeed when the remains of Czechoslovakia were taken. In Poland it had overwhelming power and faced a country with a small navy, an obsolete air force and an army that, fighting defiantly and bravely like the other services, was also short of armour and artillery. The Germans had many reservists in 'Case White', the attack on Poland, and senior officers reported that their performance was disappointing. This, of course, was no doubt because the reservists could not match the superior training of the full-time professional soldiers.

The problems of the armed services and of Germany going to war too early were not overlooked. On 24 May 1939, Major General Thomas of the Wehrmacht's military-economic office drew attention to the fact that the military spending of the USA, France and the UK for 1939-40, once adjusted for differences in spending power, would outspend Germany and Italy combined by at least 2 million Reichsmarks. If military spending as a proportion of gross national income was used as a basis for comparison, the contrast was even more worrying, as Germany planned to spend 23 per cent, France 17 per cent, the UK 12 per cent, and the USA just 2 per cent. The point was that the United States could afford a war, but for the Germans the armed forces were costing more than the country could afford. Even for the British, the problem was, in the words of one commentator, 'that the country could only hope to win a long war, but could only afford a short one'.

To Thomas and many other senior officers, these statistics suggested that Hitler should be cautious and not rush into war. To Hitler and his inner circle, the figures suggested something else. Germany could not win an arms race. Time was of the essence.

For the Kriegsmarine, as a basis of comparison, Germany would have four aircraft carriers by 1944 if Plan Z went ahead, but the Royal Navy would have six new fast armoured carriers plus the brand new HMS *Ark Royal*, while France would have two new aircraft carriers. In the air, the RAF would have large numbers of the new Supermarine Spitfire fighter and heavy bombers.

It was clear that Germany had been caught in a trap. War had come too soon.

Yet the British and French were also ill-prepared for war, and assistance from the United States was for the time-being so remote as to be almost unthinkable. The loss of France would also leave the British on their own, except for aid from an empire that was far flung and with which communications were exposed to attack by submarines and surface vessels. By contrast, the Germans had relatively few convoys to defend, and at the outset these were mainly carrying Swedish ore, shipped along the Norwegian coast as the more direct route from Sweden through the Gulf of Bothnia was impassable in winter due to ice. Later, of course, there would be convoys along the coasts of Belgium and the Netherlands, and across the Mediterranean.

The Balance Of Power At Sea

Thinly spread the Royal Navy was at the outset of both world wars, but on both occasions during the last years of peace every effort had been made to concentrate sufficient strength in home waters and what might be described as 'near' home waters. For the Norwegian campaign, the Mediterranean Fleet's aircraft carrier, HMS *Glorious*, was brought home to strengthen the Home Fleet, while a ship east of Suez was transferred to the Mediterranean to replace her. The opening months of the conflict had seen the Royal Navy beset with mixed fortunes. Two aircraft carriers had been lost and one battleship, but the Germans had also lost a *Panzerschiff*, and the Norwegian campaign had seen two German light cruisers sunk and no less than ten of the Kriegsmarine's scarce destroyers.

By the beginning of July 1940, the Home Fleet had five battleships while the Germans had none; three battlecruisers against Germany's two; eleven cruisers and fifty-three destroyers. Another twenty-three destroyers were based in Liverpool, earmarked for convoy escort duties, but available to reinforce the Home Fleet if the need arose. There were thirty-five submarines. There were also smaller and lighter vessels, such as twenty-five fast minesweepers and 140 minesweeper trawlers, which would be useless in a naval engagement but could play a vital role in keeping the sea lanes and harbour entrances clear of mines.

In command of the Home Fleet was Admiral Sir Charles Forbes, who had taken up the appointment in 1938. Forbes did not suffer fools at all, let alone gladly. Summer 1940 saw a major row erupt within the Admiralty, the sponsoring government department for the Royal Navy. Unlike its counterparts for the British army, the War Office, and for the Royal Air Force, the Air Ministry, the Admiralty was an operational headquarters. It could, and often did, send orders direct not just to its subordinate commands and fleets, but even down to the commanding officers of individual ships. The First Sea Lord, Admiral Sir Dudley Pound, and many other senior admirals, wanted the mass of the Home Fleet stationed to the south, able to protect the southern reaches of the North Sea, the Straits of Dover and the English Channel. The idea was that at least thirty-six destroyers should be placed in four flotillas as part of the Nore Command, based at Chatham and which covered the areas from the Humber to Dover. The flotillas would be based on the Humber estuary, at Harwich in Essex, and in Kent at Sheerness, at the mouth of the Thames estuary, and at Dover. These destroyers would be reinforced by five cruisers, plus a number of anti-aircraft cruisers, which had been converted from First World War cruisers, and other smaller ships. His major fleet units, the battleships and battlecruisers, would be sent to Rosyth in the east of Scotland across the Firth of Forth from Edinburgh.

Forbes realised that so many smaller ships with light armour would be vulnerable, and he saw his duty as keeping the fleet intact and ready to protect the western approaches and to continue the blockade of Germany and occupied northern Europe. He wanted to keep his fleet at Scapa Flow, its wartime anchorage on the southern coast of the mainland of Orkney. Rosyth was not only further south, it was some distance upstream from the open sea and far from the Home Fleet's gunnery practice areas. There was also the fear that a successful aerial attack on the Forth Bridge would block the Forth and hinder access to Rosyth, or from Rosyth to the open sea.

Chapter Seven

Woe to the Conquered – German Occupation in The East

As the first German occupation was that of Czechoslovakia, it is perhaps logical to look at the situation in the east of Europe first, although after the Polish campaign and before the invasion of the Soviet Union, most of the countries to fall under the jackboot were in the west.

Unwelcome though German occupation may have been in the west, and clearly harsh at times, this was nothing to the view taken in the eastern territories. In some cases, there were German, or Aryan, communities, *Ostvolk*, also known as *Volksdeutsche*, who were allowed to join the German army, but usually with German officers and with language problems often experienced by these 'Eastern Germans'. These were territories seen as being part of a future 'Greater Germany'. As in the west, the overriding German view of occupation was *vae victis*, 'woe to the conquered'. There was little attempt to soften the blow of defeat. While Jews were to be moved to camps, the mass of the local population in the Slavonic territories were to be moved eastwards leaving the most fertile land to those Germans to be settled post-war. Although viewed as superior to the Jews, the Germans still regarded the Slavonic peoples as being racially inferior. They were good as slave labour, little else.

The number of ethnic Germans in the eastern territories varied, but in Czechoslovakia they accounted for around 3 million people out of a population just in excess of 14 million in 1938: almost 25 per cent, a significant proportion of the total.

Excluded from the eastern territories was Austria, which was not treated as an occupied country but as part of 'Greater Germany'. While the *Anchluss* with Austria was not welcomed by all Austrians, and many fled rather than waiting to be rounded up and imprisoned, there was a substantial measure of popular support. Hitler had been born in Austria. Austrians joined the German armed forces and many fought with distinction and held command.

Czechoslovakia

Born out of the former Austro-Hungarian Empire, in 1938 Czechoslovakia was a democratic republic. As just mentioned above, it had a substantial proportion of ethnic Germans in its 14 million population, and there were also some 700,000 Hungarians, 500,000 Ukrainians and around 60,000 Poles. The Germans were often referred to as 'Sudeten Germans' because most of them lived in the Sudetenland, which occupied the eastern border and much of the northern and southern borders. The Versailles Treaty incorporated the Sudetenland into Czechoslovakia, but it could be argued that in a different atmosphere to that prevailing at the time the territory might have been given to Germany or Austria. The country had a significant armaments and motor industry, and on mobilisation it had a well-equipped army of a million men.

The Munich Agreement of September 1938 effectively placed the government, led by President Edvard Beneš, in an extremely difficult position. If it resisted the German takeover it could not count on support from any other nation. In the months following the Munich Agreement, Czechoslovakia started to be pulled apart. The Germans moved quickly to occupy the Sudetenland, with its heavily fortified frontier with Germany, and incorporated the territory into the Third Reich. At the same time, Poland occupied the district of Teschen, on the grounds that the local population was mainly Polish. Hungary then seized parts of eastern Slovakia, leaving just Bohemia and Moravia governed by the Czechoslovak government.

Emboldened by the appeasement of the United Kingdom and France, on 15 March 1939, the German army occupied Bohemia and Moravia. Almost immediately, the German Protectorate of Bohemia and Moravia was established with Baron Konstantin von Neurath as *Reichsprotektor*. Neurath had been foreign minister from 1932 to 1938, having been retained by Hitler to maintain good relations with the democracies, and when this was no longer regarded as essential, he was replaced by von Ribbentrop. He was soon to be replaced in his new role as his rule was regarded as being too lenient, and in September 1941 Reinhard Heydrich took over, although strangely Neurath did not officially resign until August 1943, by which time Heydrich had been assassinated. At Nuremberg, Neurath was sentenced to fifteen years imprisonment, but released in 1954. He died in 1956.

Under German control, Bohemia and Moravia retained their administrative institutions, but these operated under strict regulations laid down by the Germans. The new president, Dr Emil Hacha, was allowed a small ceremonial guard, but otherwise the army and air force were disbanded.

As elsewhere, priority was given to the rounding up and transportation of the Jewish members of the population. While considerably less harsh, certainly in the early days, than elsewhere in Eastern Europe, the Germans did lean heavily on the professional and middle classes, while courting agricultural and industrial workers. One political organisation was permitted, inevitably this was a fascist organisation, the National Co-operation, or *Národni Souručenstvi*, headed by General Rudolf Gajda.

In October 1939, on the twentieth anniversary of the country's independence from the Austro-Hungarian Empire, protests began, with university students on the streets of Prague. As a result, the universities were closed and nine students executed. No doubt partly because the country was landlocked and isolated from any allied support, armed resistance took time to develop, but by early 1940 a number of scattered underground organisations came together to form the Central Leadership of Home Resistance, *Ustředni vedeni odboje domaciho*, UVOD. Using agents trained in the United Kingdom, this was the organisation that assassinated Heydrich on 27 May 1942. In revenge the Germans killed 198 male inhabitants of the village of Lidice, imprisoned 184 women in Ravensbrück concentration camp, and abducted 98 children to be brought up as Germans. Lidice was razed to the ground, and so was nearby Ležaky as further retribution.

The main work of the Czechoslovak resistance lay in the intelligence it supplied to the Allies, and in general there was little active resistance until the Prague uprising in May 1945, which was of considerable help to the Red Army as it advanced towards the Czechoslovak capital. The uprising had its roots in a number of strikes in towns throughout Bohemia and Moravia. On 5 May, the population of Prague rose up against the Germans as Marshal Konev's First Ukrainian Front approached from the east and Lieutenant General Patton's Third US Army approached from the west. Despite an appeal for help from the Czech government-in-exile in London, General Eisenhower, who had agreed with the Soviets not to advance beyond a certain point, refused to allow Patton to help. Meanwhile, Hitler's successor, Dönitz, tried to send additional divisions to help Wilhelm Frick, who had been *Reichsprotektor* since 1943, maintain order. The German garrison in Prague was without armour or artillery. On 8 May, General Vlasov's army stopped the German reinforcements, whose 1st Division deserted the Germans to join the Czechs. Vlasov's troops then cleared Prague of German forces, leaving the way open for the Soviet forces to enter. On 11 May, the Germans surrendered.

Frick had been a lawyer and was responsible for drawing up the measures used against the Jews in Germany and the occupied zone. He refused to testify at the Nuremberg war trials but was found guilty and hanged.

Poland

Germany's invasion of Poland without declaration of war on 1 September 1939 was the spark that ignited the Second World War. Many believe that Hitler thought that the invasion would give rise to strong protests from the United Kingdom and France rather than an ultimatum and then war. There were sound reasons for his believing this. Not only had the two allies accepted the annexation of the Czech Sudetenland in 1938, but they had also allowed Hitler to take the rest of Czechoslovakia earlier in 1939. The commitment given to Poland by the UK and France was viewed by Hitler as unrealistic, which it was, unless the two allies were prepared to make war with Germany, which they did, to Hitler's surprise.

For the German people, the invasion of Poland was seen simply as a readjustment of frontiers, which had been moved westwards under the terms of the Versailles Treaty. It was a largely popular move, but even so, the Germans arranged a 'border incident' with a claimed incursion by Polish troops into German territory as a pretext for the invasion. There had been a list of demands presented to the Poles earlier in the year, including demanding that the port of Danzig be transferred to Germany and a road and a rail link built between Germany and East Prussia, with these to be regarded as German territory. These demands were rejected by the Poles. On 31 March, the British prime minister, Neville Chamberlain, promised to guarantee Poland's independence and promised aid, while France had an alliance with Poland that dated from 1921. Frustrated by Polish intransigence, in late May Hitler abandoned the German-Polish Non-Aggression Pact of 1934. On 25 August, a mutual assistance pact was signed between the UK and Poland.

Poland's value was simply to provide additional living space for Germany, *Lebensraum*. The country was one of the most backward in Europe and was virtually a dictatorship. Rather than see the alliance between the UK and Poland as an obstacle to invasion, Hitler was far more concerned about the Soviet reaction. Throughout summer 1939, Hitler courted Stalin, while the UK and France did the same. The German approach bore fruit with the signing of a pact between Germany and the USSR on 23 August 1939. Officially a non-aggression pact, this was an alliance that would allow both countries to dismember Poland, dividing the country between them.

The Soviet Union invaded Poland, again without a declaration of war, on 17 September, with fighting lasting twenty days and ending on 6 October.

In 1939, Poland had a population of 35 million. The president was Ignacy Mościcki, who ruled over a government that included many military figures, including both the prime minister and the foreign minister, who headed a movement called the '*Sanacja*', or 'cleansing', which left the four main political parties in opposition, without any real voice or influence, and with the more prominent political figures either in prison or exile. As invasion became inevitable, the opposition called for a government of national unity, but this was rejected. After the invasion, on 18 September, the Polish government sought refuge in Romania, but they were interned. Amongst those seeking to escape the downfall of their country was the head of the armed forces, Marshal Edward Śmigly-Rydz, who ordered his troops to escape to neutral countries and make their way to France, where the Polish army would be rebuilt.

Poland was poor and backward, with just 100,000 lorries in the country and many miles of unsurfaced highways.

The country was not simply divided up between Germany and Russia. Certainly most of the country was either incorporated into the Reich or into Russia, in each case these were substantial border regions, but the Germans also had a zone known as the 'General Government', most of which nestled between the German and Russian zones. The Germans named the states incorporated into Germany as the *Wartheland*, the most westerly parts of Poland, amounting to 35,000 square miles with a population of 9.5 million people. The 'General Government' consisted of 37,000 square miles with a population of 12 million people and included the capital, Warsaw, as well as Cracow and Lublin. This territory was to be used as a labour colony. Cracow became the General Government's administrative centre, and was placed under the governorship of Hans Frank, a lawyer and committed Nazi. This division of the German zone into two did not mean that the population of the *Wartheland* was to be favoured, as their territory was to be 'Germanised', with all traces of Polish culture eradicated, a task given to Heimlich Himmler. Poles considered unsuitable for Germanisation were to be removed and relocated in the 'General Government' zone.

Little time was wasted in enforcing German occupation. Following closely behind the invading German troops came the SS *Einsatzgruppen* with lists of political activists, with priority given to those who had risen up against German rule in Silesia and Wielkopolska, who were given summary execution. German supporters in Bydgoszcz, in north-western Poland, attempted to support the invaders in an uprising, but this was swiftly crushed by Polish troops who also executed the leaders. In revenge, German troops who later took Bydgoszcz treated the matter as a massacre and executed thousands of Poles. In September and October, before Wehrmacht administration ended, more than 530 towns and villages were razed to the ground and well over 16,000 Poles executed by German troops and police. Much of this was done after the fighting had stopped.

Incorporating the Wartheland into Germany was justified by Hitler on the basis that prior to 1918 and the establishment of the Polish state, the area had been controlled by Prussia. Heinrich Himmler, the Reich Commissioner responsible for the restoration and consolidation of German statehood, took charge of the Wartheland. He was responsible for the expulsion of a million Poles regarded as being unsuitable for Germanisation, with their move taking place during the severe winter of 1939-40. These victims were allowed to take very little money and few possessions, and were deprived of their homes and businesses, which were taken over by ethnic Germans from the Baltic states, eastern Poland or Romania. Able-bodied men and women were separated from their families and moved to Germany as forced labour, with a total of 2 million moved between 1939 and 1944. Of the rest, large numbers died as they were moved eastwards in unheated goods wagons into the General Government area, where they were simply abandoned.

Those allowed to stay in the Wartheland were forced to register as ethnic Germans and the use of the Polish language was banned. Schools, libraries, bookshops and museums were all closed, while signs in Polish were replaced by signs in German. More than 200,000 Polish children were taken to Germany to be brought up as Germans, while many thousands of men of military age considered suitable for 'Germanisation' were conscripted into the German army. Polish monuments were destroyed, works of art looted and taken to Germany, and the playing of music by Polish composers was banned.

At first, the Germans did not exert their authority in the General Government, but this changed on the appointment of Hans Frank as governor in late October. On 27 October, the Mayor of Warsaw was arrested and executed. On 6 November, academic staff from universities and colleges in Cracow were arrested and taken to the concentration camp at Sachsenhausen, where many died. On 9 November, street round-ups occurred in Lublin.

The Poles were to be deprived of any intellectual stimulus unless they lived in the Wartheland, where they were to become Germans. In the General Government, Frank declared that 'the Polish lands are to be changed into an intellectual desert'.

This was only the beginning. German intentions were far worse than this. The plan was to exterminate the Poles as a nation. Food was kept in short supply, with the Poles in Warsaw expected to live on 669 calories daily, with Jews on just 184 calories, while at home Germans were allowed 2,613 calories. The minimum age for marriage was raised to reduce the birth rate, which was also reduced by the numbers forced into slave labour, leaving couples separated.

Not all forced labour was deported. Instead many were committed to more than thirty concentration and forced labour camps set up in Poland, usually close to factories where the inmates had to work, regardless of whether they were Christians or Jewish. Forced labour was the lot of any Pole aged between 14 years and 60 years.

As elsewhere, the main force of the cruelty and barbarity fell upon the Jews, with around 2.5 million Jews in those parts of Poland controlled by the Germans. A small number had managed to escape, fleeing east into areas that would be occupied by the Soviet Union. Property rights were limited and then abolished completely, while in January 1940, movement was restricted and in the major cities Jews were herded into ghettos, which were sealed off and guarded by police. In Warsaw, there were 500,000 people in the ghetto, kept short of food and without medicines. The populations of the ghettos were allowed to form their own civil administrations, the *Judenrate*. Needless to say, there were extremely high death rates in the ghettos. Any Jew who left the ghetto was likely to be shot, as were any Poles, and their families, attempting to help them.

The Germans had taken control of 72,800 square miles of Poland with a population of 22 million, of whom just under a million were ethnic Germans. The Russians had taken a larger area, 77,500 square miles, but a smaller population of some 13 million, which included many Ukrainians and Belorussians. The following year, the Russians occupied the Baltic States, Estonia, Latvia and Lithuania.

Soviet occupation was only slightly less severe than German, and resistance of any kind, even before the ceasefire, was punished with summary executions. The Red Army took 200,000 Polish prisoners of war, and those from the German-occupied areas were allowed to return home. The rest were kept in PoW camps and used as labour in construction projects. The officers were taken to camps, but most of them were executed in the Katyn Forest massacre.

Local militias were raised to maintain law and order, and a civil administration was formed under Soviet control with Russians taking the leading roles, laying the basis of post-war Soviet control.

In June 1941, the Germans launched Operation Barbarossa, the invasion of the Soviet Union, and advancing quickly soon had all of Poland under their control. Poland was divided between the Reich, with 30.8 per cent, the General Government, 38.8 per cent, and the Reichskommissariats, 30.3 per cent, with the Baltic States and Ukraine incorporated into the latter. At the same time, German policy changed, with the General Government being transferred to the Reich and 80 per cent of its Polish inhabitants expelled. This was followed in November 1942 by the colonisation of the Zamość region with the settlement of ethnic Germans.

These massive shifts of population, always under German military control and direction, must have placed a considerable strain on German military resources at a time when heavy fighting was continuing inside the Soviet Union.

Much of the country's pre-war ethnic Polish population died either in the concentration camps or death camps, or when the ghettos were liquidated as the Russians approached from the east.

Yugoslavia

Created in 1918 on the collapse of the Austro-Hungarian Empire, and initially known as the Kingdom of the Serbs, Croats and Slovenes, in 1941 Yugoslavia had a population of around 16 million, and an area of 95,550 square miles. Given the ethnic composition of the country, it was far from united, and was dominated by the largest ethnic group, the Orthodox Serbs, which led to resentment by the other groups, including many Roman Catholic Croats and a substantial Muslim community. For just over ten years, between 1918 and 1929, the country was in theory a democracy, but it then became effectively an absolute monarchy, initially under King Alexander, who was assassinated in 1934. After King Alexander's death, the country was run by Prince Paul as Prince Regent for King Peter II, who was a minor and so underage for the throne.

On the outbreak of war in 1939, Yugoslavia declared itself neutral, but came under pressure from both sides in the war. The Serbs were strongly in favour of supporting the Allies, and they dominated the army's officer corps, while Prince Paul was also a supporter of the Allies. Nevertheless, the other groups were more inclined to favour the Axis powers, a situation made worse by their sense of alienation from the state. The Croats had been granted home rule in August 1939, but many saw Italy as a natural ally. In addition, there were large numbers of people with ties to Germany, Albania and Hungary, who constituted a potential fifth column that could undermine the state.

Economically, Yugoslavia was heavily dependent on Germany, which accounted for much of its foreign trade and also was amongst the main owners of its mines producing non-ferrous metals vital to the war effort. Yugoslavia became heavily dependent on German purchases of its agricultural produce, produced inefficiently by many small peasant farmers. The country's neighbours, Bulgaria, Hungary and

Romania, all gradually drifted towards allying themselves with Germany, and all had claims on Yugoslav territory. The UK was in no position to assist the country with trade or arms supplies, and while Prince Paul sought support from the Soviet Union, Stalin did not regard it as important enough to risk the non-aggression pact with Germany.

Matters came to a head when the Italian invasion of Greece in October 1940 was stalled, forcing Germany to come to Italy's aid. The Germans needed Yugoslavia to help ensure access to Greece via Bulgaria and to ensure that the British could not mount a pincer movement against German forces in Greece. Hitler began to press Prince Paul to join the Axis, signing the Tripartite Pact, but Prince Paul tried to delay matters hoping that the anticipated outbreak of hostilities between Germany and the Soviet Union would ease the pressure on him. Nevertheless, Hitler continued to demand that Yugoslavia join the Axis, and on 25 March 1941 Paul's ministers travelled to Vienna to sign the Tripartite Pact. As an incentive, a secret protocol to the pact guaranteed Yugoslavia the Greek city of Salonika when the war ended. News of the signing provoked anti-Axis demonstrations in both Serbia and Slovenia, followed by Serbian nationalists seizing power, with army and air force aid, in Belgrade early on 27 March. The Regency was declared ended and King Peter proclaimed to have come of age. Serbs celebrated the prospect of a war as allies of the Greeks and the United Kingdom, although many Communists demanded an alliance with the Soviet Union.

Opposing the popular demonstrations were the Croats, who supported the alliance with the Axis.

Another opponent was Adolf Hitler, who viewed the *coup d'état* as a personal insult. He issued Führer Directive No.25, which decreed that Yugoslavia be obliterated with Italian and Hungarian support. The invasion on 6 April 1941 took place at the same time as Germany's invasion of Greece. The invasion was spearheaded by a Luftwaffe bombing raid on Belgrade, supposedly an 'open city', in which around 5,000 people were killed, while attacks were also made on the main air force airfields. There was little attempt at defence, with the new king, his government and the military high command fleeing into exile. German forces from Bulgaria invaded Macedonia, and stopped the Yugoslav force retreating into Greece. Belgrade fell to German troops on 13 April, and on 17 April an unconditional surrender was signed.

Zagreb had already been taken by this time, and as German troops entered the city on 10 April, the Croat Fascists, under Ante Pavelić, were allowed to declare Croatia independent, which also included Bosnia and Herzegovina. Italy and

Hungary did not invade until 11 April. The following day, Hitler drew up plans for the country's dismemberment, with an independent Croatian state and other areas assigned to Germany's allies. Slovenia was divided between Germany and Italy, in each case being annexed with the territories being subjected to Germanisation and Italianisation. Dalmati on the Adriatic coast also passed to Italy. Banat, in the north-east and bordering Romania, was occupied by the Germans, while Serbia came under German administration. Hungary annexed Bačka, which adjoined its border. Macedonia was mainly annexed by Bulgaria, but the western area was annexed by Albania. Montenegro was placed under Italian administration, except for the area around the Gulf of Kotor, which was annexed by Italy.

As elsewhere, a government-in-exile was established in London, in this case under King Peter who arrived there with his ministers in June 1941. No doubt to their surprise, they were treated as heroes by their British hosts.

The Germans already had plans for the economic exploitation of Yugoslavia, not just for raw materials but for agricultural produce and also to maintain the lines of communication for their forces in Greece. The need was so great that they even demanded control over raw material output in zones occupied or annexed by other members of the alliance. Even Croatian independence was a sham, as the Germans demanded and got whatever they required. Croatia also had to meet the costs of German and Italian occupying forces. In Serbia, a similar regime applied, although the value of supplies was offset against the costs of occupation. The Croatian regime was almost Nazi Germany in miniature, with Serbs subjected to ethnic cleansing and genocide, while Jews, gypsies and communists were also targeted, to produce a racially and ideologically pure Roman Catholic Croatia.

Yugoslavs were rounded up and executed in reprisals for the major guerrilla campaign staged by resistance groups, many of which were Communist-inspired, while several hundred thousand were sent to Germany for forced labour, and in those areas annexed, many volunteered for service in Germany or in the German army. Forced labour was also used in mines operating in Yugoslavia.

While Germany profited from its annexed and occupied zones, Italy had got the worst of the bargain, finding its zones were a liability and some even had to be supplied with food from Italy.

The Bulgarian and Hungarian annexed zones were integrated with their new masters by expelling all post-1918 Serbian settlers and by taking over education and administration. This caused much resentment, especially in Macedonia, which had been annexed to Bulgaria.

In Serbia, General Milan Nedić was made the figurehead of a local government intended to help quell any Serbian opposition.

Apart from the activities of a highly-effective resistance, the Germans soon found rivalries breaking out amongst their allies, none of which was satisfied with their territorial awards, while the semi-self-governing areas were also fractious.

In short, Yugoslavia soon became a massive liability for Germany and a further strain on Germany's armed forces.

Greece

From 1453 until 1829, Greece was occupied by its neighbour, Turkey, and was effectively part of the Ottoman Empire. Shortly after gaining independence, it became a monarchy, but the monarchy was overthrown in 1924 and the country became a republic until the monarchy was restored in 1935. The country's independence was guaranteed by the UK, France and Russia, but the UK rejected the offer in 1938 of a formal alliance by the then dictator, the prime minister General Ioannis Metaxas. Nevertheless, after the Italian invasion of neighbouring Albania, in April 1938, both the UK and France undertook to guarantee the territorial integrity of Greece and Albania provided they resisted an attack. Although Greece was steadily falling under German influence, not only economically but also politically as Metaxas adopted many fascist policies, Greece continued to look towards the UK, largely due to the pro-British stance of the sovereign, King George II. The German invasion started on 6 April 1941 after an Italian invasion the previous October stalled. British forces were redeployed to Greece from North Africa, weakening the defence of Egypt and, of course, the Suez Canal. Confusion over where the Greeks and the British expeditionary force would make a stand against the Germans meant that resistance to the invasion was chaotic and failed to hold the Germans back, so that British forces had to be evacuated from the country to Crete. King George II left the country for Crete with his government on 23 April, and afterwards sought exile in London.

Greece had a small population of 7,345,000 in 1940, of whom around 70,000 were Jewish, and an area of 50,534 square miles. Sparsely populated and much of it mountainous, the country's value to Germany was for food and raw materials. Despite the country being an overall exporter of food, the immediate start of food requisitioning by the Germans soon led to shortages. As elsewhere, the Germans expected the Greeks to repay the full cost of occupation and inflation was soon on the rise, to levels seen in the last days of the *Weimar* government in Germany. As an example, an *oka*, a local measurement that equated to 1.3 kilos or almost 3 lb, of bread, was just 10 drachmas at the time of the Italian invasion in 1940, but by the time of liberation by the British just four years later, this had risen to 34 million drachmas.

The commander of the Western Macedonian Army, General Georgios Tsolakoglou, took the initiative and negotiated an armistice without the approval of the sovereign or the government. He was rewarded for his initiative by becoming prime minister of a government that collaborated with the Germans. Despite the Germans having led the invasion and wielding considerable power, the occupation was led by the Italians, although Western Thrace and part of Macedonia were occupied by Bulgaria. The premiership of Tsolakoglou was brief and he was succeeded in turn by Konstantinos Logothepoulos and by Ioannis Rallis.

As a result of German food requisitions and inflation, the severe winter of 1941/2 saw around 100,000 people die. Despite the war, the British government, under pressure from the Greek government-in-exile and the United States, allowed the International Red Cross to send supplies to alleviate the distress of the Greeks. German and Bulgarian involvement in the country increased after the Italians surrendered in September 1943, giving the increasingly hard-pressed German army yet another drain on its resources.

Armed resistance had begun as early as summer 1941, with much of it backed by the Greek Communist Party. Savage reprisals were inflicted on the civilian population. The Communist involvement grew after the launch of Operation Barbarossa, the German invasion of the Soviet Union, itself delayed by the need for the Germans to become involved with the invasion of Greece.

As the war swung in favour of the Allies, Churchill and Stalin negotiated a deal that would allow the Soviet Union to occupy Romania, and then Bulgaria, leaving the UK with Greece. This was a deal done under some pressure as Churchill was alarmed that much of Eastern Europe would pass into Soviet control as the Red Army forced the Germans into withdrawal, and Churchill saw control of Greece as being important to safeguard Britain's communications with the Empire through the Mediterranean and the Suez Canal. As civil war broke out in Greece in late 1944, the UK was forced to send troops to prevent a Communist takeover of the country.

Such was Churchill's concern for Greece that on Christmas Eve 1944 he flew with his Foreign Secretary, Anthony Eden, to Athens hoping to reconcile the conflicting parties in the civil war. His visit was unsuccessful, but British armed forces managed to prevent the Communists from seizing control of the country.

Hungary

On the outbreak of the Second World War, Hungary was in the unique position of sharing the same values and resentments as Nazi Germany. In both cases, there was a fear of Bolshevism, a distrust and dislike of Jews, and resentment over the loss of more than two-thirds of its territory in the Trianon settlement that followed the end of the First World War, which also left Magyar communities isolated from their home country. Germany had experienced a Soviet uprising in Munich; Hungary had a brief experience of being a Soviet Republic in 1919. Hungary was to be an ally of Germany and Italy, but in so many ways a reluctant ally, and was to be occupied by German forces in March 1944, at a time when German forces were under pressure in the east and being pushed backwards.

After Hitler's rise to power in 1933, successive Hungarian governments made clear that their sympathies lay with the Germans. Following the Munich Agreement of 1938, Germany presented Hungary with southern Slovakia. When Germany completed its occupation of Czechoslovakia the following year, Hungary was allowed to reoccupy the lost territory of Carpathian Ruthenia, while Romania was pressured by the Germans to return northern Transylvania in 1940. This last transfer of territory convinced Hungarian leaders that if they did not cooperate with Germany, Romania might have the area returned, and so joined the Tripartite Pact in November 1940. Further rewards came Hungary's way as a result, with Germany invading Yugoslavia across Hungarian territory and afterwards Magyar-speaking areas were transferred to Hungary.

As the Second World War approached, Hungary was governed by what almost amounted to a coalition of conservatives and the radical right, the most prominent of which was the Arrow Cross party led by Ferenc Szálasi. The Arrow Cross party forced the government to enforce land distribution, seek closer ties with Germany, and to introduce anti-Semitic measures that limited the property rights of Jews. The army's officers were overwhelmingly pro-German. The conservatives, led by Admiral Horthy, believed that war with the western allies made war with the Soviet Union more difficult and would have preferred Hitler not to engage with the United Kingdom and United States.

Despite the growing closeness of Germany and Hungary, Hungary stayed out of the war for as long as possible. Operation Barbarossa, the invasion of the Soviet Union, changed this. The view of many Hungarians was that the source of Bolshevism must be cleared, while there was also an ethnic angle as Hungarians blamed the Slavs for the loss of the country's European empire. The liberation from Austro-Hungarian rule had in fact been one of Tsarist Russia's aims in the First World War. It also seemed at the time that a German victory was certain. Nevertheless, the official reason for Hungary declaring war on 27 June 1941 was the bombing of the northern town of Kassa by Soviet aircraft. Many believe that the raid was carried out by the Luftwaffe, using aircraft given Soviet red star markings. Certainly it seems strange that the Soviet armed forces, with all their resources committed to fighting the invading Germans, would seek to attack Hungary and draw the country into war. On the other hand, the Germans would have wanted Hungary as an ally, and not just because of the extra forces it would provide but also to ensure that Romanian oil could be transported across Hungary. Oil had been found on Hungarian territory in 1938. Nevertheless, by the end of 1941, Hungary found itself at war with the United Kingdom and the United States.

The Arrow Cross party supported the alliance with Germany and the government, led by Miklos Kallay, had their support in declaring war with the Soviet Union.

Hungary had been a major supplier of food and raw materials for Germany, and had an armaments industry, producing mainly ammunition before entering the war, after which it also started to produce German aircraft, including Messerschmitt Bf109s and Me210s.

Hungary's armed forces were weak and ill-equipped. The army had 216,000 infantrymen, as well as two cavalry brigades and two motorised brigades. The infantry relied on poor quality and unreliable rifles, and there were no anti-aircraft weapons. The armoured brigades had Italian Ansaldo light tanks with fixed turrets, which were replaced by Hungary's own Toldi and Turan tanks, which did not compare with the armour being used elsewhere. A so-called Mobile Corps sent to invade the Soviet Union included six battalions using bicycles. The army had just a third of the motor transport it needed. The air force had 302 aircraft, but just 189 were operational in 1941, and all were obsolete.

Allied with Germany, Hungary sent its army and air force to the Soviet Union, and then planned a Home Army of 220,000 men due to fear of a Romanian invasion. The Germans, who were replacing the so-called Hungarian First Army's equipment losses on the Soviet Front, refused to equip the Home Army. When, as the tide turned and Soviet troops advanced towards Hungary, the Home Army did little to stop them.

In the meantime, after the massive defeat of the Axis forces at Stalingrad, Hungarian forces started to become less active. They had proven inferior to those of the Soviet Union and morale was adversely affected. Under German pressure, a Second Army was raised in 1942, included a Jewish forced-labour corps, and totalled some 250,000 men, of whom more than a tenth lost their lives as they advanced into the Ukraine. The Second Army was destroyed at Stalingrad. The defeat was down in no small part to a lack of heavy anti-tank artillery, which the Germans had only supplied belatedly.

In March 1944 German forces occupied Hungary. The main reason was to resist the advancing Soviet forces and retain access to Romanian oil production, as well as that of Hungary itself, which had only started production in 1938. Exports to Germany rose rapidly, growing from 125,500 tons in 1942 to more than 203,000 tons the following year. Another factor was that Miklos Kallay had put out feelers to the Allied powers to allow Hungary to withdraw from the war, something which Hitler was made aware of by pro-German figures in the Hungarian government.

Under German occupation, a puppet government was formed under General Döme Sztojay, who was effectively controlled by a German plenipotentiary. As elsewhere, the Hungarians had to meet the costs of occupation, but the economy was also hit by poor weather and a poor harvest. The new government suppressed anti-Nazi parties and deportation of the Jews started, with 400,000 deported between March and July 1944. Romania's switch to the Allies and an awareness of the fate of the deportees finally forced Horthy to make a stand, stopping the deportations. A new government was established under General Geza Lakatos at the end of August. It was at this stage that Horthy finally realised that negotiations for an armistice would have to be negotiated with the Soviet Union, into whose sphere of influence Hungary had been condemned by the Allies.

A preliminary armistice was signed on 11 October and announced by Horthy in a radio broadcast on 15 October, which led to a Nazi-led coup which removed Horthy and a new government was appointed under Ferenc Szalasi of the Arrow Cross. By this time, the advancing Soviet forces were closing in, having crossed the Carpathians and reached the Hungarian Plain. Surprisingly, Budapest did not fall until February 1945. By April, Hungary had lost forty per cent of its national wealth in the form of infrastructure, housing, and agricultural output.

Chapter Eight

Woe to the Conquered – German Occupation in The West

Occupation by an enemy state has always been unwelcome. There is no doubt that occupation by the Germans, the Japanese or the Russians was severe at best, and brutal at times. These powers differed in their style of occupation. The Russians looked for sympathisers, which meant Communists, amongst the occupied peoples. The Japanese didn't worry too much about this. Uniquely, the Germans were intent on what would today be described as 'ethnic cleansing'. Yes, they did look for sympathisers, but the extent of this varied widely depending on the territory, or, more correctly, the ethnic grouping of the peoples of the occupied territory.

There were certain elements of occupation that were common to all of the occupied territories, at least in the west, where some semblance of civilised existence was allowed. Adults once they left their homes were expected to carry an array of identification documents. Prominent amongst these was an identity card with the holder's name, date and place of birth, parentage, and marital state; but the Germans also wanted to be able to check a work permit, which gave the employer's name and address; a ration card; a tobacco card, even if the individual was a non-smoker; males had to have a demobilisation card stating which unit had discharged them; males also had to have a medical certificate stating the reasons why the holder should not be deported for forced labour, although this was something that only became widespread in late 1942. Those living near the coast or a frontier also had to have a permit allowing them to be in the area.

Nazi hatred of the Jews is well known, and many realise that they also hated the Romany people, or gypsies, as well as homosexuals and people with disabilities. Not being liked by the Nazis, let alone being hated, was nothing short of a death sentence, although if such people were fit enough, the Germans would try to exact forced labour from their victims first, often through working for the Organisation Todt, which handled construction projects throughout the occupied territories.

There was nothing short of a pecking order in the way the Germans viewed foreigners under the Nazi regime. The regime regarded Slavs as subhuman, or

Untermenschen, fit only to be slaves. This accounted for the brutal manner in which Russian prisoners of war were treated, and the situation was not much better for those in other smaller Slavonic states. By contrast, the Germans saw the Scandinavian peoples as being not too unlike themselves, and German oppression only began to bite harshly with the experience of resistance in Norway. This is not to say that the Norwegians and Danes were treated gently, as any sign of opposition, even written or verbal, was dealt with by the secret police, the Gestapo, who must have been the most high-profile and visible secret police of all time.

In a number of territories the Germans sought to recruit personnel for their security services. There were Russian fascists, as well as *Osttruppen*, Russian troops who had volunteered to escape the harsh prisoner-of-war camps, and in Poland former soldiers had been forcibly conscripted. Generally those from the occupied territories, even if sympathetic to the German cause, were treated as second class.

There had been in effect an earlier German Diaspora, and the many ethnic Germans had provided an excuse for the occupation first of the Czech Sudetenland and then the rest of Czechoslovakia. These people were encouraged to volunteer to join the German armies and were known as the *Volksdeutsche*, but so *Deutsch* were many of these *Volk* that many did not speak German. The numbers of these different groups were so significant to the German war effort that they accounted for some twenty per cent of the defenders of the Normandy beaches.

There were also volunteers from Luxembourg, and the French territories of Alsace and Lorraine, whose history was one of being part of France or of Germany, depending on who had won the last war.

In occupied France, there was both resistance and there were collaborators. After the armistice in June 1940, many senior military figures in the Vichy regime wanted to continue the war as allies of Germany, but this was rejected. The French held true to their promise not to allow the French navy, the *Marine Nationale*, to be taken over by the Germans, although the British refusal to believe this had led to bombardment and bloodshed at Oran and Mers-el Kebir, and later at Dakar, which had resulted in outrage and much ill-feeling amongst many French people. The Germans had shown little interest in acquiring French ships, although they had shown much interest in gaining captured armour, artillery and motor vehicles from the armies they had defeated. This could have been because of a shortage of manpower and fuel, while the French ships had different calibre guns from those used by the Kriegsmarine. It was not until the invasion of Vichy France in late 1942 that an attempt was made to capture French warships at Toulon, which was foiled by the French scuttling many of them while others escaped to join the Free French or seek refuge in neutral Spain.

It can be fairly said that the only occupied territory treated as an equal was that of Austria, where Hitler had been born and which had always had close links with Germany, so much so that the victorious allies had to intervene after the First World War to prevent the country becoming *Deutscheösterreich*.

The Germans also adopted a superior attitude towards their allies. The Italians, for example, had disappointed by not joining the war until after French surrender on 10 June 1940, gaining the title of the 'harvest hands', meaning that they were only there to reap the benefit of German achievements.

Hitler had professed his admiration of the British Empire. Further back, at the outbreak of the First World War, many Germans had been shocked to find their country at war with the United Kingdom as they felt that they were 'at war with a cousin' as one German put it. Times had changed, however, and many Nazis regarded the British working class as being considerably inferior in health, physique and education to their German counterparts, and as we will see later, a booklet, *German Invasion Plans for the British Isles 1940*, also described the Welsh in terms that were unflattering: 'Unlike the bright English, they are dark and small in stature.'

Not only did occupation vary in severity, so too did resistance. Resistance was strong in France, Norway and Yugoslavia, and varied for a number of reasons. Resistance needed access to arms and explosives, terrain which offered good cover, and a population willing to take risks to support it. There was something else as well: there needed to be a political philosophy that was opposed to Fascism. Despite many similarities between Fascism and Communism, this was the divide that provided the strongest resistance. Where Communism was strongest, resistance was strongest.

Generally, government structures were left in place and expected to continue functioning. Vichy France was even allowed an army of 100,000 personnel. Policing continued, although subservient to the rules and regulations introduced by the Germans, and expected to provide support for the Gestapo.

We will look at the experience of those western territories occupied by the Germans, in order of occupation.

Denmark

Denmark was probably the easiest of all the German invasions apart from Austria. A small country with a population of 3.85 million and poor defences, the

Germans basically just walked across the frontier. The Danes had had a policy of neutrality since 1815 and Scandinavian unity failed during the 1930s. Alone amongst the Scandinavian countries, Denmark had accepted Germany's offer of a non-aggression pact in spring 1939. The country had already fallen under German influence following Hitler's rise to power, but continued to trade with other countries until the German occupation on 9 April 1940. At the time of the German occupation, the army consisted of just 14,000 personnel, and of these, more than half, 8,000, had been conscripted during the previous two months. The Royal Danish Navy had two coastal defence vessels, one dating from 1906 and the other from 1918. Air power was split between these two services with a total of fifty aircraft, mainly obsolete.

Reports of German intentions were not believed, largely because they were contradictory. It was not until 8 April that any attempt was made to prepare the border defences, and so the Germans entered the country at 0415 hours the following morning without any resistance apart from in North Schleswig, which only lasted for a few hours. The navy made no attempt at all, and a German troopship entered the harbour at Copenhagen without any resistance.

At 0600, the government accepted the German occupation 'under protest'. The monarch was allowed to retain the throne throughout the occupation, and until late August 1943, the government maintained a pretence of neutrality to prevent German interference. The armed forces remained, but their activities were much reduced. A coalition government was established and despite fears that Fascist political groups would attempt to seize power, the coalition survived with strong public support. Nevertheless, the 'neutral government' could not prevent the introduction of censorship and a complete ban on political activity.

Denmark was seen mainly as a stepping stone to Norway, and occupation eased German communications with Norway.

Most of the Danish merchant vessels that were outside territorial waters at the time of the German invasion transferred of their masters' own accord to the British merchant fleet, giving it another 230 ships and around 6,000 seamen, but in the Battle of the Atlantic and the Arctic convoys, 1,500 Danish seamen were killed and 60 per cent of the fleet was lost. Two British minesweepers were manned by Danish personnel, and provided the nucleus of a post-war Royal Danish Navy.

Henrik Kauffmann, the Danish ambassador to the United States, declared himself in charge of Danish territory outside German control, and in April 1941 signed a treaty allowing the United States to assume control of Greenland, while the United Kingdom took control of the Faeroes in April 1940 and Iceland in

May, although later the United States took over the occupation of Iceland, which declared independence in 1944.

After the occupation started, all of Denmark's agricultural exports were to Germany, supplying ten per cent of that country's meat, mainly pork and bacon, as well as butter and eggs.

In return the Germans had promised no interference, but before long started to demand the removal from office of difficult officials and politicians, and pressed for more active Danish support, leading the government to urge around 100,000 Danish workers to volunteer to work in Germany rather than risk conscription. After the start of Operation Barbarossa, the invasion of the Soviet Union, in June 1941, the Danes were forced to ban the Communist Party and create a Danish Free Corps to fight alongside the Germans on the Eastern Front. Despite this, the government managed to get the Germans to agree that Denmark would not be directly involved in the war between Germany and the USSR.

Hitler replaced the initial Nazi officials and German military commanders in 1942 with a strict Nazi, Werner Best, and an army officer, Lieutenant General Hermann Hanneken, who was another staunch supporter of Hitler, with orders to rule 'with an iron hand', although they stopped short of taking absolute control. The objective was to ensure that the Danes remained compliant and continued to export much needed food supplies to Germany. Despite the ban on political activity, Best allowed a general election to be held, in which there was a record turnout of 89.5 per cent of the electorate, with 94 per cent voting for the governing coalition parties.

As the tide turned for the Germans in the East, the Danish mood also changed, becoming more militant and resistant, with encouragement from the BBC in London and aided by the Special Operations Executive, SOE. The Germans demanded that the Danish government declare a state of emergency, which it refused to do, and on 29 August 1943 the Germans dismissed the government and took over the country's administration, as well as arresting influential citizens. Danish military bases were attacked prior to being taken over by the Germans, but there was resistance and ships were scuttled, while many naval personnel escaped to Sweden.

What had started as a peaceful occupation became increasingly brutal, leading to a general strike in Copenhagen in June 1944. A Freedom Council had been organised in September 1943, supported by the SOE, but strongly influenced by Communists. The Freedom Council initiated an underground press, and by 1944 was publishing no less than 254 newspapers producing a combined total of 11 million copies a year. Local resistance groups sabotaged railway lines in Jutland, while also sending the first details of the V-1 flying bomb to London after one had crash-landed on the island of Bornholm during test flying.

As the German grip on Denmark tightened, attention finally turned to the country's Jewish population and these started to be rounded up on 1 October 1943. Before this, the King and the Prime Minister had agreed that deportation of the Jews would be a 'red line' in the relationship with the Germans. But by this time the Germans were firmly in control. Fortunately, Werner Best's shipping attaché, G.F. von Duckwitz, was anti-Nazi and he tipped off the Freedom Council that arrests and deportations were planned, giving the Council time to organise the escape of some 5,500 Jews to Sweden in just one night. Of 472 Jews who were caught by the Germans and deported to Theresienstadt, 52 died. The Germans also started to attack the Danish resistance movement, arresting many of its leaders, but highly accurate bombing by the RAF destroyed the Gestapo headquarters in Copenhagen and destroyed records as well as enabling many resistance members to escape custody. In September 1944, the Germans disbanded the Danish police service and arrested 2,000 of its personnel.

After the German surrender on 4 May 1945, the Danish resistance took control of the country the following day, but the German commander on the island of Bornholm refused to surrender until the island was bombed by Russian aircraft, killing a number of civilians. The remaining Germans surrendered when Soviet warships arrived at Bornholm on 9 May, and Soviet troops remained there until the following April.

Post-war, 34,000 collaborators were identified, arrested and punished.

Norway

As with so many elsewhere, the Norwegians expected the Second World War to follow the same pattern as the First World War when the country was neutral. Heavily dependent on foreign trade and with one of the world's largest merchant fleets, neutrality was not without problems, but the country had a population of just three million and small armed forces. There was a belief that the United Kingdom would protect the country, and the Royal Navy would keep its shipping lanes open, but this did not stop the Norwegian government from protesting over the *Altmark* incident when the British destroyer HMS *Cossack* intercepted the Panzerschiff *Graf Spee*'s supply ship to free British merchant seamen imprisoned aboard.

For the Germans, invading Norway was far more challenging than Czechoslovakia, Poland or Denmark. It had to be an amphibious operation, and the country had a difficult mountainous terrain, with few good airfields. Yet Norway was important to Germany's war effort in several ways. One of the most important was to protect the passage of Swedish iron ore as the Gulf of Bothnia froze in winter, meaning that the ore had to be transported by railway to Norway for onward coastal shipment. The other was that Hitler, even at this early stage in the war, was planning to invade the Soviet Union, and the occupation of Norway would hamper any attempt by the Allies to send supplies to northern Russia. Of course, at this time, Germany and the Soviet Union were allies, and the United Kingdom was an enemy of both, while the United States was still, officially, neutral.

The Germans regarded the Norwegians as a related folk that could be persuaded to become part of the 'Greater Germany'. There was even a Norwegian Nazi Party led by Vidkun Quisling. The party was far from popular as in elections it never gained more than three per cent of the vote. Nevertheless, the Germans were prepared to let Quisling and his party play a role in government, albeit under the control of the *Reichskommissariat*.

Quisling could be said to have overplayed his hand, showing ill-judgement on the day of the invasion, 9 April, by attempting a *coup d'état*, calling for a government of national unity in opposition to the elected Norwegian government. All this did was strengthen national resolve, as the Norwegians were rapidly creating resistance to the German invasion boosted by the landing of British and French troops. King Haakon VII refused to abdicate and remained in the country while fighting continued, not leaving for exile in the United Kingdom until the fighting ended with a British and French withdrawal on 7 June, then becoming a figurehead for Norwegian resistance while a government-in-exile was created in London.

On 15 April, a non-political administrative council was established under the *Reichskommissar* Josef Terboven, who spent that first summer trying to suspend the exiled king and the government while turning the administrative council into a government of occupation and collaboration. Over the period of occupation attempts to use as many as possible of Quisling's party as ministers and local government leaders were hampered by the shortage of numbers and their lack of experience. While many national and local government officials resigned, others felt that the best way forward was to remain in post and attempt to soften the impact of German rule rather than see Germans replace them. It was not until 1 February 1942 that Quisling was given a prominent role, when he was installed as Minister President, in an attempt to show Norway as having self-government, but Quisling's attempts to promote the German occupation as a New Order, initially through changes to the school curriculum, not only resulted in letters of protest from the parents but also the refusal of the majority of school teachers to cooperate. The result was that Quisling was forced to operate under tight control from the Reichskommissar, with the commander of German forces in Norway maintaining order.

Given the small population, the gulf between the Norwegians and the Germans can be measured by the fact that around 40,000 Norwegians were imprisoned or sent to concentration camps, where around 2,000 died, including 700 Jews. Another 500 Norwegians were killed while fighting with the resistance or executed for their resistance activities.

The Germans were quick to acquire any useful assets that fell into their hands. On paper, Norway's great contribution would have been the fourth largest merchant navy in the world, with mostly modern ships, but 85 per cent of them evaded capture, in part because many were away from Norwegian waters, often in the so-called 'cross trades', meaning trades between countries other than their home country. The ships the Germans did take were mainly small and designed for the coastal trades. Incredibly for such a small country, Norway provided around twenty per cent of the world's tanker tonnage. The ships that did not fall into German hands, about 1,000, were requisitioned by the Norwegian government-in-exile for service with the Allies.

Despite Nazi ideology seeing the Norwegians as virtually cousins, from the start the relationship was uneasy. The Norwegians had been in a union with Sweden until 1905, when the link was broken, and they were keen to maintain their independence. The problem was that the country depended on imports for most agricultural foodstuffs and, unable to have its ships moving freely, became dependent on Germany for its supplies, including fuel.

The Germans had originally planned to exploit Norway's natural assets in building the economy of a 'Greater Germany', utilising the country's mineral resources, expanding hydro-electric power and aluminium production, but from 1942 onwards, as the tide of war turned, the priority was to meet Germany's short-term needs. The cost of occupation for Germany was high with a large occupation force approximating to one German soldier for every ten Norwegians. As elsewhere, most consumer goods were severely rationed, and the standard of living plummeted. A third of the country's income was taken to support the costs of occupation.

Resistance in Norway started almost as soon as the British and French forces left, with a number of Norwegians joining them to continue the war. Initially the groups were widely scattered and mostly unarmed and it was not until spring 1941 that links were established with the SOE in London. What amounted to a headquarters emerged in Oslo, and in October the Norwegian government-in-exile recognised the resistance as being the fourth arm of the country's armed forces. The following year, 1942, SOE started to provide arms and instructors, and this was helped by what became known as the 'Shetland Bus', a clandestine operation formed by SOE, the Admiralty Naval Intelligence Division and the Norwegian government-in-exile's Military Intelligence Division. This initially used Norwegian fishing boats to maintain supplies for the Norwegian resistance, but towards the end of the war these were replaced by three ex-USN submarine chasers. As the name implies, it operated from Shetland, the most northerly island grouping in the United Kingdom, and it was most active during the winter months when the nights were longest. Civilians under risk of being detained by the Germans were also evacuated by the 'Shetland Bus'.

The Norwegian resistance suffered badly from penetration by German agents, and it became clear that the best use of the organisation would be to hamper the Germans when the time came for liberation. By this time the resistance had become known officially as *Milorg*, and by the time of German surrender had some 40,000 personnel. It provided reliable intelligence for the Allies, and aided, but did not take the lead, in the successful sabotage of the heavy water plant at Rjukan, Operation Freshman, which was carried out by Norwegian special forces landed from the UK after an earlier attempt by British special forces, landed by glider, failed and the personnel involved were executed.

In 1941, the Germans confiscated all radio receivers, and the resistance responded by providing newspapers and newsletters, with more than 300 different titles being produced overall, but many of these were not published for long as those who produced and distributed them were often quickly identified and arrested.

Liberation came with the advance of Soviet troops through Finnmark in late 1944. As they retreated, the Germans applied a scorched earth policy, destroying infrastructure and industrial assets, as well as agricultural holdings and food and fuel stores as they withdrew. On German surrender, Norway had lost a fifth of its pre-war capital stock.

Complete liberation did not come until German surrender, although Norwegian troops entered the north of the country from the UK and Sweden before this. On 8 May 1945, the German forces holding the southern part of the country surrendered, with the Norwegian government returning on 31 May and King Haakon VII on 7 June.

Belgium

As in the First World War, Belgium was seen as the route into France. Belgium fully expected that if war started, the country would be invaded, but there was no attempt at liaison or joint exercises with the United Kingdom and France. Belgium believed in neutrality, and after the treaties of Versailles and St Germaine had redrawn many of Europe's borders, a series of military alliances had been agreed with the major western powers which were thought to ensure protection from future aggression. In 1935 and 1936 these treaties were repudiated by the Socialist-Catholic-Liberal coalition government with the support of the sovereign, King Leopold III, and neutrality was combined with a policy of national defence, in an attempt to unite the Belgians, who were divided between the Flemish-speaking north and the French-speaking south or Walloon area. The capital, Brussels, was also Francophone, but this contributed to tensions between the two communities and pre-war a Flemish Nationalist Movement, the *Vlaamsch Nationaal Verbond*, VNV, had agitated for greater powers.

Belgium had a population in 1939 of around 8.2 million people, which did not provide much scope for strong armed forces, especially since the country had a substantial colonial commitment in the Belgian Congo. Mobilisation started early, on 25 August 1939, and continued into 1940, so that by May 1940 the army had 600,000 personnel, with 18 infantry divisions, 2 divisions of mountain troops who were partly mechanised, and 2 cavalry divisions. There were considerable weaknesses in this force, with just ten tanks, and no anti-aircraft artillery at all.

In the air, the situation was no better. Out of a total of 250 aircraft, there were only 50 that could be regarded as modern. There were just 90 fighters and 12 bombers, compared to which the 120 reconnaissance aircraft appeared excessive. At sea, a handful of fishery protection and patrol craft sufficed.

The winter of 1939-40 had seen limited discussions with the commanders of the British and French forces, but nothing more. This inaction was surprising as there had been warnings of invasion in late 1939 and again in January 1940, including captured documents. Even before this there must have been an indication that Germany might invade as once war had broken out in September 1939, King Leopold III was joined by Queen Wilhelmina of the Netherlands in appealing to the governments of France, the UK and Germany to make peace.

The forward line of defence against invasion was the Albert Canal, based on the fortress of Eben-Emael, which commanded the bridges over the canal. The army was deployed along the borders with Germany and France as the Maginot Line did not extend along the Belgian border.

Barges assembled at a port in northern France or the Low Countries. These are clearly river and canal barges hastily adapted for landings and would have been unstable in the open sea. The box structures on several of them are probably for anti-aircraft guns. (*Bundesarchiv*)

A barge converted with a ramp for loading and unloading vehicles. This would not have been able to handle a heavy tank, and here it is seen with a half-track edging its way towards the beach. (*Bundesarchiv*)

A light tank being moved by crane from the dockside to the sea. The long flexible hose is to provide air for the engines and the occupants as it makes its way towards the beach. This must be a trial, judging by the number of onlookers and their uniforms, with both army and navy officers present. (*Bundesarchiv*)

General Franz Halder, chief of the army general staff, who frequently discussed the possibility of the invasion with Adolph Hitler. At the beginning the Führer was in a buoyant mood, describing the army's successes in the first nine months of the war as little short of a miracle. He could not understand the British refusal to surrender. (*Bundesarchiv*)

Field Marshal Walther von Brauchitsch, another of the senior officers close to the Führer. He would have played a commanding role in any invasion, but instead found himself leading Operation Barbarossa, the invasion of the Soviet Union, where German forces scored massive early successes against largely unprepared Soviet forces. (*Bundesarchiv*)

Joachim von Ribbentrop was Germany's foreign minister from 1938 to 1945, and acclaimed by Hitler as being 'greater than Bismarck'. Fluent in English and French, Ribbentrop was from a middle-class family and in 1925 added the aristocratic '*von*' to his name. He was one of the two men that Hitler considered for the post of *Reichskommissar für Großbritannien*, 'State Commissar for Great Britain'. This individual would have had near dictatorial powers. His most outstanding achievements in the run up to the Second World War were the Anglo-German Naval Treaty which opened the way for further German naval expansion and the Nazi-Soviet Pact, signed with his Soviet counterpart Molotov in August 1939. His wartime career was less successful, failing to persuade Italy to join the war immediately and failing to gain Spanish support. (*Bundesarchiv*)

General Gerd von Rundstedt, later Field Marshal, had been brought out of retirement on the eve of the Second World War. He impressed during the invasion of Poland and was to command the ground forces for Operation Sea Lion, for which he had little enthusiasm or confidence. He explained that at one stage he could no longer follow Hitler's thoughts, and so asked at what points on the south coast the landing was to take place, but Hitler kept strictly to his order that operations were to be kept secret and said, 'I cannot tell you yet'. He nevertheless served with distinction in the early stages of Operation Barbarossa, until dismissed by Hitler for making a strategic withdrawal. (*Bundesarchiv*)

Heinrich Himmler became the head of the SS, the *Schutzstaffel*, or protection squads, which developed into a force of its own, playing an important part in the administration and control of the occupied territories, even engaging in business in its own right using slave labour. Himmler discussed the possibility of moving all able-bodied workers to Germany after the success of Sea Lion. (*Bundesarchiv*)

Ernst Wilhelm Bohle, an undersecretary in the Foreign Office who had previously been promised by Hitler that if the British 'behave sensibly' he would be the next German ambassador to the Court of St James. He was also considered for the role of *Reichskommissar für Großbritannien*. He is seen here at the Nuremberg war trials. (*Bundesarchiv*)

Adolf Hitler frequently expressed his admiration of the British Empire. He had not at the outset planned to invade, only coming round to the idea after the United Kingdom refused to surrender after the fall of France. He allowed what many called the 'Führer system' to evolve, with his ministers and senior officers competing for his ear rather than working together, while others started what was known as 'working towards the Führer', trying to gain favour by enacting policies that they thought would find his favour. (*Bundesarchiv*)

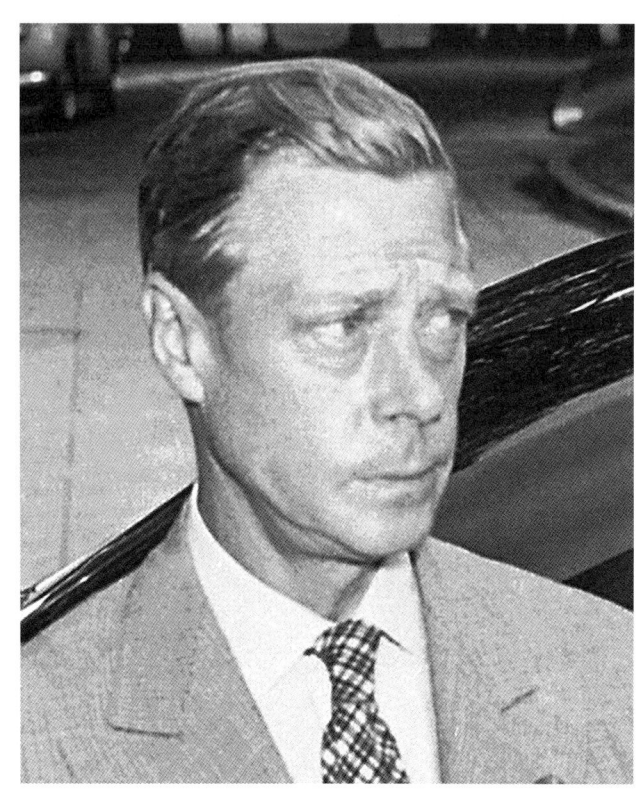

The Duke of Windsor, the former Prince of Wales who turned down the British throne as King Edward VIII due to his involvement with an American divorcee Wallis Simpson. He had visited Germany and was believed by many, including Hitler and his entourage, to be sympathetic to the Nazis. He actively sought a position within the UK during the war years, but instead was awarded the governorship of the Bahamas. Debate about his opinions continues to this day. (*Bundesarchiv*)

An aerial view of the barges assembled in the enclosed dock area of a port in mainland Europe. Many of these were already loaded with equipment and munitions, something which was realised as they often blew up when bombed by the Royal Air Force. There was in fact little secrecy about German intentions. (*Bundesarchiv*)

The barges in close-up, with men working aboard completing loading and covering the cargo from the elements. There can be no doubt that the Germans were in earnest about the invasion, but time was not on their side, and they lacked the equipment necessary for a successful invasion, while the winter weather was imminent. (*Bundesarchiv*)

A close-up of a barge in dry dock, possibly after having had the bows modified to include a landing ramp. Even so, the result did not compare with the landing craft developed by the Allies which were capable of dealing with the open sea while the craft selected by the Germans came from inland waterways, the rivers and canals of continental Europe and would have been difficult to steer and unstable in the open sea. (*Bundesarchiv*)

German troops making a river crossing in an inflatable craft. This was about the limit of their capabilities, a continental nation with a continental army, a navy that was insignificant apart from its submarines, but with great ambitions encouraged by the early successes of the war against opponents who had less manpower as well as poorer equipment and not enough of it. This inflatable would have been vulnerable to well directed machine gun fire. (*Bundesarchiv*)

An amphibious tank being prepared for sea trials. These were highly vulnerable and, with clumsy flotation devices, could only operate in calm waters. They were no substitute for battle tanks rolling off a tank landing ship. (*Bundesarchiv*)

Coastal artillery was, on the other hand, one of the strengths of the German armed forces. This piece was mainly for defensive use, but the Germans did possess guns that could fire across the Straits of Dover, forcing that town to be largely evacuated during the war years. The drawback of such guns was that they did not provide cover for troops advancing inland from the coast. (*Bundesarchiv*)

(*Right*) This large railway gun was mobile and could fire over long distances, although the rate of fire would have been slow. (*Bundesarchiv*)

(*Below*) In Norway, the Netherlands and Crete, the Germans combined their frontal assaults with the use of paratroops, who were part of the Luftwaffe rather than the army. These paratroops dropping onto the island of Crete give an idea of what the situation in the countryside inland from Dover might have looked like had the invasion gone ahead. (*Bundesarchiv*)

(*Left*) German paratroops getting ready to board their aircraft, a Junkers Ju52/3m trimotor transport. Originally designed as a bomber-transport, it was outdated in the former role during the Spanish Civil War, and by 1940 was also outdated as a transport. One of the weaknesses of the Luftwaffe was transport aircraft, while the USAAF and RAF were developing stronger and more modern transport elements. (*Bundesarchiv*)

(*Below*) A German soldier leaves a glider after it has landed. The advantage of glider landings was that the troops were ready to fight as soon as they landed, while paratroops had to get their equipment together and were vulnerable for the first couple of minutes. (*Bundesarchiv*)

Another image of paratroops dropping, again probably in Crete. The soldier nearest the camera is going to unpack his equipment, including a rifle and ammunition. (*Bundesarchiv*)

The *Scharnhorst*, one of two German battlecruisers which were the largest ships in the Kriegsmarine in 1940, and which would have had to provide gunnery cover for the landings and the advance inland. But these ships were outgunned by the Royal Navy's battleships and battlecruisers. (*Bundesarchiv*)

Between the wars, restricted by the Treaty of Versailles and the Washington Naval Treaty, the Germans built a fleet of three *Panzerschiffe*, but these were intended for commerce-raiding and one of them, the *Graf Spee*, had already been scuttled after an encounter with the Royal Navy and Royal New Zealand Navy in December 1939. The four 12-inch guns in two turrets would have been helpful in support in the south of England, but would have been hopelessly outgunned by the Royal Navy. In fact *Graf Spee* was crippled by a heavy cruiser with 8-inch guns and two light cruisers each with 6-inch guns. (*Bundesarchiv*)

The first German battleship, *Bismarck*, was not ready for service in 1939, and her first operational cruises was also her last. (*Bundesarchiv*)

The second German battleship, *Tirpitz*, was not available in 1940 or the following years, and spent most of her existence hiding in a Norwegian fjord. Here she is camouflaged. Hitler had ordered her to seek shelter and not to venture out if there was any chance of her encountering a British aircraft carrier or battleship. (*Bundesarchiv*)

A convoy of Allied landing craft, which were purpose-designed vessels unlike the German conversions of river and canal barges. They were uncomfortable in the open sea. (Imperial War Museum)

This was the way to do it. The British battleship *Nelson* fires her 16-inch guns, of which she had nine in three turrets. A 16-inch gun had a heavier warhead and a longer range than a 12-inch. Most British battleships had 14 or 15-inch calibre guns. After D-Day, the availability of such firepower seriously affected German troop and armour movements, even twenty miles from the coast. (Imperial War Museum)

The British and Canadians learnt the hard way at Dieppe that beach reconnaissance was important, and took no chances for D-Day, using midget submarines such as *X-24* for beach reconnaissance, and also, on D-Day itself, to guide the landing fleet to the right beaches in Operation Gambit. (Imperial War Museum)

Modern warfare requires vast volumes of fuel, for aircraft and armoured vehicles, and for transport and electricity generation, which is why the British laid 'Pluto', pipelines that ran from Shanklin on the east coast of the Isle of Wight to Normandy. This also saved a considerable amount of shipping and reduced the need for harbours to be captured and secured. The laying of the pipelines is shown top, and below is the end result. The Germans had nothing planned like this. (Imperial War Museum)

Two Mulberry harbours were needed, each equivalent in size and ship handling capacity to the port of Dover, one for the British forces and the other for the American. A severe storm wrecked the American harbour before it was completed, and the British harbour, shown here, was badly damaged. The Germans had plans for floating wharves, but no coherent plan for a harbour. Anyway, where would they have located it? (Imperial War Museum)

Pre-war, the Prince of Wales visited Germany with his fiancée Wallis Simpson, and the three of them got on well together, but would this image have been repeated after an invasion? The debate continues. (*Bundesarchiv*)

Senate House, University of London, was intended to house the civilian administration staff after German occupation.

Blenheim Palace was to be the headquarters for the German military in England, and for Hitler when he visited, in preference to any of the Royal palaces or houses. No doubt this was due in part to it having been the ancestral home of Winston Churchill.

On 10 May, Eben-Emael was neutralised by a sudden German airborne attack with commandos landed by glider on the top of the fortress and its occupants imprisoned until the Germans had taken the bridges and advanced across the canal.

It was not until 28 May that King Leopold negotiated a surrender of Belgian forces. Between the start of the invasion and surrender there had been a strong disagreement between the government and the monarch. The former believed that King Leopold should move to France with the government and continue the war, but Leopold argued that the impossibility of continuing fighting on Belgian soil, as had happened during the First World War, should mean that Belgium was out of the war and that he should remain in the country with his defeated troops. He spent the next four years of the war as a voluntary prisoner at his palace at Laeken, near Brussels. The government moved to France and declared that Leopold could not abdicate as he was a prisoner. The government then managed to improvise a meeting of the Belgian parliament at Limoges on 31 May. At Limoges the government and members of parliament deplored Leopold's actions, but he in turn had long deplored their lack of strong government and their failure to make provision for adequate defence.

The fall of France led the parliamentarians to return to Belgium and seek to repair relations with Leopold, but they were rebuffed.

Leopold and many of his subjects hoped that with the country out of the war, they would be able to negotiate an understanding with the Germans and Belgium would be granted internal self-government. Leopold did in fact leave his palace for a meeting with Adolf Hitler on 19 November 1940 at Berchtesgaden. This should have been Leopold's opportunity to press for a general political settlement between the two countries, or at least discover Germany's plans for the country, but unfortunately Hitler was preoccupied with the continuation of the war and the meeting was inconclusive, leaving Leopold to remain in Belgium until moved to Germany in June 1944.

For the rest of the war, Leopold considered the Belgian government-in-exile, based in London, as traitors. He was not alone in this, but his own authority and popularity was also diminished as the war progressed. Very popular at the start of the war, his lack of authority under German occupation became an embarrassment. There were even those advocating a 'New Order' for Belgium; possibly a republic.

The Germans meanwhile had hastened to ensure that Belgium was occupied and under their complete control. Three frontier cantons that had been transferred from Germany to Belgium under the Treaty of Versailles were taken back into Germany by a Führer decree of 18 May 1940. The rest of Belgium and the French departments of Pas-de-Calais and the Nord were governed by a Wehrmacht military administration, headed by General Alexander von Falkenhausen, but actually run by Eggert Reeder, who was president of the military administration. Falkenhausen was one of the more lenient occupation commanders, so much so that he was recalled to Germany in June 1944 because he was regarded as not being strong enough with the resistance movements in Belgium and northern France. He was sent to Dachau after being implicated in a plot to assassinate Hitler. Post-war, he was sentenced by a Belgian court to twelve years imprisonment with hard labour (at the age of 73) for the execution of hostages and transporting Jews to Auschwitz, but was released soon afterwards as it was recognised that he had also safeguarded many Belgians from the SS. The military administration itself survived until July 1944, when as the Germans were being forced out of Belgium, it was replaced by a German civilian administration.

Under occupation, the Germans favoured the Flemish population, who were seen by Hitler as being 'Germanic', at the expense of the French or Walloon population, and within Flanders pro-German groups emerged, of which the most important was the VNV. Nevertheless, the need to keep Belgian agriculture and industry contributing to the war effort and the need to minimise the deployment of German armed forces in the country meant that the Germans were forced to try to work with the existing Belgian authorities, and in the absence of their political masters, senior civil servants had wide powers, so that German rule was for the most part indirect. The Roman Catholic Church and its clergy enjoyed considerable freedom from interference and this extended to education.

Much of Belgian business was left to continue, although one exception was the defence equipment industry, which, surprisingly given the weak state of the country's armed forces between the wars, was fairly substantial.

For the population as a whole, after some serious food shortages in the early stages, the occupation was less onerous and demanding than elsewhere, although there were still some shortages of food and fuel, and clothing, but a thriving black market existed, largely unchecked. Some 70,000 French-speakers were detained in prisoner-of-war camps for the duration of the war, while civilians were encouraged to volunteer to work in German industry as only Flemish personnel were released after the Belgian surrender. The exception to this was, of course, the small Jewish population which was rounded up and transported to Auschwitz.

Inevitably, resistance emerged after the occupation started. Many personnel who had fought in the First World War were active early in the occupation and, as elsewhere, in addition to the armed resistance and sabotage, an underground press also came into existence. The Belgian Communist Party organised a wave of strikes, which reached a peak in May 1941 as Germany prepared to invade the Soviet Union, although it is unlikely that they were aware of this. The communists formed the *Front de l'Indépendence*, FI.

A distinctive feature of the Belgian resistance was the establishment of escape networks for downed Allied airmen, who were protected and then sent back to the UK by a lengthy escape line through France and into Spain. The resistance also provided intelligence. Armed groups emerged, some operating within the FI, but others were led by former army officers, notably those of the *Armée Secrète*, AS, which supported King Leopold III. Recruitment was boosted when in 1942 the Germans started to conscript workers to be sent to Germany.

In Belgium, as in France, relations between the government-in-exile and the resistance were not always harmonious, especially as many in the resistance did not want to be dictated to by the Belgian politicians sitting safely in London. For their part, the members of the government-in-exile distrusted the communist FI and the pro-Leopold AS. Allied liberation of Belgium was rapid and did not allow the resistance much opportunity to seek direct combat with the retreating German forces, although they did manage to seize the port of Antwerp and prevent its destruction by the Germans.

The Netherlands

Along with Denmark and Norway, the Dutch expected to be allowed to remain neutral, as during the First World War. This was another country that had neglected its defences, and the best equipped of its armed forces were far away in the colonies, especially in the Netherlands East Indies, a large and prosperous colony with substantial and valuable oil and rubber production. In 1940, the population of the Netherlands totalled less than 9 million.

The Dutch placed their hopes for security first in neutrality, which had worked well during the First World War, with food supplies and fertilizer for Germany passing through Dutch ports, and then in flooding, so much so that in 1937 the prime minister declared that he could foil any invasion simply by pressing a button. Some have compared this approach to the French Maginot Line. In addition, there were three fortified lines, the Ijssel, the Grebbe north of the Meuse, and to the south of the Meuse, the Peel-Ramm. There was also a water line which was meant to act as a last ditch defence of what was known as 'Fortress Holland'. None of these fortifications was adequate or modern. There must have been some inkling that Germany might invade, as once war had broken out in September 1939, Queen Wilhelmina joined King Leopold III of Belgium in appealing to the governments of France, the UK and Germany to make peace. Hitler sent Wilhelmina a personal assurance that he would respect Dutch neutrality.

The creation of strong armed forces that could at least have discouraged the Germans and ensured that neutrality was respected had been hindered by the existence of a strong pacifist movement between the wars, with ironically a broken rifle as its symbol.

The mainstay of the Dutch armed forces was the army, which when mobilised consisted at the time of four corps each of two divisions, totalling 400,000 personnel. While the numbers seem good for a small country, it lacked tanks and had just 26 armoured cars, while the artillery, with a total of 656 guns, was largely obsolete. This was bad enough, but there was an absence of operational experience or of effective exercises, and little understanding of the concept, let alone the potential, of airborne warfare. In effect, this was an army suited to fighting colonial wars, but ill-equipped and unprepared for a major European war, or for the Japanese when they turned their attention to the Netherlands East Indies.

The air force was still part of the Dutch army in 1939. It had 175 aircraft, of which only 132 were operational and of these just 72 could be regarded as modern. There was a separate Netherlands East Indies Air Force.

A maritime nation, but not really a maritime power, the Netherlands had a small but modern navy, mainly deployed in the East Indies. It had nothing more powerful than light cruisers, of which there were five, while there were eight destroyers, twenty-four submarines, attractive because of their small crewing requirements, sixteen minesweepers and a number of small gunboats, torpedo boats and other assorted small craft. There were about fifty aircraft, all obsolete. Apart from a solitary light cruiser and a single destroyer, as well as some minor warships, the bulk of the fleet was based in the Netherlands East Indies and the Caribbean.

Invasion did not come as a complete surprise. Colonel Oster, deputy chief of German military intelligence, the *Abwehr*, was one of the first to be opposed to Hitler and was also a friend of the Dutch military attaché in Berlin, Major Sas. On 9 May Oster warned him that his country was about to be invaded the next morning. Sas immediately passed this information on to his superiors at The Hague, but it seems that little of this went any further as the commanders at the main strategic points were largely taken by surprise. German forces included the 22nd Airborne Infantry Division, which seized vital points in South Holland, but were put under extreme pressure by the defenders. The airborne troops who had seized the important bridge across the Waal at Moerdijk, managed to hold on until relieved by the 9th Armoured Division on 12 May, and then headed for Rotterdam. The Dutch were left isolated as French forces to the south were too weak to provide any support.

To break any resistance by the Dutch, despite being declared an open city, Rotterdam was heavily bombed on 14 May. Later that day, the Dutch government surrendered.

Surprisingly, given staunch resistance and heavy fighting, the Dutch army's losses were relatively low, at just 2,100 dead and 2,700 wounded. Yet out of 72 modern aircraft, the air force lost 62 on the first day.

Some warships were scuttled and the destroyer was sunk by German aircraft, but several ships did manage to escape to British ports.

The substantial merchant marine was largely at sea or in port far from home, and this also escaped. Some 640 ships were thus available to the Allies.

Queen Wilhelmina and her government went into exile in the UK.

While the Nazis officially regarded the Dutch as cousins, fellow members of the Aryan race who could be incorporated into a greater Germany, after surrender the policy was placed on hold, partly because the Germans believed that the defeated nations should be in no doubt of this diminished status, but also because the Germans needed to ensure that their new possessions were as productive as possible. The Netherlands was treated as a province of Germany under the control of the *Reichskommissariat Niederlanden*, headed by Artur Seyss-Inquart, who had experience in this role having previously been installed as chancellor of Austria the day before Germany annexed its neighbour.

Clearly not recognised as being related to the German people were the Dutch Jews, whose numbers had been swollen by those who had fled persecution in Germany. Out of an estimated 140,000, 117,000 died in the death camps. Many of those who survived owed this to the efforts of Dutch people who, at great risk to themselves and their families, provided a safe hiding place out of sight of the Germans and also ensured that they were fed, despite a worsening shortage of food.

Before the war the Dutch had created a considerable export market for agricultural produce, especially dairy products such as cheese and butter, as well as fruit and vegetables. Dutch agricultural produce was desperately needed by Germany, but only at prices which the German population could afford. This meant that there was little chance of prosperity for Dutch farmers as their produce was requisitioned by the Germans who dictated the price that would be paid.

The Germans did not hesitate to impose their racial and political regime on the Netherlands, with Nazification of the professions and academic institutions. Jews were initially banned from the professions or from owning a business, before being deported. The professors at the University of Leyden protested at the treatment of their Jewish colleagues, and the university was promptly shut down. Elsewhere, many in the professions refused to join new Nazified organisations, seeking employment elsewhere, or went into hiding.

The severity of the initial round-up of the Jews in Amsterdam in 1941 led to a strike in February. The reaction by the Germans was to execute seventeen Dutchmen already held in prison, an action that sent shockwaves through a society that had abolished the death penalty as long ago as 1870. Some of those executed had originally been arrested for sabotage, having tried to destroy a cruiser under construction for the Kriegsmarine at a shipyard near Rotterdam.

As in many other countries that were occupied, there was a local Nazi party, although in the last general election before the war, in 1937, it had polled just 4 per cent of the vote, the same percentage as for the Communist Party. Membership was around 30,000 before the occupation, during which it rose to 50,000. Its leader, Anton Mussart, communicated with Hitler, reminding the Führer that the Dutch were Aryans, although this point did not need to be made, and pressing for a post-war Greater Netherlands, incorporating the Flemish areas of Belgium. Instead of receiving any special position in the administration of the Netherlands, Mussart was treated as unimportant. For his pains, he was executed in 1946.

More than 5,000 Dutchmen joined the Waffen-SS, and another 54,000 joined other Nazi organisations. Nevertheless, the police and civil service tried to continue as before, without being too zealous about obeying orders.

A number of Dutchmen escaped to join the British armed forces, but not in great numbers. Airmen were assigned to the RAF's 320 Squadron, while the soldiers formed the Irene Brigade, which took part in the Normandy campaign and continued to fight afterwards as the Allies advanced towards Germany. Warships fought alongside the Royal Navy.

Queen Wilhelmina broadcast on Radio Orange to her people and became the symbol of the Dutch in exile. In May 1944 an agreement was reached with the British for a Dutch military government after occupation, while the Dutch created the Netherlands Forces of the Interior under the command of the queen's son-in-law, Prince Bernhard. This combined three existing resistance groups, in Zeeland, North Brabant and Limburg.

On 17 September 1944, the start of the Arnhem raid, the prime minister of the Dutch government-in-exile broadcast, calling on Dutch railwaymen to strike, which they did. In retaliation, the Germans stopped the movement of food by canal. This was a contributory factor to the starvation that followed in the winter of 1944/5, often known as the 'Hunger Winter', when in some parts of the country there was no food at all and 16,000 people died of starvation, and most farm animals were killed for food. The situation was made worse as the Allies, intent on pressing towards Germany, bypassed much of the Netherlands. The situation was only relieved by an air drop of essential supplies by RAF Bomber Command.

France

The French were under no illusions about the progress of any war with Germany. They had been invaded by Prussia in 1870 and Paris besieged. During the First World War, the Germans were stopped near Paris. The view amongst politicians and senior military figures in both France and the United Kingdom was that the Second World War would be almost a rerun of the earlier conflict, with the opposing sides facing each other. The French hoped that their Maginot Line would hold the Germans back from actually invading France, but it only ran from the Belgian border to that with Switzerland and, as before, the Germans planned their invasion through Belgium. The refusal to accept the neutrality of Denmark, Norway and the Netherlands came as a shock, and a costly shock in the case of Norway, as British and French forces were deployed in a futile attempt to rescue the country.

As elsewhere, the mass of the French people had no enthusiasm for war, although a public opinion poll in July 1939 had shown 76 per cent support for the use of force if Germany tried to seize Danzig. While many in the UK had welcomed Chamberlain's Munich Agreement in 1938 with relief and were optimistic about the future, the French had been under no such illusions at the time. Under Prime Minister Deladier's leadership the nation's defence budget had been trebled. In short, they did not trust Germany, having been invaded twice during the previous seventy years. However, the French government was not united in this stand, and the foreign minister, Georges Bonnet, believed passionately in appeasement. While pacifism was popular with many during the interwar period, there was still pride at the victory in the Great War and the French nation did not go to war in 1939 expecting defeat, although many were astonished at how their government had changed from attempting to reach an accommodation with Germany to preparing for war. Some blamed the United Kingdom for this dramatic about turn in policy. German propaganda played on this, telling the French that the 'British would fight to the last Frenchman!'

After eight months of the 'phoney war', or the *drôle de guerre* to the French, or *Sitzkrieg* to the Germans, the invasion of France started on 10 May 1940. The French had high expectations of the Maginot Line, but they were to be disappointed and it took just six weeks for the Germans to overrun northern France and force a surrender. The German concept of *Blitzkrieg*, with armour and strong tactical air power operating together, was too much for the two allies, the United Kingdom and France. It should not have been this way, as one young French army officer, Charles de Gaulle, had written a book in the 1930s advocating strong armoured forces, but his superiors ignored his ideas.

Daladier had resigned on 20 March and been replaced as prime minister by Reynaud, who lasted until 16 June when he was replaced in turn by the 84-year old war veteran Marshal Philippe Pétain. By this time, the Germans were south of Paris and the government had been evacuated to Bordeaux in the south-west. An offer by Winston Churchill of a political union between the United Kingdom and France instead of French surrender, was rejected by the French.

During the First World War, Pétain had been due to retire as a colonel in 1914, but the start of the war meant he remained in office and was promoted. Later in the war, as the 'victor of Verdun', he was elevated to become a Marshal of France in December 1918. By 1940, the fight had gone out of the elderly Pétain, and a mood of defeatism had taken hold. He started negotiations for an armistice and moved his government to Vichy on 1 July. On 11 July the National Assembly transferred all of its powers to Pétain as *Chef d'État*, making him head of state as well as prime minister. He surrounded himself mostly with military men as ministers, although his deputy prime minister, Pierre Laval, was a civilian.

After the cease-fire, Pétain remained popular and was seen as a truly national leader, but strangely the Vichy government which he headed was regarded with contempt.

The cease-fire was very welcome to many French people. Poor information and propaganda, including German radio broadcasts claiming that 'the British will fight to the last Frenchman', resulted in panic and a mass exodus from areas close to the front. Exact figures do not exist, but it is widely believed that between 8 and 10 million, out of a total population of around 41 million at the time, left their homes and headed west once the invasion started. Rather than place the burden of conscription on the peasants, many industrial workers had been called up during the early months of the war, but the alarming drop in output that resulted forced the government to bring back two million men from the front and reassign them to the defence equipment industry, which made a bad situation on the front even worse.

Uniquely, the Germans allowed the French to retain a substantial area unoccupied (until late 1942), which became known as Vichy France after its seat of government, although this was more a form of internal self-government and was not truly independent. It was allowed to keep an army of 100,000 personnel and retained control over the navy, as well as France's colonies. Vichy France was not allowed its own air force, at least not in France itself as it had fighter squadrons in North Africa. Pétain's government decided to revitalise the nation, and with Germany's approval it launched a 'National Revolution' using the slogan, 'Work, Family and Country'. The adult male population was encouraged to volunteer to work in Germany, although as the war continued, volunteering was to prove insufficient to provide the numbers needed by the Germans.

A priority for the Germans was to reverse the decisions imposed on them by the Treaty of Versailles. Alsace and Lorraine immediately became German once again, although those inhabitants deemed to be French and not suitable for 'Germanisation' were deported to France. Those regarded as being sufficiently German were allowed to stay, while those of military age were conscripted into the German army. The departments of Nord and Pas-de-Calais were governed from Brussels under direct German rule. The main *zone occupée* was governed from Paris, where the Germans established their Military Administration, *Militarbefehlshaber in Frankreich*.

As in the other occupied territories, the Germans were obsessed with the Jewish question, diverting scarce resources to their removal and internment, and eventual extermination. The deportations started in earnest in 1942, and by 1944 more than 75,000 Jews had been removed from France. Even those in Vichy territory were not safe as the regime collaborated with the Germans even before occupation was extended.

Laval persuaded Pétain to go further and arranged a meeting between Pétain and Hitler at Montoire in October 1940, where Pétain offered Hitler the full collaboration of Vichy France. Nothing came of this, and Pétain blamed Laval for this humiliation, dismissing him in December. Nevertheless, at the end of 1941 Pétain met Goering, where the subject was raised again. Pressed as to what he meant by collaboration, Pétain told Goering that it meant Vichy France and Germany acting as equals, which prompted a furious Goering to ask, 'Who are the victors, you or us?' It seems that it was not until this point that Pétain realised the true implications of French surrender. He was not the only French leader to think that the way ahead lay in collaboration. So did Admiral Darlan, who could have provided Germany with a much strengthened navy, continuing the war against the British Empire in partnership with Germany.

Laval was replaced by Pierre Flandin, who was unacceptable to the Germans, as was his successor, Admiral Darlan, and in April 1942 the Germans forced Pétain to have Laval back, giving him increased power. It was an unhappy working relationship, with Pétain trying to replace Laval and then attempting to revive the National Assembly and make it his successor, but the Germans wouldn't allow it. By this time, Germany had occupied the whole of France, shocked at the speed at which the Vichy forces in North Africa had switched their allegiance to the Allies after Operation Torch, the invasion of North Africa, in late 1942.

Pétain did little from this time on, although he was treated by Parisians as a hero when he visited the city in April 1944 and never suffered the contempt afforded other collaborators. After the Allied landings in France, he resigned, and was moved by the Germans, initially to Germany and then to Switzerland, but returned home of his own accord despite de Gaulle, by this time leader of the Free French, having asked the Swiss not to agree to any demands for extradition. Placed on trial, despite mounting a robust defence, he was sentenced to death, but this was reprieved and he spent the last few years of his life as a prisoner on the Île d'Yeu, dying in 1951.

In France, after the surrender, there was the gradual development of a strong resistance movement which was soon in contact with the Allies, and which itself was split into communist and anti-communist groups. Many French workers were employed by the Germans, and often worked reluctantly, doing as little as possible as badly as possible, with strikes, go-slows, sabotage and other forms of non-cooperation. For others, it was possible to conceive of a French economy within an overall economy, with many trading locally. Nevertheless, as elsewhere the Germans requisitioned agricultural produce and mineral production, taking as much as 75 per cent in the case of aluminium production, but just one per cent of sugar production, and two per cent of potatoes. They took 56 per cent of champagne production and 25 per cent of spirits, but clearly had little taste for French beer as they took just 10 per cent. These figures could have been higher, but many farmers worked hard to undermine the German requisitions. Attempts to bring more land into agricultural production were hampered by the climate in the main wine and citrus fruit producing areas which meant they were unable to switch and produce extra vegetables.

Clothing and shoes were soon in short supply, as were many household items, especially after the shops had sold their stock, often to German servicemen anxious to buy goods that were no longer available in Germany to take to their families when they returned home on leave. Eventually, with an absence of leather for re-soling shoes, wood had to be used, so that the streets resounded to the sound of wooden soles clattering on the pavements and the cobbles.

Of all the occupied territories, France had the largest industrial base and the most diverse. It also had the largest population of the western occupied territories, although the breakdown between those in occupied France and their fellow countrymen in Vichy France is not known. French economic planners prepared a ten year plan in 1942 that placed the emphasis on agriculture, reflecting the German view of France's role in post-war German-dominated Europe.

As a result of acting as Germany's larder, the strict rationing forced on the French meant that an adult was entitled to just 1,200 calories daily, which was insufficient, and the poorer sections of society received much less. To maintain a reasonable standard of health and fitness, it was necessary to make use of the black market, which was easier for those living in rural areas than for their urban counterparts. In Vichy in early 1942 there were food riots, led mainly by women whose earning power had been curtailed by the regime's objections to mothers working. Vichy farmers also refused to supply the towns with food because of the uneconomic prices being enforced by the Vichy authorities.

Planning was pointless given the disruption in the country, and the absence of 1.6 million men in German prisoner-of-war camps. Many others were in French colonies and unlikely to hasten homeward in the circumstances, while a smaller number were in the UK with the Free French forces. No doubt planning helped the French feel that they still had some control over their affairs. There were other problems, including a shortage of raw materials and fuel with France cut-off from its peacetime sources. All this is, of course, not forgetting the disruptive tactics employed by many French workers, and the constant threat of bombing by first the Royal Air Force and then the combined Royal Air Force and United States Army Air Force, with French factories being so much closer and easier to get to than those in Germany.

Germany soon became France's largest market, and in 1943 Germany was taking no less than 40 per cent of the country's industrial production, including 80 per cent of vehicle production, 100 per cent of aircraft and aero-engine production, and 78 per cent of shipbuilding. As elsewhere, the French were expected to pay the costs of occupation, taking more than 55 per cent of the government's revenue.

The Germans set the actual cost of occupation at 20 million marks daily, after the enforced exchange rate devalued the French franc by 20 per cent. In all, under occupation France provided goods, raw materials, foodstuffs and services equal to 25 per cent of Germany's gross national product.

Vichy introduced voluntary service in Germany in June 1942, before the German occupation, but on 16 February 1943, the Compulsory Labour Service, *Service du Travail Obligatoire*, STO, was introduced, which resulted in 600,000 men being sent to Germany while others were sent into French industry and the mines to fulfil the country's obligations to Germany, while others worked on the defensive Atlantic Wall, which was at its strongest in north-western France, and worked for the Todt construction organisation. The STO acted as a spur to the resistance, with many going underground to escape being sent to Germany.

Forced labour did not increase industrial production and indeed had the opposite effect. In the mines, coal production ran at 68 per cent of pre-war output, while industrial production dropped to 38 per cent of the 1938 level, and agricultural production was just 70 per cent of pre-war levels. What did go up was the cost of living, which rose by 270 per cent.

While initially the Germans were seen as being correct and in some cases lenient, as resistance mounted there were severe punishments, hostage-taking, torture and executions. In areas where resistance was strong or especially successful, entire communities were punished. On the night of 1/2 April 1944, an explosion halted a German troop train, although there were no casualties; eighty-six civilians were massacred in the village of Ascq as a consequence. Worse was to follow after the Normandy landings, with 99 men hanged at Tulle, and more than 600 local people shot or burned alive at Oradour-sur-Glane. The German desire for revenge intensified after the landings, and often reflected their frustration at the lack of assistance from local officials.

The Channel Islands

The one part of the British Isles that did fall under German occupation was the Channel Islands. The third largest island, Alderney, was completely evacuated, but in Jersey, the largest, Guernsey and Sark, many of the local population stayed. Some of these did not feel able to leave their homes or farms, but others simply could not get on the evacuation ships for one reason or another, often because they did not have enough time or the ships were already overcrowded. Some, of course, wanted to stay behind in their homes or on their farms. Senior members of the civil administration generally remained, these included the bailiffs, the heads of government, in both Jersey and Guernsey. The Dame of Sark, Sibyl Hathaway, also stayed, but her American husband was deported by the Germans.

The two main islands, Jersey and Guernsey, had their own territorial battalions of the British army, and these troops formed a battalion of the Hampshire Regiment after evacuation, but individual soldiers were given false names and addresses to prevent reprisals against those of their families still resident in the islands should they become prisoners-of-war.

The Germans bombed the two largest islands, Jersey and Guernsey, before landing, inflicting casualties, killing 44 people, despite having been told that the islands had been demilitarised. Whether this was a failure of communication or simply a show of strength is not clear.

As elsewhere, the Germans seized anything of value, and the best motor vehicles were seized and shipped back to Germany. An acute shortage of fuel meant that bus services were severely curtailed, leading to overcrowding. In some cases horses were harnessed to buses to enable them to move, although soon the horses were also starving. German soldiers were banned from using public transport, but when one inspector for the main (there were several operators on the two largest islands at the time) bus company on Jersey, appropriately enough JMT, Jersey Motor Transport, ordered two German soldiers off a crowded bus, he was arrested shortly afterwards and sent to a prison camp in Germany. Agricultural produce was commandeered by the Germans and rationing introduced, while fishing vessels could only leave port if permission was granted and then with German personnel aboard to prevent any escape.

The authorities on the islands tried to establish a working relationship with the Germans, but their only significant success was to prevent the Germans from forcing members of the small Jewish population to wear the yellow badge with the Star of David. This was to prove to be a hollow victory and soon became immaterial when the Jews were eventually gathered up and sent to Germany. The rest of the population was spared slave labour or deportation to Germany and not even asked to volunteer for work in Germany. But the Germans still had to be obeyed. All radios were supposed to have been handed in to the authorities, and anyone found in possession of one, let alone actually listening to one, was imprisoned.

Organisations of almost every kind were banned, excepting the Company of Foresters as the Germans believed it was a union for woodsmen. The ban even extended to the Salvation Army, which possibly the Germans viewed as a paramilitary organisation. A Salvation Army major, Marie Ozanne, defied the ban and continued to wear her uniform and preached against the treatment of slave labourers used by the Organisation Todt, until she was arrested, held without trial and imprisoned, where eventually she died of peritonitis.

There was no armed resistance on any of the Channel Islands because the possibility of making a successful attack and then escaping and evading capture on such small territories was almost impossible. The chances of obtaining arms and ammunition were also remote. Islanders did resist in several ways, including feeding and sheltering escaped slave labourers.

Following the British victory at El Alamein, a commando raid was made on Sark, mainly to gain intelligence about the German defences, and this led to an accelerated programme of construction as substantial fortifications were built by slave labour, with an estimated 15,000 sent to the islands from Eastern Europe: many of these fortifications remain today. The police were enlisted not only to continue their peacetime duties, but to chauffeur senior German officers. Where possible, German officers were billeted on local households. To improve communications and make the most of the available fuel, a substantial narrow gauge railway network was created in Jersey, where the two railway companies, the Jersey Railway and the Jersey Eastern Railway, had both closed between the wars. This prompted some amusement amongst the locals, for as one put it, 'We had done away with the railways thinking they were old fashioned.' Of course, in peacetime the problem had been that the railways were too short to be viable once roads improved and motor vehicles appeared, with the Jersey Eastern running for just over six miles from St Helier to Gorey and the Jersey Railway which was not much longer running westwards from St Helier to Corbiere, via St Aubin. The new German system was far larger and more extensive than the former Jersey railway network with many new lines feeding gunnery positions around the coast.

The Royal Air Force did not bomb the Channel Islands because of the very real risk of civilian casualties, leading one German soldier to remark that he was in 'the safest air-raid shelter in Europe'. Many writers of fiction like to pretend that the Luftwaffe mounted bombing raids against southern England from the Channel Islands, but bases in France were far more conveniently placed, closer to the south of England, and much larger. The only offensive forces based on the Channel Islands were E-boats, but these were there to enforce a blockade against British ships and also to ensure that no one escaped, which few did as apart from a distance of more than eighty miles from the Hampshire coast, the route also had to pass round the exposed Cherbourg peninsula.

Channel islanders had to suffer severe shortages. As early as 1942, the butter ration was cut to two ounces a week and tea to one ounce. The local newspapers even ran news stories when leather was available for re-soling or re-heeling shoes. Perhaps here too wood was used to make soles, although the islands were not heavily forested. Under strict censorship, the newspapers were mainly used for conveying orders from the German occupiers to the local population. There was little paper anyway, so the newspapers usually consisted of no more than four pages.

Ironically, the situation on the islands became much more serious after the Normandy landings in June 1944. The German governor was a committed Nazi and a fanatic who refused to consider surrender, even though the islands were cut off from German supplies and German personnel were as much captives as the islanders. Before the final German surrender, some relief was provided when the Red Cross negotiated for a Swedish ship, the SS *Vega*, to carry supplies for the civilian population.

Despite the many problems, and the harsh treatment sometimes handed down by the occupiers, this was one of the least oppressive of all the occupations inflicted by the Germans on the countries of Europe. The question is, of course, would the mainland have been as fortunate?

Italy

Many comparisons can be drawn between Italy and Hungary. Both countries had pre-war governments sympathetic to Germany, and both had resentments over the outcome of the First World War, although in Italy's case it was because of the poor share of the 'spoils of war'. Both entered the Second World War on the side of the Axis, but only after the war had started. Both sent forces to join the Germans in the invasion of the Soviet Union. There were differences, however. Italy could fairly claim to be the birthplace of Fascism, and for some time Hitler was an admirer of the Italian leader, Benito Mussolini. As with Hungary, Italy tried to come to terms with the Allies, but although Italy managed this, it resulted in German occupation of the northern part of the country including the capital Rome. While both countries were monarchies, Hungary had what amounted to a regency.

Italy entered the war on 10 June 1940 only after the fall of France (which resulted in the Germans describing the Italians as the 'harvest hands'). Italian troops invaded the south of France, although this was a temporary measure with the creation of the Vichy zone. Certainly Hitler was disappointed that he had not been joined by Mussolini at the outset as both countries were founder-signatories of the Tripartite Pact. Hitler was to be further disappointed as he expected an early invasion and occupation of the island of Malta, a major British naval base just eighty miles from Sicily. Italy's failure to take Greece without considerable German help was one of the factors that delayed the start of Operation Barbarossa and contributed to its failure to take its primary objectives before the onset of the harsh Russian winter.

At the outset, the Italians felt that ultimate German victory was inevitable, even though German successes in the Balkans meant that the outcome would not be a partnership of equals but with Italy as a junior partner or even a satellite of Germany. This mood did not last long. The failure to take Moscow in December 1941, combined with the entry of the United States into the war, meant that German defeat would be inevitable. There were other problems, such as shortages of food. Many started to worry about Soviet expansion that might even go as far west as Italy, and amongst the working classes an interest in communism started to emerge.

Marshal Badoglio and the king's daughter-in-law sought to make contact with the United Kingdom and the United States as early as August 1942. Meanwhile, a number of opposition groups started to become more active, including those sponsored by the Roman Catholic Church and the Communist Party, while others were movements that had been banned by Mussolini. As the year progressed, pressure on Mussolini's leadership began to grow with Operation Torch (the Allied landings in North Africa), and the defeat of Axis forces outside Stalingrad, as well as RAF bombing of the major industrial cities in the north of Italy. Despite this, in January 1943 the British Foreign Secretary, Anthony Eden, rejected an Italian approach that came via Switzerland for deposing Mussolini.

By this time, Mussolini's ministers had started to jostle for the position of a replacement. Mussolini himself pressed Hitler to arrange a separate peace with the Soviet Union in late 1942 and spring 1943. February 1943 saw strikes in Milan and Turin, the same month that Mussolini sacked most of his government, including his son-in-law, Count Ciano, who had been foreign minister.

After the Allied landings in Sicily, Mussolini called a meeting of the Fascist Grand Council for the first time since 1939, but the meeting ended with lengthy quarrels leaving Mussolini isolated. Unknown to Mussolini, King Victor Emanuel had arranged for Mussolini to be arrested and replaced with Marshal Badoglio on 25 July 1943.

At first, Badoglio was popular with the masses as well as with the Roman Catholic Church and the military. Widespread demonstrations in support of the new order were tolerated for a few days until they started to demand social change and peace, upon which they were put down with brutal force. The Germans, meanwhile, had been watching developments in Italy carefully. Badoglio hoped to keep the Germans assured of Italian support until he could negotiate an armistice with the Allies, and then support an Allied landing with Italian troops. The Germans played a similar game, waiting patiently without taking action until they would increase the number of troops in Italy, which went from six divisions in July 1943 to eighteen by September, with four more divisions on their way to join them.

A truce was signed in secret between the Allies and the Italians on 3 September 1943, the day that the Allies crossed the Straits of Messina from Sicily to mainland Italy. The Allied landings at Salerno, Operation Avalanche, followed on 9 September. When signing the armistice, the Supreme Allied Commander, General Eisenhower, agreed to send an airborne division to help the Italians defend Rome, but this plan had to be abandoned because the Italians could not secure a landing ground. Badoglio and his staff quickly headed south, leaving Italian forces in the north of Italy without leadership and without orders.

Chaos resulted, but not without moments of bravery against heavy odds. There were several instances of Italian units resisting the Germans, but these were all doomed to failure. At Cephalonia, in mid-September, 1,250 Italian troops died in the battle and afterwards, the Germans shot 4,750. For the most part, the Italian Army was broken up within twenty-four hours, and around 650,000 soldiers were taken prisoner and moved to Germany. More fortunate were the sailors as the bulk of the Italian fleet left its home ports and sailed to Malta where they surrendered to the Royal Navy, although the battleship *Roma* was lost to a German guided bomb. The air force saved 400 aircraft, flying to Allied airfields, while in the south and in Sardinia the army saved sixteen divisions.

The north then became German occupied territory, with the area under German control initially stretching as far south as the River Volturno, some forty miles north of Naples, but this was pushed back. When the advances slowed, the Allies tried to land at Anzio in Operation Shingle, but this failed to meet expectations and it was not until June 1944 that Rome fell to the Allies. The single major obstacle to the advance was at Monte Casino, an old monastery set high above the plain to the south of it, with the fortified town of Casino occupied by the Germans. The 'Battle of Monte Casino' actually consisted of four battles between January and late May 1944. During this period the monastery was heavily bombed and post-war the Allies attempted to prove that the monastery itself was part of the Germans' defences, but no such proof materialised.

The occupied area of Italy became the Italian Social Republic, RSI, or *Republica Socialiste Italia*, with Mussolini, who had been rescued by the Germans, installed as leader. The RSI did not settle on Rome but instead based itself at Gargnano on Lake Garda. A challenge was mounted by the Committee for National Liberation which was opposed to the RSI, the Germans and the monarchy. The RSI instigated a propaganda campaign intended to convince the population of its socialist credentials, and at first was widely supported, with young men volunteering to join the revived armed forces. Nevertheless, it soon became clear that it was being used by the Germans to enforce the occupation. Mussolini's aim of 'socialisation' was suppressed by the Germans as they conscripted more than 100,000 able-bodied men to work in German industry, while Italy's own manufacturing industries, which were mainly in the occupied zone, were directed towards supporting the German war effort, with the occupation authorities taking control of industry. As elsewhere, the Germans took the country's gold reserves. Anything of value was moved to Germany. The fact that the country was a former ally counted for nothing, despite efforts to rebuild the armed forces, which were not very successful, with just four divisions raised by the RSI and the men trained in Germany. Conscription of one kind or another simply encouraged many young men to drop out of sight and join the growing number of partisan organisations. It has been estimated that as many as 200,000 of Rome's population of around 1.5 million were being hidden, many in churches, monasteries or large rambling buildings. As elsewhere, hostages were taken and partisan or resistance successes were followed by German revenge: on 30 March 1944, 335 hostages were shot in the Ardeatine Caves near Rome.

When liberation came, the Italians celebrated by hanging the bodies of Mussolini and his mistress over the concourse of the main railway station in Milan.

Chapter Nine

The Lessons of Crete

Operationally, Crete was the closest parallel to an invasion of the British Isles by the Germans. Of necessity, it had to be an amphibious assault with supporting paratroops and air-landed troops. It was the paratroops and air-landed troops who ensured success in Crete, but at a high price and it was a close run thing.

The British Amy had been doing well in checking Italian attempts to invade Egypt and take the Suez Canal. Unfortunately, many troops were taken away to help defend Greece from the German invasion which started on 6 April 1941. This weakened the British forces in North Africa, and despite the British reinforcements, once again the Germans pushed through Greece, overcoming desperate efforts by British and Greek troops, even with support from shore-based Fleet Air Arm aircraft using a secret RAF base that was behind enemy lines at Paramythia in Albania. The Germans were supporting the Italians whose venture into the Balkans had been unsuccessful, and such was the pressure on German military resources that after the surrender of Greece, Italy was officially the occupying power until the Italian armistice of September 1943.

By 23 April, resistance to the German invasion had collapsed and the Greek government and the country's sovereign, King George, were evacuated to Crete.

British forces were also evacuated to Crete, and in a repeat of the evacuation from Dunkirk, did so leaving most of their heavy equipment behind in Greece. Distances were greater in the eastern Mediterranean than across the English Channel, so, while evacuating British forces to Crete was sensible and eased the evacuation of Greece, attempting to establish Crete as a base was over-optimistic. It was fine as a staging post, on the way back to Egypt, but the British forces in Crete were in no state to defend the island when, on 20 May, the German airborne invasion started.

Few could have foreseen that the German assault would come by air, despite earlier experience in Norway and the Low Countries.

As they arrived, the Germans were helped by the fact that most of the British and Greek forces defending the island had been deployed to the coast, expecting a seaborne invasion. Goering had persuaded Hitler that the Luftwaffe's paratroops should mount the invasion with the army and the navy playing a supporting role. The army used barges, *caigues*, for the invasion and suffered serious casualties, with the Royal Navy completely wiping out one convoy.

A Pyrrhic Victory

It should have been clear that, after taking Greece, the next German objective would be to seize the island of Crete. This was not just a case of pursuing the Allied troops; Crete had a strategic value of its own, centrally placed in the eastern Mediterranean and a possible stepping stone for an invasion of Cyprus, which would have given the Axis forces aerial supremacy over the approaches to the Suez Canal and helped Rommel and his *Afrika Korps* in his advance into Egypt in a bid to close the Canal. Crete also offered the important naval base at Suda Bay and three airfields, at Heraklion, Retima and Maleme.

Capturing both Crete and Cyprus might also have convinced Turkey that it was worth joining the Axis powers, further tipping the balance of power in the Middle East and placing another ally close to the frontier with the Soviet Union, with only Romania and Bulgaria between Turkey and the USSR, while Turkish warships could have bombarded Soviet ports from the Black Sea.

This was clearly an important operation and one that had the potential to change the balance of power in the Mediterranean and perhaps determine the outcome of the wider war. The Germans were still disappointed that their Italian allies had not invaded Malta, which would have been another great gain and which could even have meant if not ultimate victory at least forcing the British to negotiate, something that was supposed to have been one of Hitler's main aims. An Italian attack on Malta, using the country's six battleships as well as bombing, stood a good chance of success in June 1940, when Italy had belatedly entered the war, and many Germans could not understand why this was not done.

Despite the importance of the operation, the invasion of Crete was conceived by the Luftwaffe, and the army's high command was not consulted about the feasibility or the desirability of the invasion. Possibly this was because of Hermann Goering's involvement and his still strong influence over Hitler. The army commanders might have preferred a seaborne invasion, although this would have been difficult given the Royal Navy's control of the seas, and there would have been opposition from the Kriegsmarine, especially since the Italian navy, the *Regia Marina*, had already suffered at the hands of the Royal Navy in the attack on the major naval base at Taranto on the night of 11/12 November 1940, that had put three of Italy's six battleships out of action.

The Luftwaffe had both aerial supremacy and its own paratroops, giving it the opportunity to show just how significant a force it had become. Once again this was an example of the inter-service rivalry that had run out of control, and showed how the 'Führer system' had allowed the individual service chiefs to run their own fiefdoms without coordination or cooperation.

The fault for this situation was down to just one man, Adolf Hitler. Goering was to blame, but his leader should have reined him in.

Goering had failed to destroy the British Expeditionary Force on the beaches at Dunkirk, and then failed to destroy the Royal Air Force in the Battle of Britain. The RAF had even reached Berlin, despite his promise that this would never happen. Goering, and the Luftwaffe, needed a resounding success.

On a more positive note, perhaps the Wehrmacht high command had another reason for invading Crete, delaying, even cancelling, the proposed invasion of the Soviet Union, which would have meant a new front in the war and what is now known as 'overstretch' of Germany's armed forces. Until Britain was out of the war, the German high command rightly feared a second front. Hitler wanted to strike east, however, for a number of reasons, including not just *Lebensraum*, but also for food, raw materials and fuel.

Hitler's acceptance of the need to invade Crete meant that the army had no choice but to support the operation. Even so, this was the first major airborne assault in history, and not to be compared with the landings in Norway and the Low Countries in which airborne forces had merely played a supporting role. The main thrust would be by paratroops, with air-landed troops following as soon as airfields were captured, landing in gliders as well as transport aircraft. For the first time in warfare, seaborne forces were to play a supporting role.

Codenamed Operation *Merkur*, Operation Mercury, the invasion was the idea of General Kurt Student, who quickly assembled three airborne regiments, each of three battalions and each with its own support units, from the 7th Parachute Division. A total of 22,750 men were involved, of whom 10,000 were to be parachuted into Crete, another 750 to be landed by glider, 5,000 were to be flown in by aircraft, while just 7,000 were to be landed by sea. In theory, 6,500 troops could have been flown in, but the need to fly in equipment limited the numbers to 5,000.

A force of 500 Junkers Ju52/3m transports was assigned to the Luftwaffe's *Fliegerkorps XI*, plus eighty DFS 230 gliders, while air cover was to be provided by

280 bombers, 150 dive-bombers and 180 fighter aircraft. This force overwhelmed the RAF strength in the eastern Mediterranean, which had never been very strong but also suffered from the exposed position of the three airfields on Crete, which had led the RAF and Fleet Air Arm to withdraw to Egypt for fear of their aircraft being wiped out on the ground by a surprise German aerial attack. Crete did not have the benefit of an integrated radar system on the lines of the Chain Home network that had so ably alerted and directed the RAF during the Battle of Britain.

German intelligence failings misled Student, who expected his forces to be facing just 15,000 British and Empire troops, while there were around twice that number and another 11,000 Greek troops. Yet the defenders were badly equipped with little artillery, almost no radios, and ammunition was in short supply. Poor roads and mountainous terrain also made it difficult for the defenders to respond effectively.

The German invasion troops assembled in Athens, having arrived there by road, rail and air, before being deployed to airfields at Elevis, Tatoi, Megara and Corinth. This was a difficult undertaking with poor road and rail networks within Greece, whose railways were metre gauge, that is much narrower than in the rest of Europe, and Student was forced to postpone the assault from 16 May to 20 May.

Maleme would be the objective for the Western Group in the first airlift, accompanied by half of the Central Group, which would take Canea, while the rest of the Central Group would take Retimo. The rest of the airlift would carry the Eastern Group which would take the capital, Heraklion. The 7th Division's paratroops would be joined by the 5th Mountain Division, which had four regiments each of three battalions, plus its own parachute battalion. A weakness in this plan was that the two airlifts could not be less than eight hours apart, giving the defenders time to respond and get their forces into position, but the Germans might have thought that the defenders would not be expecting a second airlift.

Early in the morning of 20 May 1941, the first lift took off from its airfields in Greece, with 493 Ju5/3m transports and 53 gliders, of which five carried headquarters units. One of the headquarter's gliders broke up in mid-air, possibly due to being overloaded, and amongst those lost was Sussman, the commander of the Central Group. The poor state of the anti-aircraft defences on Crete meant that only seven of the transport aircraft were lost, but the gliders suffered serious losses, with seven of those in the Western Group crashing, while others ran into heavy machine gun fire.

As a result of having lost the element of surprise, many of the paratroops were shot while they dropped, so that before the day was over many of the olive trees on the island were festooned with the bodies of dead paratroops, still in their harnesses. Many more were killed as they attempted to reach their weapons containers after disentangling themselves from their parachutes. Air-landed troops were killed as they left their gliders. Despite their considerable experience of airborne assaults in Norway and the Netherlands, German paratroops dropped without strapping rifles or light machine guns to themselves, and only had small arms to defend themselves during the vulnerable first few moments of landing.

After landing in a light haze at Maleme around 0800, the men of the Western Group were able to take the bridge over the Tavronitis River, knocking out the anti-aircraft batteries close to the mouth of the river, while others attempted to take Hill 107, overlooking the airfield. The airfield itself was soon taken. The Central Group, with more than 2,000 paratroops and more than 270 glider-landed troops, occupied the Akrotiri Peninsula and also cut the Canae–Akikianou road, but a well-organised counter-attack by British troops almost wiped out many units. By nightfall, the invaders were badly scattered and fighting in small isolated groups.

While the departure of the first airlift from its Greek airfields had gone smoothly, the second airlift was hampered by serious congestion at these same airfields, so its departure was slow and, worse, scattered. The remainder of the Central Group did not start to drop onto the airfield at Retimo until 1615 and, while only a little later than planned, the drop was slow and scattered. In the meantime even the limited anti-aircraft fire available to the defenders had become more concentrated and effective. The ground forces had been expecting a second drop. The Eastern Group also faced strong defences, with the final aircraft not dropping their paratroops until 1930, by which time it was dark and all element of surprise had been lost. Casualties were extremely heavy as a result.

The Germans were saved by confusion amongst the defenders, without radio communication to convey information and assemble an effective defence. The difficult terrain, poor roads, and shortage of transport, also hampered the defence. Even though the Germans were pinned down everywhere, the defenders were unable to assess the true position, and moved off Hill 107 to regroup. Student and General Meindl gambled everything on seizing Maleme airfield, gaining an air bridgehead into which reinforcements could be flown.

At 0800 on 21 May, six Ju53/3m transports landed on the beach near the mouth of the Tavronitis River, while paratroops were dropped to the rear of the defenders, although some landed amidst them and suffered heavy casualties. By 1700, Maleme airfield was secured and reinforcements were flown in the following day.

Fighting continued for several days so that all but 5,000 of the defending troops could be evacuated by the Royal Navy. More than 4,000 German troops were killed and another 327 were drowned as aircraft or gliders ploughed into the sea. The Germans lost 40 combat aircraft, and another 170 transport aircraft, while many more were seriously damaged.

This was another Allied defeat in difficult circumstances. It was small comfort that the German invasions of Yugoslavia and Greece, followed by that of Crete, were to be a major part of the ultimate undoing of the German army and of the Luftwaffe, delaying the planned invasion of the Soviet Union, Operation Barbarossa, by a vital two months and ensuring that the Germans could not secure their main objectives before the onset of the severe Russian winter, for which the German forces were so ill-prepared (these campaigns were only part of the problem, as a wet spring in Poland and Russia also meant that the ground was not ready for heavy armour and artillery movements).

The fighting continued at sea. During the night of 21/22 May, the cruisers HMS *Ajax*, *Dido* and *Orion* with four destroyers completely destroyed one convoy carrying troops and munitions. The Luftwaffe responded on 22 May with a crippling attack on the Mediterranean Fleet, sinking the cruisers *Fiji* and *Gloucester*, and badly damaging the battleship *Warspite* and the cruisers *Carlisle* and *Naiad*. Cunningham sent the battleships *Queen Elizabeth* and *Barham* with nine destroyers to attack Axis airfields in the Dodecanese, aided by aircraft from *Formidable*, but by this time the carrier's air power was extremely limited due to a shortage of aircraft after suffering heavy losses, and she could do little to defend herself when the Luftwaffe turned its attention to her, causing serious damage. Even so, the British Mediterranean Fleet continued to evacuate British, Empire and Greek troops from Crete long after the deadline set by the Admiralty.

The stark truth was that for the second time in five months during the war in the Mediterranean, an aircraft carrier was damaged beyond local repair and had to be sent away. This time, there was no replacement available.

Chapter Ten

Barbarossa and Deliverance

In modern times, the most famous invasion of Russia was by Napoleon in 1812, when the French armies were defeated in battle and then ruined by the horrors of the Russian winter.

Often forgotten, however, were the invasions towards the end of the First World War, orchestrated by the victorious allies anxious to support the White Russian counter-revolutionary forces and reverse the Bolshevik revolution while also pulling Russia back into the war against Germany and the Austro-Hungarian Empire. 'Invasions' rather than 'invasion' is really the correct term as the Allies entered Russia from four directions: through Finland; from the Black Sea through the Caucasus; from what was then known as the Persian Gulf; and from the Far East through Siberia. These invasions consisted of different armies depending on their geographical location, so the invasion through the Caucasus was largely a British affair and known as 'Dunster Force' after its commanding officer, Major General L.C. Dunsterville. That through Siberia included United States, Canadian and Japanese troops.

Although these various forces were intended to join up, the vastness of the country, war weariness, a lack of overall command and strategy, and the differing aspirations of the national contingents, all conspired to ensure failure. These problems were compounded by the poor communications technology of the day.

The First World War had seen Russian troops facing German and Austro-Hungarian Forces on what the Germans described as the 'Eastern Front'. Austria-Hungary was weak militarily and suffering from serious internal problems, not least of which was the very real risk that the Austro-Hungarian Empire might split in two, or even worse become fragmented as rising nationalist sentiment undermined effective governance. For Tsarist Russia, freeing the Slavonic countries from Austro-Hungarian domination was a vital war aim. For Germany, the strain of fighting a major war on two fronts was taking its toll, hence the support for the Bolsheviks, on the basis that 'my enemy's enemy is my friend' and certainly not through any sympathy with the revolution. Germany after all was at this point still a monarchy.

The Soviet Union

Although media reports on Operation Barbarossa almost always described it as 'the invasion of Russia', the Soviet Union actually consisted of sixteen republics with no less than seventy officially recognised languages. The Germans invaded the Soviet-occupied Baltic States of Estonia, Latvia and Lithuania, as well as Belorussia and the Ukraine. Very little of Russia itself was ever occupied by German forces. One British field marshal, Lord Montgomery, once said, 'On page one of the Book of War, it says: never march on Moscow.' Like Napoleon before him, Hitler was soon to realise the wisdom in this statement.

Unlike the invasion of the United Kingdom, or in effect southern England, Hitler had long seen war with the Soviet Union as inevitable. Indeed, one of his many concerns over the invasion of England was that it would encourage the Soviet leader, Stalin, to seize the opportunity to strike west and invade Germany. The two nations were not just politically opposed, but racially as well. Hitler, and many Germans with him, despised the Slavonic races. The result was that Operation Barbarossa was to result in savagery unmatched in any of the earlier German campaigns, and once the Soviets managed to fight back and go onto the offensive, the same could be said about their treatment of the Germans and their allies.

The invasion was not unpopular. In the BBC publication *War of the Century* by Laurence Rees, Major Hubert Menzel of the Wehrmacht's General Operations Department recalled that there was a clear logic to it: 'We knew that in two years' time, that is by the end of 1942, beginning of 1943, the English would be ready, the Americans would be ready, the Russians would be ready too, and then we would have to deal with all three of them at the same time... We had to try to remove the greatest threat from the east.'

This meant that Hitler had a clear alternative to invading the United Kingdom, and one that had the advantages of securing vast areas of land, ample food supplies and raw materials. It would also mean extinguishing an ideological foe and eliminating a substantial Jewish population, while providing Slavonic slave labour.

Stalin's refusal to believe warnings about German intentions meant that his forces were unprepared and poorly placed, and this was compounded by the pre-war purges of senior officers in the Soviet armed forces so at first there was a dearth of leadership. The final order for the invasion was given by Hitler on 20 June issuing the code word 'Dortmund'.

At 0315 on 22 June 1941 the German invasion of the Soviet Union began, without declaration of war, along a line from the Baltic in the north and the

Carpathian mountains in the south. Stalin at the last moment ordered his units to be scattered and camouflaged, but the headquarters received the message too late to pass to all units at the front.

The Soviet Union had around 18,000 aircraft, but no more than a fifth could be classified as modern. Only half of the aircraft were based in the west. The Luftwaffe had 1,945 aircraft against the 9,000 Soviet. The difference lay in the quality of the aircraft and the combat skills and experience of the aircrew. Another thousand aircraft came from Germany's allies, Romania providing about 400, Hungary 200, Finland 300, and Italy, larger, more industrialised and prosperous than either of these, just 100. This was due in no small measure to the country's involvement in the Balkans and North Africa, as well as the air campaign against Malta and the convoys to Malta.

There was also the element of surprise, with most of the Soviet aircraft being caught on the ground. The sixty-six Soviet airfields which had seventy per cent of the Soviet air strength in the west were overwhelmed. One senior officer, Lieutenant General Kopets, lost 600 aircraft without making any impact on the Germans, and committed suicide on 23 June. Some believe that half of Soviet aircraft were non-operational on the day of the invasion.

The Germans were not without their problems. The launch of the operation had been delayed by the invasion of Greece, with one German general stating that the invasion had cost the Germans five weeks. This may have been academic as a wet spring had left much of the ground too soft for tanks, and many rivers were still swollen making crossing more difficult. Another problem had been getting transport to the right place in time. The delays were to mean that the Germans were going to have little time to reach their objectives before the onset of the Russian winter, for which they were fatally ill-equipped.

The cold weather meant that tanks were to slide helplessly on the ice, while bombs broke up on the ice rather than exploding. Aircraft had to have fires lit under their engines before they could be started. German leather boots were too brittle and provided little grip on the ice, proving far inferior to the felt boots worn by Soviet troops.

At the start, all had gone well. For Operation Barbarossa, the Germans had assembled the largest armed force in European history, with almost 3.6 million Axis troops, some 3,600 tanks and almost 2,900 aircraft. The commander was Field Marshal von Brauchitsch. He had his forces divided into three army groups: North, commanded by Field Marshal von Leeb; Centre, commanded by Field Marshal von Bock; and South, commanded by Field Marshal von Rundstedt.

These had air support from three tactical air forces, commanded by General Alfred Keller in the north, Field Marshal von Kesselring in the centre, and in the south by General Lohr. This overwhelming force achieved its initial objectives, and within one week more than 150,000 Soviet troops were dead or wounded, a higher attrition rate than during the five months of the Somme offensive of the First World War.

Stalin was in such a state of denial that it took some time before he could bring himself to address the Soviet people, who learnt of the German invasion from the foreign minister, Molotov. He recovered enough by 3 July to proclaim the defence of Soviet territory as being a 'Great Patriotic War', calling for sacrifice and for the implementation of a scorched earth policy.

The German invasion of the Soviet Union was far more brutal and bloody than any that preceded it. This was due as much to Stalin as to Hitler. Everything that lay in the path of the invader was to be destroyed, including livestock and food stores, as well as whatever was growing in the fields. Buildings were to be razed to the ground and any machinery that could not be moved destroyed. Major towns and cities were not to be surrendered but to fight to the last person, which in the Soviet armed forces meant women as well as men. Anyone who was taken prisoner-of-war was to face punishment once liberated, even if they had escaped on their own initiative. Worse, their families would also be punished. When Stalin's son, a fighter pilot, was shot down and taken prisoner, Stalin disowned him so as not to be implicated in his son's failure.

A million Soviet troops were positioned to augment the defences of Kiev, capital of the Ukraine, which Kleist's First Panzer Group reached on 11 July and started the encirclement of the city. During the first week of August, German Army Group South was closing in, facing four Soviet armies with two more moving to reinforce them. Hitler ordered a stop to the advance on Moscow on 25 August and sent additional Panzer units south to Kiev, where, despite an orderly retreat being possible, this was forbidden by Stalin. The result was that in early September Kiev fell, and 665,000 Soviet prisoners were taken by the Germans. Overall, by the end of October 1941, some three million Soviet personnel had become German prisoners-of-war.

Soviet rule was harsh, but the German attitude to those in the occupied territories in the east was far worse than in the west. According to Erich Koch, the *Reichskommissar* of Ukraine, 'the lowliest German worker is a thousand times more valuable' than the entire population of the Ukraine. The local people were kept short of food, which was commandeered and either used to feed the occupation force or sent to Germany, so that in the Ukraine and in other Soviet occupied territories, the population was forced to eat whatever they could find. Dogs were the first victims, until there were none left, and rats, crows and birch bark had to be resorted to. In Kharkov, 100,000 Ukrainians died from starvation and associated diseases. One woman working in a slaughterhouse in Kharkov considered herself lucky as she was able to collect blood, smuggle it home and make a 'blood omelette'. No explanation was given for where she found the eggs.

Life as a German prisoner was not easy anywhere, but the treatment of Soviet prisoners was far harsher than for British and American PoWs. The provision of food was erratic, and accommodation was inadequate. Red Cross parcels which helped sustain morale amongst the Western Allied troops in the PoW camps as well as providing some comforts and variety in their diet, were unknown to Soviet prisoners. This was not so much the fault of the Germans but because of the shortages endemic in the Soviet system which meant that there was nothing to send.

Despite fighting a desperate war against a numerically superior enemy, a priority for many Germans was the extermination of the Jewish population of the Soviet Union, added to which was the execution of all Red Army commissars (despite this being against international law). Not all German officers agreed with this, or the extermination of the Jews, and often Slavs as well, so the slaughter was patchy. *Waffen-SS* and *Einsatzgruppen* units followed the combat units, who supported them with fuel and food, although these units were under the direct control of the Reich Main Security Office (RSHA), whose chief was Reinhard Heydrich.

The *Einsatzgruppen* were also to deal with any partisan activity, taking whatever action they saw fit.

Paradoxically, the first reaction of many Jews in the Soviet Union was to welcome the German invasion. Jews in Eastern Europe, and especially Poland and Russia, had been accustomed to centuries of pogroms, usually violent, which resulted in the loss of property and often life as well. They were soon to be disillusioned. Many historians in the West now believe that the Germans had initially simply wanted to rid Germany of its Jewish population by forcing them to leave, but under wartime conditions this was impossible, and hence the death camps of the so-called 'final solution'. German thinking was that exterminating the Jews would also end Bolshevism.

Different Strands of Socialism

Hitler's Nazi Party was officially the National Socialist Party. It has been said that the difference between Fascists, such as the Nazis, and Communists, who ruled the

Soviet Union, is that Communists nationalised property while Fascists nationalised people. Hitler and his supporters were extremely anti-communist, largely because of the several attempts to establish Bolshevik uprisings in Germany as the First World War came to an end. What developed was a power struggle between the Fascists and the Bolsheviks, with the former's appeal and power base enhanced by many who feared a repeat of the Russian Revolution in Germany itself.

As early as 1925, Hitler had advocated the invasion of the Soviet Union in his book *Mein Kampf* (My Struggle), published that year. This was his reaction to the rash of Bolshevik uprisings across Germany, including the short-lived creation of a localised Soviet in Munich, and a similar attempt by disgruntled ratings at a naval base, which he saw as being inspired by the Soviet Union.

The irony was that after Hitler came to power and as German rearmament gathered pace, the dire state of the German economy and the resistance from those opposed to Hitler meant that increasingly the German economy was adopting features more usually aligned with those of the Soviet Union. Businessmen who did not follow Hitler's lead had their businesses confiscated, in other words, nationalised. One of the most prominent early victims was the aeronautical expert Professor Hugo Junkers, who refused to collaborate with the Nazis not long after Hitler took power and had his business taken from him in 1934. Within Germany, political direction and restraints on holding precious metals also meant the running of the economy was becoming almost Soviet in style.

Post-First World War Germany and the Soviet Union were politically opposed, but these two countries needed each other. The Russians needed German expertise so that the country could industrialise and move forward from being a backward state, especially since so much of its scientific and engineering talent had fled the revolution, including Igor Sikorsky, the talented aircraft designer and later, working in the United States, pioneer not only of the helicopter but also of flying boats and amphibians. In the 1920s, the Germans, faced with the restrictions imposed on them by the Treaty of Versailles, needed somewhere to develop and continue their work on such matters as aircraft and submarine design. The Treaty had banned Germany from operating aircraft, although eventually civil aviation was permitted, and also banned the country from possessing submarines.

The Germans were not the only odd bedfellows for Soviet Russia. The United States, the bastion of capitalism and one of the countries that had tried to keep Russia in the First World War, and then tried to reverse the Bolshevik Revolution, helped improve Russian lorry production.

Short of natural resources, especially oil, and incapable of feeding its own population, Germany needed Russia. Russia in turn needed foreign currency, although even before the war broke out in 1939 this was also an increasing problem for Germany, which grabbed the gold and foreign exchange reserves of Austria and Czechoslovakia to pay for its growing deficit.

To Hitler and many of his supporters, there was another bone of contention. They equated Bolshevism with the Jews, and the Jews with Bolshevism. In fact, both countries persecuted their Jewish communities, although in Russia this almost amounted to a tradition so that Jews in Russia, and in Poland as well, had a history of suffering from frequent violent pogroms. In Germany it was more recent, although prejudice was notable even before and during the First World War.

Germany Prepares to Open a Second Front

To the average German, even those involved in fighting the war, the outlook in early 1941 looked good. True, the British were still in the war, and despite having been pushed out of Norway and then France, still capable of fighting. On the other hand, nothing could disguise the fact that Germany had now incorporated Austria, had seized Czechoslovakia, and then occupied much of Poland, including territory lost as a result of the Treaty of Versailles. By mid-1940, Germany controlled territory from the North Cape to the Bay of Biscay, and Italy had finally entered the war. Then Germany was victorious in Yugoslavia and Greece, and had taken the island of Crete, while winning a battle against the British at Tobruk.

Those with a deeper understanding of the economy, and especially those with what might be described as inside information, knew that all was not well. Germany needed to secure its supplies of oil and other essential materials, and food was becoming a problem, at least for the civilian population, despite supplies being commandeered from the occupied territories and sent to Germany.

After the Russian-German truce of August 1939, the two sides had toned down the rhetoric and the gullible could even have thought that they were now friends; but despite Russia and Germany in effect sharing Poland, the truce was a temporary expedient, a case of Germany covering its back while it attacked north and then west. In fact nothing had changed, as behind the scenes the two leaders did not trust and certainly did not like each other, and each vied for the unsavoury distinction of being the more evil. Both believed in expansion. Hitler followed Bismarck and the Kaiser in wanting a greater Germany, a *Mitteleuropa*. Stalin wanted a greater

Russia, despite his belief in 'Communism in one country', which incorporated countries such as the Ukraine and Georgia, his birthplace. This had already been achieved during the early years of the Soviet Union, but the Soviet Union had lost Poland, which had seized its independence after the Bolshevik Revolution, and Finland which had done much the same, and had managed to hold on to most of its territory during the Russo-Finnish War, or 'Winter War', of 1939-40.

Neither leader trusted his subordinates and both interfered in military matters. Neither understood maritime affairs. One big difference was that Stalin kept those close to him under control by placing their families in the notorious 'Gulag' prison camp system on near starvation rations, effectively holding them as hostages, while Hitler was far more relaxed and even generous in his dealing with his inner circle.

While Germany and the Soviet Union were allies, many in the western democracies with left-leaning political views objected to the war with the United Kingdom and France fighting Germany, the Soviet Union's ally at the time. Attitudes amongst such people changed virtually overnight when Germany launched Operation Barbarossa. More importantly, once Germany had started on this course, any prospect of an invasion of England was impossible. Germany had more than enough to contend with.

By 1941, Germany's armed forces were nearing the zenith of their capability and confidence. By contrast, those of the Soviet Union were at a low ebb. The armed forces had seen as much as half of their officer corps purged before the war by Stalin. Just five of the eighty members of the Military Soviet in 1934 were still alive in 1938. None of the military district commanders had survived the purges, often accompanied by show trials. At all levels, Russian military commanders shared their command with a political commissar, often lacking military experience but who could, nevertheless, and often did, countermand their orders. The political commissars could report the military commanders for inefficiency, regardless of whether or not this was justified, and had the power to second guess them. This obviously undermined the confidence of the commanders and their ability to respond quickly and effectively.

The equipment situation was no better. Despite the earlier associations with German and American industry, most of the Soviet Union's industry was obsolete and inefficient to the extent that it was often primitive. As mentioned earlier, out of a total of 18,000 aircraft in the armed forces, only a fifth could be regarded as modern.

By contrast, most German military equipment was a match for the best that any other country could provide. But there were some serious omissions. The Luftwaffe lacked a truly heavy bomber in 1941, which was to prove to be as much a drawback during Operation Barbarossa as it was during the blitz on British cities because the one precaution that Stalin had taken against the possibility of invasion by the Germans was to position most of the country's heavy industry to the east of the Ural mountains, out of reach of the Luftwaffe. This was an exercise similar to the British 'shadow factory' concept, which had factories from what, in wartime, were regarded as non-essential industries converted to work on military essentials, with railway workshops producing tanks, for example.

The second omission was the absence of a truly modern and well-equipped air transport force. Whenever transport aircraft were needed, they were the obsolete Junker Ju52/3 *Tante Ju*, the 'Iron Auntie', rather than newer types such as the Ju252. Aircrew for the transports were drawn from the instructors of the bomber training schools, rather than having trained and dedicated transport pilots, so that bomber aircrew training ceased during major operations, and then was affected afterwards by the inevitable losses.

The third problem was that the German army was not fully mechanised, apart from the armoured divisions, depending on horses for transport and much of its artillery limbers. This was a problem given the vast distances of the Soviet Union, and one that was made worse by the railway track gauge of the Soviet Union being different from that used in Germany and much of western Europe (Greece, operating on a narrow gauge of just one metre, and broad-gauge Ireland, Portugal and Spain were other exceptions). Once the invasion started, time had to be wasted re-gauging lines as the Germans advanced, and there was a dire shortage of dual-gauge rolling stock.

The fourth problem comes as a shock to anyone believing in German efficiency, preparation and thoroughness: the Germans were unprepared for the harshness of the Russian winter. They not only lacked the technology to ensure that aircraft and armoured vehicles could operate in extreme cold, which might be excused due to the limitations of the technology available at the time, but what was inexcusable was the failure to provide warm winter clothing for the men in either quality or quantity.

Some have argued that the Germans had expected to have reached all of their objectives before the onset of winter, but this ignores the inconvenient fact that conquering armies do not return home during the winter months.

Barbarossa

Planning for the invasion of the Soviet Union began as early as August 1940, even while the Germans were still contemplating the invasion of England. One senior officer, General Marcks, produced a plan that he believed would result in the defeat of the Soviet armed forces in no more than seventeen weeks. He envisaged using 146 divisions, which at the time was virtually the entire strength of the German army. Given the number of troops tied down in the occupied territories, it was clear that the Germans were expecting a considerable contribution from their four allies, Italy, Finland, Hungary and Romania.

Finland, of course, was almost an ally by default as the country had spent the previous winter locked in combat with the Soviet Union in the so-called 'Winter War' as the Russians tried to retake Finland which had been part of Tsarist Russia. While the Russians failed, Finland did have to cede some territory, mainly parts of Karelia, in the eventual peace agreement.

Marcks proposed a two-pronged assault, with the northern prong aimed at Moscow, the capital, and the southern pointed at the resources of the Ukraine.

This might have worked, but after discussion and war games the Germans settled on a three-pronged attack. While there would still be a southern force heading for the Ukraine, there would be two prongs to the north, one encircling Leningrad (now St Petersburg) and then moving on to take Moscow, while the other was intended to cripple Russia's communications, especially those leading into Moscow, the centre of the country's railway system, so that the city would be isolated until the Leningrad force was ready to take the city. Hitler was the determining influence in these changes as he believed that Moscow was not the centre of power and did not wish to repeat Napoleon's mistake by concentrating on Moscow.

Ideally, the Germans should either have concentrated on Leningrad and Moscow, hoping to force Stalin to cede the Ukraine, or they should have ignored the northern cities and instead concentrated on taking the Ukraine, simply containing Soviet forces in the north, and gaining the vital supplies that the Ukraine had to offer. At the same time, the Soviet Union would be denied these supplies.

Of the 146 divisions, 19 would be *Panzer* divisions, 9 lines of communications troops, and 116 would be infantry, but of these only 14 would be motorised: a fatal flaw given the vast distances to be covered. A larger territory with a far higher population than Germany, the Soviet Union had more men than Germany and her allies combined.

The original plan had been to mount the invasion in April, but the Italians were in trouble in Yugoslavia and Greece, so the Germans had to rush troops and aircraft to reinforce the invasion of these two countries. Then the Germans had to take Crete, at some considerable cost in manpower as the seaborne element of the invasion was savaged by the Royal Navy, and the paratroops and glider-landed troops also suffered heavy casualties, to the extent that for a time Hitler forbade any airborne assaults.

On 22 June when the invasion started, the ground was dry and firm, but it gave the Germans just fourteen weeks to gain their objectives. The Germans and their allies at least had the advantage of surprise. This shouldn't have happened as Stalin had received numerous warnings about German intentions from diplomats, and from agents in other countries, including Japan. Had Stalin reacted to intelligence reports and organised a robust and well-prepared defence, he might have been able to hold off the Germans. At one stage he is reported to have even considered ceding some territory to the Germans. Some believe that Stalin was expecting a last-minute reconciliation with Hitler. He did, eventually, panic and order his armies to disperse and use camouflage, but the order was issued too late for divisional headquarters to pass it to frontline units in time.

Despite the losses in the campaign for Crete, the eventual force sent forward comprised 153 divisions. They were facing Soviet forces organised into 140 divisions and with a total of 2.9 million men, with between 10,000 and 15,000 tanks, and 9,000 aircraft. Not just the aircraft, but many of the tanks were obsolete. The Luftwaffe achieved aerial supremacy within a couple of days with many Soviet aircraft destroyed on the ground.

On the ground, the operation was conducted with unprecedented brutality. All captured Red Army commissars were executed, while the 'Barbarossa Jurisdiction Decree' exempted all German soldiers from prosecution for any crime committed against Soviet citizens. Captured Russian soldiers were kept under severe conditions in prison camps, with little food and no medical provision.

On 3 July, Stalin finally broadcast to his people. He declared a 'patriotic war' against the Germans and urged a scorched earth policy so that the advancing Germans would not be able to live off the land, and would not be able to use anything left behind. Resistance warfare behind German lines was expected of all Russians.

To the Germans, the Russians were regarded as being *Untermenschen*, and Soviet armed forces were assumed, wrongly, to have little military potential. On taking Leningrad and Moscow, both cities were to be razed to the ground. Their populations were to be slaughtered, forced to move or face starvation. The vast Jewish population of Russia at first welcomed the Germans as liberators, but they were soon disillusioned as the plans for the occupation of Russian territory called not simply for their removal, but their elimination. Once the fighting ended, the best agricultural areas were to be offered to German servicemen and their families for resettlement.

The harshness of the Soviet regime and the way in which so many had been deprived of property and freedom meant that there were Russians willing to fight alongside the Axis forces. Many Soviet troops in German prisoner-of-war camps volunteered to join the German army in the hope of getting better treatment.

There were major battles of encirclement at Bialystok-Minsk and Smolensk, as a result of which the Germans soon realised that they had underestimated their enemy. Not only did the Russian troops fight fiercely and with growing skill, their equipment was better than the Germans had assumed, and the relocation of the major factories east of the Urals also meant that equipment losses were made good quickly.

The encirclement at Bialystok-Minsk destroyed the Soviet West army group and after having advanced almost 300 miles since the start of the invasion, the Germans arrived at Smolensk on 6 July. This was the traditional gateway to Moscow, a gap some fifty miles wide between the Dnieper and Western Dvina. Here the Germans found a new Soviet West army waiting for them, commanded by Marshal Timoshenko. Repeated attacks by Timoshenko showed the Germans that they were to encounter stronger resistance than previously. By 11 July the German Panzers had seized Smolensk, but advancing further eastwards two additional Panzer divisions could not join up because of fierce resistance by Russia troops. The encirclement of Smolensk could not be completed until 5 August. It yielded more than 300,000 Russian prisoners.

Instead of continuing towards Leningrad and Moscow aided by the Panzer divisions of Army Group Centre, on 21 August Hitler ordered most of these divisions to assist Army Group South advance into the Ukraine. This resulted in the capture of Kiev, along with more than 600,000 Russian prisoners, but it delayed the attack on Moscow for six weeks, until early October when the Panzer divisions returned north. In the meantime, the defenders of Moscow put the time to good use, while on the other hand, the Germans had expended fuel and ammunition reserves in the Ukraine and stretched their supply lines as well as wearing out tanks and other vehicles.

The result of the diversion into the Ukraine was that it took the Germans longer to reach Moscow in 1941 than Napoleon's Grand Army had taken in 1812. Operation Barbarossa was now stretching into winter without having taken its key objectives. Now the Germans had to face temperatures dropping to between -30 and -50 degrees centigrade for long periods, and occasionally dropping to as low as -70. Snow and ice affected mobility, with tanks skidding and slipping, while aircraft engines froze. Another unforeseen problem was that there was more than three feet of snow: the impact of shells and bombs was muffled, while on ice, shells and bombs shattered without exploding.

Such had been the optimism at the outset in late June that many German troops were still in summer uniforms. Even German winter clothing was not warm enough for the Russian winter. Around Moscow, the Germans suffered 10,000 cases of frostbite while supplies of food and fuel were rapidly exhausted.

The Germans never managed to take Moscow. The anti-tank trenches that the residents had dug in the main streets were never needed. First, the position stabilised, and then in fierce fighting the Germans were forced to retreat, so that by late January 1942 they had been pushed back some forty miles from Moscow. Suitably encouraged, Stalin started to plan the relief of Leningrad and the retaking of the Ukraine.

By spring, the Germans still had a chance of reversing the position and making further advances. They had occupied the Ukraine. They had managed to secure their front at Moscow, and managed to keep Leningrad under siege. If the Finns had been persuaded to renew their offensive against Leningrad, the city might have fallen. Instead, the siege continued until January 1944, by which time more than 200,000 civilians had been killed in German air raids and artillery bombardment, and another 650,000 had died from starvation.

With renewed optimism and vigour, the Axis forces planned further advances. The next priority was to take the oilfields of the Caucasus, while Hitler also demanded that they capture Stalingrad (now Volgograd) on the River Volga. The Caucasus on their own might have been achievable, but the longer lines of communication were now proving to be too much. There was a need for more railway regauging. While initial Russian partisan resistance had been weak, this was becoming stronger. As the Germans entered mountainous territory, the terrain favoured the defence. By this time, the increasingly successful Soviet strategy was beginning to work. Rather than fight the Germans in open country where Panzer units could be used to good effect, they fell back towards the mountains and Stalingrad. In the mountains, the well-tried Blitzkrieg tactics were useless. In the cities, as at Leningrad in 1941 and then at Stalingrad a year later, the German advance was brought to a stop in street fighting.

The Battle for Moscow

It had been thought that Moscow would be reached in September, before the onset of the Russian winter. Hitler had even hoped for a grand victory parade in Moscow at the end of August. At the start of the German invasion, Stalin himself had kept a train ready to make his escape eastwards. The diversion of strong forces to ensure the seizure of Kiev made Hitler's dream unobtainable. Instead, by late August the German advance was being countered by the refusal of Soviet defensive formations to break, and by desperate counter-attacks.

Moscow was regarded as important by Hitler who placed great emphasis on taking capital cities, a case of cutting off the head. In fact, the city was a centre of transport, especially railway, and of industry, although the Soviet Union, in general so ill-prepared for war, had taken the precaution of moving as much industry as possible east of the Urals, outside the limited range of the Luftwaffe bomber force. Governments[1] as well could, and did, relocate to safer areas to continue the business of administration and leadership. Yet Hitler had diverted his forces towards Kiev rather than persisting with the drive towards Moscow. This seems perverse, but the Ukraine was a great centre of agricultural production, and through it lay the way to the vital oilfields of the Caucasus.

It was only on 2 October that Moscow once again became the prime objective. Eight days later, Stalin appointed General Zhukov to command the West Front army group, which consisted of eight armies with around a million men spread along a 174-mile front running north-south to the west of the capital and centred on Mozhaisk. Once again Stalin was slow in acting, and clearly failed to anticipate the speed of the German advance. Bock's Army Group Centre, with a similar number of men, broke through the Soviet defences at Kalinin on 14 October, taking the northern end of the defensive line, while Mozhaisk itself, in the centre, fell on 18 October. At this stage it was decided to place Moscow under martial law, and government departments started to evacuate eastwards to Kuibyshev. Fate then intervened. The autumn rains turned the unmetalled Russian roads into mud tracks and halted the German advance for three weeks. The Luftwaffe remained operational but there was little bombing of Moscow as the Germans preferred to attack Zhukov's armies. The Russians maintained that just 229 German sorties were made over Moscow at this time, and gave the credit to the capital's air defences.

With the German advance checked by the weather, Zhukov acted decisively. He restored order to the frontline while Stalin organised nine reserve armies behind the River Volga (although these only totalled around 100,000 men and consisted of poor quality troops too young, too old or too unfit to have been conscripted already). Meanwhile, stronger units with seasoned and well-trained troops were being hurried from Siberia, despite the limitations of the Trans-Siberian Railway.[2] The Germans were alarmed at the change of fortunes that would follow. A direct assault on Moscow itself seemed unlikely to succeed, but an alternative seemed possible, forcing a way past the city and then surrounding it, which would undermine Soviet morale and would be better for that of the Germans than sitting out the harsh Russian winter forty miles from Moscow.

The advance resumed on 15 November. Heavy frosts had frozen the ground and provided a firm base for the tanks to operate, and the Germans moved out of the forests into open ground, better suited for armour and artillery.

Morale was boosted further when on the first day an entire Soviet Army was crushed by the German Ninth Army. The Third Panzer Group reached the Moscow-Volga Canal, 37 miles north of Moscow, on 27 November, while Fourth Panzer Group was just 12.5 miles outside the city. On the other side, south-east of the city, lay the Second Panzer Army at Kashira on the River Oka. This situation made Stalin change his mind about committing valuable reserves to the battle, but Bock had run out of reserves and his Fourth Army, to the west of Moscow, had finally been checked by Soviet forces which was preventing his other forces from completing the encirclement.

On the outskirts of Moscow, Soviet forces had no option but to stand their ground regardless of cost. Soldiers who attempted to leave the front line found that they faced special detachments with orders to shoot deserters on sight, while Soviet partisans infiltrated behind enemy lines were instructed to shoot anyone deserting. The partisans took full advantage of this, imposing their will on villagers. Inside Moscow itself, some 8,000 inhabitants were executed for what the authorities perceived as cowardice. Outside Moscow, the partisans did not hesitate to loot, beat, rape or kill villagers. The residents remaining in the occupied territories, having been forced to do as the Germans wished, and then as the Soviet partisans wished, then had to suffer further as a third force emerged in the shape of nationalist partisans who were fighting both the Germans and the Soviet forces, wanting their territory to be freed from the Soviet Union.

As for the German Army, as elsewhere, the distinction between a partisan and an ordinary citizen was not rigidly observed. On one occasion 1,900 partisans and their 'helpers' were killed in one engagement, but only thirty rifles were recovered, suggesting that the force of partisans was indeed small.

On the night of 4/5 December, a heavy snowfall brought all hopes of any further German advances to an end, while temperatures plummeted to minus 34 degrees centigrade. Most German equipment was immobilised, and the troops did not have suitable clothing. Hitler had planned to have seized his objectives in the Soviet Union before the worst of the winter weather set in, and this would have allowed two-thirds of the invasion force to have been withdrawn. Clothing for those troops set to remain had been brought forward and stored in Poland, where most of it stayed due to transport difficulties. The Germans had in any case come to realise that much of their equipment was unsuitable. The German predilection for leather notwithstanding, Soviet felt boots provided more warmth and a better grip in the icy conditions.

Realising the German predicament, Zhukov ordered a counter-attack on 6 December, with Stalin releasing the newly-arrived reserve units. Ill-equipped to handle the difficult weather, the Germans started to fall back. The counter-attack became an offensive. Unable to move much of their equipment, the Germans had to abandon it, setting fire to it whenever they could. Communications all but collapsed as the heavy snow brought down telephone lines, while rear-echelon troops in full retreat blocked the roads and hindered reinforcements and supplies moving forward.

The situation was aptly described by the chief of the German General Staff, General Franz Halder, as the 'greatest crisis in two world wars'. On 18 December, Bock took sick leave, and the commander-in-chief of the German Army, Field Marshal von Brauchitsch, offered his resignation. Hitler assumed the role of commander-in-chief and appointed Field Marshal von Kluge as Bock's replacement. Next, Hitler demanded 'fanatical resistance' and banned retreats for any reason, sacking officers who disobeyed, and for some the consequences were worse. Rank and previous esteem were no defence, as one of the first victims of this harsh regime was the Second Panzer Army's commander, General Heinz Guderian, who had previously been a favourite of the Führer.

On 7 January, Zhukov had pushed the Germans back to the point where they had restarted their advance on 15 November. He intended to go further, as far west as Smolensk, but Stalin was taken with the idea of encircling German Army Group Centre. This was a manoeuvre beyond the forces available, and in the chaos that ensued, the Germans managed to regain control of their forces. When spring came, the Germans had been pushed back to 93 miles from Moscow, but Army Group Centre had recovered and remained a cohesive force.

Leningrad

Formerly St Petersburg, and briefly after the revolution Petrograd, Leningrad was at the mouth of the Neva River on the Gulf of Finland, and was the second largest city of the Soviet Union. A ship canal linked it to the naval base at Kronstadt, while another canal linked it to the River Volga. The city was an important manufacturing centre as well as a port.

Leningrad was cut off from the rest of the Soviet Union on 8 July 1941 after the German Fourth Panzer Army reached the old fortress of Shlisselburg, which guarded the River Neva at the point where it flows out of Lake Ladoga. North of Leningrad, Finnish forces were advancing towards the River Svir and the city. The German commander, Marshal von Leeb, was confident that his Army Group North and the Finns could take the city quickly, but problems soon arose. The first was that the Finns refused to go beyond the Svir, their boundary before the Finnish-Russian War, or 'Winter' War, of 1939-40, leaving them standing twenty-five miles north of Leningrad. Leeb then had the Fourth Panzer Army staff and half of its tanks removed and transferred to the attack on Moscow. Hitler then demanded that Leningrad should not be allowed to surrender, but should be obliterated by bombing and shelling while its population was to be allowed to starve and succumb to disease.

Leeb had little choice but to settle his forces around the fortress complex of Oranienbaum, including the Kronstadt naval base, and along a line close enough to Leningrad for all of it to be within artillery range. On the south shore of Lake Ladoga, German forces placed a stranglehold on the city, known, from the shape of the troop dispositions, as the 'bottleneck'. In mid-October, Hitler overruled Leeb and insisted that Army Group North should sweep around Lake Ladoga to meet with the Finns on the Svir, a distance of 155 miles, which left Leeb's forces over-extended. As it happened, Leeb's men got halfway, to Tikhvin, before in mid-December Stalin, by this time confident of ultimate victory at Moscow, sent reinforcements. On 18 December, Hitler had no option but to allow Leeb to withdraw and return to the 'bottleneck'.

Leningrad was highly vulnerable to any siege or blockade (the difference being that a siege was designed to bring about surrender). The winter of 1941-42 started early and was exceptionally severe even by Russian standards. Nothing had been done to alleviate the problems the city was to encounter even though the danger had been obvious since July. No attempt had been made to evacuate the civilian population or transfer factories and their machinery further east. The only action taken had been to remove some, but by no means all, of the Hermitage Museum's art collection. The problem arose because the Communist Party chief in Leningrad, Andrei Zhdanov, and the army chief, Marshal Voroshilov, who had been appointed directly by Stalin to defend the city, did not wish to do anything that could be construed as defeatist. What this meant was that there were 2.5 million civilians to feed within the blockaded area, as well as the Red Banner Fleet in the Baltic and the Red Army troops. By November, there was no option but to cut civilian rations to starvation levels, and here again dogs and horses were slaughtered and butchered.

Lake Ladoga was the one route available to bypass the blockade. It was navigable by boat in the summer but in winter the ice had to be strong enough for lorries to use an improvised road. Yet communications across the lake did not provide sufficient supplies to sustain the minimal rations imposed on the population, and there was an increasing fuel shortage, affecting transport, lighting and, of course, heating. Freight had to be transported by road from the railhead at Tikhvin, 175 miles away. Even when the Germans withdrew from around Tikhvin, there was little improvement in the city's plight until February 1942, when the railway reopened. The supply lorries carried evacuees on their return journeys across the lake, but travelling in unheated vehicles, frail due to lack of food, and often suffering from illnesses brought on by starvation, many did not survive the journey.

Soviet figures claim that 850,000 civilians were evacuated between January and July 1942, leaving around 800,000 in Leningrad, but that suggests that almost a million were unaccounted for. It seems likely that those buried in mass graves were not counted. There was also another more sinister reason for so many to be missing, which was that once the supply of animals was exhausted, many resorted to cannibalism. While the Soviet Union has never officially recognised this problem, the records of the NKVD, the People's Commissariat for Internal Affairs (Komissariat Vnutrennikh Del), not released until 2004, noted that some 2,000 people were arrested for cannibalism, usually eating the flesh of dead bodies rather than having first murdered the victims.

On 7 January, Stalin ordered General Meretskov's Volkhov front to advance and eliminate the German line running 120 miles between Lake Ladoga and Lake Ilmen. Despite the harsh weather, Meretskov managed to create a narrow passage north of Lake Ilmen, through which General Vlasov's Second Shock Army advanced 37 miles north-west before being halted by the start of the thaw in March, when roads turned to mud and swollen rivers burst their banks, flooding the flat land around Leningrad.

Once again, Hitler demanded the complete blockade of Leningrad as soon as adequate forces were available. Army Group North prepared Operation Northern Lights, as well as a number of other plans. In late July, Hitler changed his mind. Leningrad was to be destroyed and the area between Lake Ladoga and the Baltic occupied so that Finnish troops could be switched to an operation against the

Murmansk railway, which was carrying supplies from the UK and US landed by the Arctic convoys. For this, Hitler was sending five divisions as well as large-calibre siege artillery and additional aircraft. Field Marshal Georg von Küchler, in command of Army Group North, protested that Leningrad was too solidly built to be burned or blasted, and on 24 August he was replaced by Field Marshal Erich von Manstein, who had conducted an effective destruction of the fortress of Sevastopol.

Meanwhile, Meretskov had planned an attack on the 'bottleneck', which he launched on 27 August against the eastern side. Manstein succeeded in stopping the assault, and on 4 September counter-attacked. Meretskov obtained reinforcements but Manstein succeeded in encircling two Soviet armies and two corps before Hitler, concerned about the winter that lay ahead, cancelled Operation Northern Lights.

The problem for the Germans was that until Lake Ladoga froze, small vessels were still able to supply the city, and the Russians had taken the opportunity during the summer to lay fuel pipelines and electricity cables on the lake bed. The Germans brought in E-boats while the *Regia Marina* provided midget submarines. The Luftwaffe was to provide floating anti-aircraft gun positions, with AA artillery mounted on catamarans, but they were delayed and arrived too late.

It was not until October that the Leningrad front received substantial reinforcements, enabling it to reorganise from three armies into four. On 12 January 1943, the Soviet front commanders, Generals Govorow and Meretskov, launched Operation Spark, simultaneous assaults on opposite sides of the bottleneck meeting east of Shlisselburg on 19 January. The blockade was broken and in Moscow Stalin ordered the firing of artillery salvoes in celebration. A German counterattack narrowed the corridor into Leningrad to just over six miles. By this time, railway tracks had been laid over the ice and on 7 February the first train crossed into the city. Despite these gains, the city continued to be racked by artillery fire and air raids.

Soviet attention was elsewhere during the summer and the Germans had time to rebuild and reorganise their forces at Leningrad, but much of their strength was being taken away to meet more pressing demands elsewhere. As a result, it was not until October that Army Group North was ready to launch Operation Blue, the first step in building an 'East Wall', Hitler's belated attempt to hold back the growing strength of the Soviet armies. The idea was that the operation could, under pressure, become a planned retreat, but Army Group North continued to be weakened by the transfer of further divisions and Hitler failed to make up his mind and support Operation Blue. On 14 January, Govorow and Meretskov attacked, by which time they had double the number of men available to the Germans, and four times the number of tanks and aircraft. Hitler's response was to order the positions to be held, with his men suffering heavy casualties in a pointless battle, until, on 27 January, Stalin declared the blockade ended.

Stalingrad

Spring 1942 heralded the start of the massive reversal of fortunes that would come with the Battle of Stalingrad. The advance to the very edge of Asia was vital for Hitler as the rich oil resources of the Caucasus beckoned, bringing much-needed relief for the Third Reich. The Germans already controlled the rich farmlands of the Ukraine.

Despite the heavy fighting and heavy losses suffered around Moscow and Leningrad, most of Army Group Centre's infantry had seen little combat, while Army Group North and Army Group South had advanced almost unopposed and had suffered relatively little over the winter. Despite the failure to take Moscow and the hardships of the winter, confidence and morale were high, while that of their Soviet opponents was low. Operation Barbarossa might have failed to crush the Soviet Union, but the Germans had made vast territorial gains, capturing the Ukraine, the Baltic republics and Belarus. The front in the east had been stabilised and ran from Leningrad in the north southwards to Rostov. The line was far from straight and there were several salients, but none of these was viewed as serious.

Stalin expected the summer offensive of 1942 to target Moscow once again. For their part, the Germans preferred to divert their attacks towards the south. Stalingrad offered substantial industrial capacity, the loss of which would severely damage the Soviet war effort, while it would also give the Germans the opportunity to block the Volga River, cutting traffic from the Caucasus and the Caspian Sea to Moscow and making the movement of supplies provided by the Allies through the Persian Gulf difficult.

General, later Field Marshal, Friedrich Paulus, was given the task of seizing Stalingrad, with the support of General Hermann Hoth, commander of the Fourth Panzer Army, after which they would extend the territory occupied to Astrakhan.

Once again, the summer campaign started well. On 23 July, Rostov-on-Don was captured and the pipeline carrying fuel from the oilfields of Baku was cut. That same day however, Hitler intervened and insisted that Stalingrad itself be occupied. This had strong propaganda value as it bore the name of the Soviet leader.

Describing the population as 'thoroughly communistic', Hitler demanded that all of the city's men were to be slaughtered and the women and children deported eastwards. Stalin was horrified at the thought of 'his' city being taken and hastened to send reinforcements and the order was given that anyone strong enough to fire a rifle was to fight. On 19 August 1942, the Germans reached Stalingrad, and by 13 October they were on the Volga, with the Russians squeezed into a narrow perimeter, but on this occasion still receiving supplies from across the river.

Inside Stalingrad, the defenders were desperate. Prisoners were armed and put into punishment regiments which were to be given the most exposed and difficult tasks, sparing other troops from the most risky fighting. A new strategy was adopted by the Soviet troops: instead of standing firm and risking capture, a fighting retreat was introduced, which started to wear down the German assailants. The Luftwaffe dropped a thousand tons of bombs on Stalingrad, but Stalin insisted that the city was not to be surrendered and its defenders were to stand firm.

This gave the Germans the problem of having to take the city street by street, a time-consuming form of warfare, costly in terms of casualties, which most soldiers hate. Instead of bypassing the city, German forces entered it on 12 September, and Stalin decided that at least some part of the city must be saved, regardless of what it might take. Stalingrad was being held by a veteran of the Soviet Polish campaign, Major General Vasili Chuikov, in command of the 62nd Army. Chuikov started receiving substantial reinforcements, while the Don Front Army Group to the north and the Stalingrad Front Army Group to the south started to apply strong pressure on the Germans. On 30 September, with Paulus and Hoth having taken two-thirds of the city, Hitler broadcast telling the world that Stalingrad would be taken.

At this stage, the Germans had been fought to a standstill. General Weichs, in overall command, had to increase the number of troops fighting to take Stalingrad, and had little option but to give half of Paulus's front on the Don to the Romanian Third Army, which had to its left the Eighth Italian Army, and to do the same with half of Hoth's front south of Stalingrad being passed to the Romanian Fourth Army, but both the Romanian armies had performed badly in the Soviet Union. The Soviet commanders, Zhukov and Vasilevsky, seized the opportunity to mount Operation Uranus, building a new South-West Front with four field armies and a tank army facing the Romanian Third Army and the Italian Eighth Army, while a tank army was added to the Stalingrad Front's 51st Army, which was facing the Fourth Romanian Army.

These changes took place over a period of seven weeks, but progress was hampered by the autumn rains, which also prevented the Germans from managing to complete the seizure of Stalingrad, or discovering the new Soviet dispositions and taking action against them. The final two weeks saw ice floes begin to block the Volga. This was the occasion when the Germans had reached what was in affect a 'city too far', and as winter approached quickly, the besiegers soon became the besieged.

On 19 November, Lieutenant General N.F. Vatutin, in command of the South-West Front, sent two field armies and his tank army against the Third Romanian Army, while the next day on the Stalingrad Front, Lieutenant General Andrey Eremenko attacked the Fourth Romanian Army with his 51st Army supported by a tank army. The Romanian armies collapsed and by 23 November the Soviet armies had achieved an almost complete encirclement of the German forces and what remained of their allies.

One of the German generals, Weichs, withdrew his forces in time. Paulus, with twenty divisions of which six were Panzers, and around 250,000 troops in all, sought permission to break through the Soviet lines and abandon Stalingrad, but Hitler demanded that he hold his position until relief could be made from the outside. Hitler also promised a relief air supply. To relieve Paulus, Hitler created Army Group Don, with two Panzer divisions and an infantry division, as well as some Romanian troops, and handed the command of this improvised force to Field Marshal von Manstein. To a great extent, Hitler's attitude was strongly influenced by Goering, who maintained that the Luftwaffe could deliver 500 tons of fuel and food daily to Paulus's troops, even though this was just a third of the daily requirement. Less than half the available aircraft were transports, others were bombers, but supplies needed more space than bombs. In the air resupply operation that ensued, the best daily total of supplies delivered was just 289 tons, while the average was much less.

The Germans did not have to wait long. On 19 November Soviet forces mounted a strong counter-attack, and by 23 November the Germans were in retreat. In heavy snow and with many still fighting in their summer uniforms, before long twenty German and two Romanian divisions were trapped.

The Soviet commanders, Zhukov and Vasilevsky, had expected Paulus to surrender, and while they decided what to do next they gave Manstein time to enlarge his force with Hoth in command, giving him three Panzer and two infantry divisions. The relief operation, code-named 'Winter Storm' started on 12 December from a point 62½ miles south of the beleaguered Germans. On 16 December, Zhukov mounted an opposing operation, Little Saturn, to force Army Group Don away from Stalingrad. The Soviet South-West Front Army overran the Eighth Italian Army and then struck south, forcing its way behind Manstein's flank.

The Axis situation soon became critical. The best hope lay in a relief operation, but as this advanced towards the besieged troops, it was checked by the Russians while still 25 miles away. The Russians seriously underestimated the number of troops trapped outside Stalingrad, and so failed to attack in sufficient force, and instead of overwhelming the Germans and Romanians, they simply chipped away at the edges, making small gains and tightening the circle around them. These troops were fighting for survival on less than starvation rations. Part of the problem was that the German quartermasters did not know how long the siege would last and doubted the Luftwaffe's ability to provide sufficient supplies, so tightened rations more than was necessary. When surrender eventually came, as well as soldiers suffering from starvation the Soviet forces discovered large quantities of supplies.

On 23 December, after Hoth's armour had been held up for four days on the River Mishkova, still 35 miles south of Paulus, Manstein informed Hitler that he would have to move at least one Panzer division away from the river and that Paulus would have to attempt a breakout despite being short of food and fuel. Meanwhile, the airlift promised by Goering had delivered no more than an average 90 tons per day, with part of the problem being the shortage of transport aircraft, which forced the Luftwaffe to use bombers which took longer to load and unload, and which did not have the space of a transport aircraft. Some 30,000 sick and wounded troops were evacuated by air. Hitler dithered and by 28 December Hoth's entire force had been surrounded and Manstein had no option but to allow him to make a withdrawal.

The main German force remained in a pocket about 37 miles east to west and 28 miles north to south. Lieutenant General Rokossovsky in command of the Don Front Army was ordered to launch Operation Ring to break the Germans. The Luftwaffe managed to raise its daily deliveries to the encircled troops to 120 tons a day. Against strong German resistance, Rokossovsky started his advance on 10 January, moving from east to west, and by 17 January his forces were halfway across the pocket before pausing for four days to regroup. On 22 January, Paulus lost his last airfield and suggested to Hitler that he surrender. Hitler refused permission, and on 29 January the Germans were squeezed into two small zones at Stalingrad. On 30 January, Hitler promoted Paulus to field marshal. The following day Paulus surrendered his zone with its headquarters, but refused to order the other pocket to follow. Hitler demanded that the six divisions in the other pocket fight to the last man, but contact was lost on 2 February.

The final fatal blow to Axis hopes was the loss of the airstrip at Pitomnik on 16 January 1943. Eventually more than 94,000 German and Romanian troops surrendered. Estimates vary but it is generally accepted that more than 147,000 died inside Stalingrad and more than 100,000 outside it.

The defeat led to a second battle for the Ukraine, which started in December 1943, and continued until May 1944, when the Axis forces were defeated. By this time, the siege of Leningrad had also been lifted. Such heavy losses of men and equipment meant that the demoralised Axis armies were forced back into a long and cruel retreat.

The Germans had given no quarter during their advance, slaughtering civilians and maltreating Russian prisoners of war, and they received none in return. Typical of the times was the fate of a German army chaplain at Stalingrad, who was bending over a seriously wounded soldier, but was shot in the back of the head by a Russian officer. Axis prisoners were left to starve after being robbed of personal possessions, especially their watches. There were few attempts to help the sick, wounded and dying, of whom there were many due to the poor diet and unsanitary conditions. The cruelty displayed by both sides helped to prolong the conflict. In particular, those Russians who had thrown in their lot with the Axis forces knew that a cruel fate awaited them and their families once captured, and this prolonged the fighting.

There was another aspect that encouraged many Russians to join the Germans. Russians taken prisoner were regarded as suspect by Stalin and faced punishment once liberated. The punishment did not stop with the liberated prisoners, but was extended to their families, unless, of course, the prisoner was a member of Stalin's family.

The Balkan campaigns had delayed the launch of Operation Barbarossa for too long, but the overriding reason for failure was that in invading the Soviet Union, the Germans had fatally overreached themselves. Losses could not be replaced. Supply lines were far too long. In the west, Allied bombing raids increased in intensity, with more aircraft per raid, larger aircraft and heavier bombers, and countermeasures and fighter cover for the bombers. Then the pressure began to mount as Italy surrendered and the Germans had to take the burden of attempting to hold back Allied forces moving up the leg of Italy, and this was followed by the Allied invasion of Normandy, and then of the south of France.

The once mighty German war machine was falling into disrepair, just as the country was fighting battles in Italy, and then France and the Low Countries, trying to withdraw from the Balkans, and seeing its gains in the east ebbing away.

The German Red Cross estimated that 200,000 German troops were lost at Stalingrad. Yet, for the Soviet forces, victory had come at a high price, for by the time the siege ended, a million Soviet troops were estimated to have died at and around Stalingrad.

Failure at Stalingrad proved to be the final roll of the dice for the Germans. The year 1943 was to see Germany in retreat with all hope of winning the war lost. From this time onwards, the Germans were fighting for their existence. Hitler was to insist that the capital city of each occupied country was to be defended to the end, and in so doing weakened the German resistance. Refusal to countenance a planned withdrawal meant that any hope of defending the Reich itself was lost.

Chapter Eleven

What Would German Occupation Have Meant?

It seems clear that Hitler had not envisaged the invasion of the United Kingdom as one of his war aims, which could be summed up briefly as finding '*Lebensraum*' in the east, of recovering territory lost after the end of the First World War, and of securing the return of her colonies.

The Germans were very short of gold and foreign exchange by this time, and Hitler's reluctance to invade the United Kingdom may also have lain in the recognition that the country lacked significant foreign exchange or gold reserves as the years of the great depression and then the cost of hastily preparing for war had seriously affected the economy. It was also the case that the UK imported half of its food at the time, and so would not have made a significant contribution to Germany's wartime food supplies, unless the indigenous population was starved.

Hitler had once confessed to a confidante that while 'on land he was a lion, on sea he was a coward'. He had the continental's ignorance of the sea. He could happily direct ground and even air operations, overruling his generals, but was far less comfortable attempting the same thing at sea. He would have been all too aware of the Kriegsmarine's inauspicious start to the war. True, they had sunk the battleship *Royal Oak* at Scapa Flow and the two aircraft carriers, *Courageous* and *Glorious*, but had suffered heavy losses, including two light cruisers, ten destroyers, and the Panzerschiff *Graf Spee*.

As the war continued, Hitler became increasingly concerned about the fate of his major fleet units. Once the battleship *Bismarck* was lost on 27 May 1941 on her maiden operational voyage, he refused to allow her sister ship, *Tirpitz*, to go to sea unless there was no doubt that she would not meet a British battleship or aircraft carrier. In another relatively rare intervention in the war at sea, he ordered home the two battlecruisers *Scharnhorst* and *Gneisenau* and the heavy cruiser *Prinz Eugen*, and insisted that instead of taking the safer route around the west of Ireland, that these three ships should take the risk of running through the English Channel and up the North Sea, a gamble that paid off due to excessive British secrecy and poor planning. From May 1941, the war at sea was left almost entirely to the U-boats.

There was also the argument, voiced by many including General Alfred Jodl, the German army's chief of operations throughout the war, that a less risky alternative to invading the UK would be to seize certain strategic points that would hinder the British war effort so severely that surrender, or at least a negotiated peace, would be inevitable. These were regarded as being Gibraltar, Malta and the Suez Canal.

Taking these vitally important areas would indeed have made sense, yet the United Kingdom remained in the war even though the Mediterranean was all but impassable from early 1941 until summer 1942. Far from being a short cut to the Gulf, to India and Australia, during this period the Suez Canal remained the only way supplies and reinforcements could reach British forces fighting in North Africa, meaning that shipping had to go the long way, via the South Atlantic, the Cape of Good Hope and the Indian Ocean.

The Italians had been held in North Africa by British and Empire forces until their numbers were severely depleted in a desperate and unsuccessful attempt to save Greece. With German reinforcements in the form of the *Afrika Korps*, the battle to save the Suez Canal became much more difficult. But despite losing Tobruk the British held the line and eventually won their last victory to be achieved solely by their own forces at El Alamein.

An early Italian invasion of Malta had been expected by the Germans when Italy entered the war on 10 July 1940, but it was not to be. Italian heavy bombing was not accompanied, as it could have been, by heavy shelling by the *Regia Marina*'s six battleships. One reason for Italian slowness to invade Malta was that they believed that air power, and especially the use of the heavy bomber, combined with a highly effective blockade of the Maltese islands, would force a surrender.

There was also the question of suitable landing grounds on islands with small fields surrounded by drystone walls. Maltese beaches are generally small, and most are dominated by high cliffs which provided a good defensive position. There was little pro-Italian feeling amongst the Maltese, whose language originated with the Phoenicians, and the small number with such sympathies were detained and eventually moved to East Africa for the duration of the war.

Governing the British Isles

There has ever since the end of the Second World War been speculation over how the Germans would have run the United Kingdom. There seems little doubt that they would not have tried to occupy the entire country, but as with France leave much of it under local rule. Yet, as in Vichy France, the local civilian administration even outside the occupied zone would be very much influenced by the Germans. Not only Scotland and Wales, but Ireland would also be treated in this way, with the island reunited and ruled from Dublin, but still under German guidance.

Under German plans created for the planned post-invasion administration, Great Britain and Ireland were to be divided into six military-economic commands, with headquarters in London, Birmingham, Newcastle, Liverpool, Glasgow and Dublin. Hitler himself decided that Blenheim Palace, the ancestral home of Winston Churchill, was to serve as the overall headquarters of the German occupation military government. Many believe that the Germans intended to occupy Southern England only, and that draft documents existed on the regulation of the passage of British civilians back and forth between the occupied and unoccupied territories. Some Nazi planners envisaged the institution of a nationalities policy in Western Europe to secure German hegemony there, which entailed the granting of independence to various regions, breaking up the United Kingdom. In the British Isles this involved detaching Scotland from the United Kingdom with an autonomous status as well as the creation of a United Ireland, and an autonomous status for the West of England and Wales.

The occupation civil government was to be based in Senate House, the tall administration building of the University of London. This was a modern building, having been built in 1933.

As for the monarchy, King George VI and his family were generally presumed to have departed for Canada in an attempt to continue the war from there, although whether or not Canada would have wanted to remain in the war is open to question.

Over the years, many have claimed that the Germans would have installed as sovereign the Duke of Windsor, who as Edward VIII had surrendered his throne in 1937, and this question remains unresolved to this day. The Foreign Office has always maintained that the Duke of Windsor never wavered in his loyalty to the United Kingdom. Even so, there were concerns about the reliability of the Duke, and it was perhaps for this reason that the British government put him as far out of the way as possible, so that getting hold of him would have been difficult for the Germans. After the fall of France he spent the rest of the war as governor of the Bahamas.

The Duke of Windsor and the American Wallis Simpson had visited Germany in 1937 and many senior Nazi Party figures believed that he was sympathetic to Hitler and his government. Just how sympathetic he was remains open to question. One likely explanation was that as Prince of Wales he had toured the United Kingdom extensively during the years of the great depression and had been appalled at the unemployment and misery suffered by many. On one occasion he was reported as saying, 'Something must be done.' This, however, was only a remark of despair and sympathy. He would have been impressed at the way full employment was being created in Germany, although perhaps not so much had he realised that the rearmament drive was responsible. Being impressed by Germany's economic revival was one thing, accepting Hitler's expansionist policies would have been something else, even without the persecution of the Jews. The economic revival was of course all show, as behind it was increasing loss of German gold reserves and foreign currency, while the country was failing to meet its reparations for the cost of the First World War.

On the outbreak of war, the Duke and his wife were living in Paris where he was appointed a member of the British Military Mission, dropping in rank from field marshal, as the sovereign traditionally held five-star rank in all three of the UK's armed forces, to the two-star rank of major general. The French were secretive about their defensive preparations, but the Duke made goodwill visits to a number of military installations, including touring the Maginot Line, and reported back on these to the War Office in London. On the fall of France, the Duke and Duchess moved first to Madrid and then to Lisbon. While in Iberia the German foreign minister, Ribbentrop, attempted to detain them there, with Colonel Walter Schellenberg of the *Reichssicherheitshauptamt*, RSHA, or State Security Main Office, attempting to kidnap them and take them to Germany as they were about to embark at Lisbon for the Bahamas. The Duke and Duchess remained unaware of the plot, but British intelligence warned London and their departure was brought forward. On several occasions, the Duke sought an appointment within the UK, but these requests were always refused.

Nevertheless, files released in London by the National Archives in July 2017 have shown that post-war both Churchill and Eisenhower tried to suppress captured Nazi documents regarding Edward VIII discussing his desire for peace with Adolf Hitler. The files came from the UK government's secret basement storeroom in the Cabinet Office where papers deemed 'too difficult, too sensitive' for the regular filing system were hidden away. They include a 1953 memo from Churchill, marked 'top secret', explaining the existence of a series of German telegrams carrying reports of comments by the Duke of Windsor, as Edward VIII was known after he abdicated in 1936: 'He is convinced that had he remained on [the] throne war would have been avoided and describes himself as a firm supporter of a peaceful compromise with Germany,' reported a telegram from Lisbon in neutral Portugal, where the duke was staying in July 1940. 'Duke believes with certainty that continued heavy bombing will make England ready for peace.'

The *Oberkommando der Wehrmacht*, OKW, or High Command of the German Armed Forces, and the RSHA, joined the Foreign Ministry in preparing lists of those they regarded as sympathisers who would be able to run a government on behalf of the Germans, similar to that they put in place in occupied Norway. Sir Oswald Moseley, founder and leader of the British National Union of Fascists, headed the list, and Harold Nicolson was another regarded as being suitable to join a puppet government. Also included was the broadcaster William Joyce.

To drive home the point that any government run by Britons would be a puppet administration, it was also planned to have a governor, or *Reichskommissar für Großbritannien*, 'State Commissar for Great Britain'. This individual would have had near dictatorial powers. Two candidates made what would today be called the short list, Joachim von Ribbentrop, the German Foreign Minister and previously an ambassador to Great Britain, and Ernst Wilhelm Bohle, an undersecretary in the Foreign Office, who had previously been promised by Hitler that if the British 'behave sensibly' he would be the next German ambassador to the Court of St James.[1]

If Operation Sea Lion had succeeded, the Germans intended to waste no time in establishing their new order. Five task forces, or *Einsatzgruppen*, were to be established under Dr Franz Six, with a headquarters in London and regional offices in Birmingham, Edinburgh, Liverpool and Manchester. The task forces were to be given a list, known as the 'Black Book', with the names of 2,820 people who were to be arrested immediately. After this, they were to turn their attention to the UK's Jewish population, which at the time numbered more than 300,000.

Six and his teams would not simply be concerned with dealing with people, as they also had to secure research establishments and important items of equipment, which were to be transported to Germany.

The British Ministry of Information was to be taken over and the major national and international news agencies closed down. All newspapers were to be controlled by the Commissar, and those which had adopted an anti-German tone, which by this time was all of them, were to be closed down.

In addition, the country was to be stripped of everything of economic, industrial, military or cultural value. This was not unique to the UK as the same treatment had been inflicted on Germany's earlier conquest, and although Austria was different, even there the national treasury had been seized.

Fate of the Civilian Population

Some German plans indicate that the occupation would only have been temporary, but the commander-in-chief of the German army, the *Heer*, Feldmarshal Walther von Brauchitsch, seems to have had a different idea. Even before the invasion date, he issued a directive: 'The able-bodied male population between the ages of 17 and 45 will, unless the local situation calls for an exceptional ruling, be interned and dispatched to the Continent.'

There were also plans to move all women of child-bearing age with the right Aryan characteristics to Germany where they would be sired by the best examples of German manhood to add to the numbers of the 'Master Race'.

The deportation of able-bodied men to Germany was not only intended to provide Germany with additional slave labour and, if necessary, hostages, but was also aimed at reducing the danger of extensive guerrilla activity during the occupation. Even passive resistance was to be punished by the death penalty. Between a quarter and a third of adult males would have been affected by the German plan.

These plans give the lie to any hope that because of racial similarities between the English and the Germans treatment would have been much different from that suffered by other European populations. Many have, nevertheless, surmised that the treatment of British slave workers would have been less harsh than that given to the '*Untermenschen*' of eastern Europe, who could be worked to death. But it is questionable whether the Germans would have shown any racial preference for the English as on one occasion Hitler had described the English lower classes as 'racially inferior'.

Just how bad could it have been? A member of the Reich Ministry for the Occupied Eastern Territories claimed he had seen a personal report in early 1943 of a discussion between General Eduard Wagner and Heinrich Himmler, Germany's Minister of the Interior and Head of the SS, in which Himmler stated that he had planned to kill some 80 per cent of the populations of both France and England using specially-trained SS squads.

In fact, it looks as if the Germans were not firmly decided on just how to occupy the United Kingdom. In recent years, in addition to the German booklet *Invasion Plans for the British Isles 1940*, another dossier has emerged, with the title *Militargeographische Angaben über England* (*Military/geographical information about England*), which was preserved in an Austrian library until 2014. This suggested that London would have been heavily controlled and occupied, but that senior officers and officials would have been able to occupy country homes in the New Forest. For the lower ranks, Hitler seemed to have regarded Blackpool as the ideal resort for his troops to have rest and recreation, which many believed was one reason why it was not bombed, although the town had little military value anyway.

It is not clear why Hitler was attracted to Blackpool as he never went there. His own official residence in England was to be the headquarters for the German military occupation force, Blenheim Palace, away from the ruins of London and so much more to his taste as the conqueror than Windsor Castle or Sandringham. Blenheim was the ancestral home of the Churchill family, which added to its appeal.

The dossier also implies a period of destruction, including the iconic Clifton Suspension Bridge over the Avon Gorge at Bristol. This might not have been a loss in other than architectural or engineering terms, or as an inconvenience to the local population, because of the narrow roadway and weight restrictions, but other items on the list for destruction included the Tyne Bridge in Newcastle, which would have given the occupying forces communications problems of their own. The destruction of the Manchester Ship Canal was less important, as most of the port capacity the Germans would have found useful would have been on the east and south coasts of England.

As for people to be arrested and either detained or executed according to the 'Black Book', these included Winston Churchill, Labour leader Clement Attlee, feminist author Vera Brittain and Jewish psychoanalysis pioneer Sigmund Freud. Freud would have been doomed anyway, along with the rest of the country's estimated 300,000 Jews.

The population could expect an acute shortage of food once the occupation started. In the other occupied territories, priority was given to feeding the occupation forces and then to sending food back to Germany. The United Kingdom pre-war had only managed to provide half of its food, with the remainder imported, preference given to imports from the Empire. These imports would have ended once the occupation started. Certain items, such as tea, coffee and sugar, would have disappeared. Even in Germany, 'coffee' included ground and roasted acorns, and this would have been the best the British could have expected.

Fuel, other than coal, would have been in short supply, so motor bus services and road haulage would have become rare. As for private motoring, one could forget it. Electric power generation using coal meant that electric trams and trolleybuses, as well as electric railways, could have continued to run. In the south there were many miles of electric railways, including the London Underground, the Southern Railway's London suburban network, its main line and some branch lines stretching along the south coast all the way from Eastbourne to Portsmouth. Most of the remaining railway network used steam traction except for the Glasgow underground, known locally as the 'Clockwork Orange', and there were some isolated electrified lines in the north-west of England.

The Germans would have acted quickly to seize key manufacturing centres, but to what extent factories would have been taken over, as in France, or simply stripped of their equipment, which would then have been shipped to Germany, is a matter for conjecture. Indeed, keeping the factories intact and operating them (probably after essential repairs as it is fair to believe that they would have been sabotaged to stop worthwhile industrial assets falling into German hands) would have been far better than wholesale removal of equipment (although that would have gone against the plan to move able-bodied adults to Germany for forced labour).

One is left wondering whether some of the more extreme German plans would have come to fruition. Would they really have wanted to kill 80 per cent of the population of France and England, as per the discussion between General Wagner and Himmler? The only benefit would have been many fewer mouths to feed and more space for Germans to settle post-war, which may have been benefit enough, but a country normally has a match between its population and its facilities, which means that losing 80 per cent of its population would have left too few people to maintain the infrastructure. Would there have been enough Germans to fill the gaps, the vacancies? Almost certainly not.

This raises another point. As the chapters on occupation in eastern and Western Europe show, occupation varied between countries and much also depended on the attitude of the governor or *Reichskommissar für Großbritannien*. The Kommissars varied in character, but the more lenient were often removed from their posts. The Germans liked the populations of their conquered territories to know that they were indeed conquered. The signing of the French surrender in the same railway carriage that had seen the Germans sign the Armistice in 1918 was a good example of this, and the fact that they wanted to use Churchill's ancestral home as a military headquarters and base for Hitler during his visits was another.

In short, the Germans might not have murdered 80 per cent of the population, or sent so many to work in Germany, but it would not have been an easy relationship. If resistance had been strong, as it probably would have been, harsh and repressive measures with the taking of hostages and brutal retaliation against the civilian population would have been the order of the day.

Chapter Twelve

The Lessons of Normandy

Invasions take considerable planning and vast resources if they are to be successful. One Soviet-era Russian general believed that it was essential for the attackers to have a 3:1 superiority in numbers over the defenders. The challenge is all the greater when amphibious landings are being planned. Much also depends on the defences. Fixed defences such as the French Maginot Line are often disparaged, and with good reason as the Germans simply went around it. But fixed defences along the coast can be an asset, just so long as the enemy does not have the chance to bypass them.

The arrangements for the Normandy landings (the Allies discouraged the use of the term 'invasion' for the landings in Normandy as France was an ally) tell us much about the planning and the resources needed for a successful amphibious assault on a well defended coast.

The so-called 'Atlantic Wall' built by the Germans in northern France did not mean that there were no gaps or opportunities for the Allies to go around, but the extra distance involved would have made doing so more difficult and dangerous, leaving the landing fleet vulnerable in the southern end of the North Sea or further west as the English Channel becomes wider. In that sense, the Atlantic Wall worked, up to a point, as the Allies had to devote considerable resources to overcoming it.

Unlike Germany in 1940, by 1944 the allies had the resources. Had Churchill not objected strongly to landings in 1943, Normandy could have been a costly failure. Waiting until June 1944 meant that the Allies had gained further experience in amphibious assault and, no less important, had the time to produce additional equipment and assemble extra men, ships and aircraft. Nevertheless, there were also some hard lessons along the way. Churchill's reluctance to support landings in Normandy was not solely down to the time needed for preparations, but also because his original idea once Italy was invaded was to advance through Italy and then into Austria, taking Germany from the south. This plan ignored the great challenge presented by the mountainous terrain of Austria and southern Germany, but in any case, the advance through Italy towards Rome proved much more difficult than the Allies had anticipated with many strong defensive positions to overcome even before they reached the Italian capital.

So much specialised equipment had to be developed, even invented. There was a need for landing craft of all sizes; plus prefabricated harbours so that normal cargo vessels could unload; a need for fuel pipelines to meet the great thirst of armoured vehicles, aircraft and the many lorries needed to keep a modern mechanised army on the move.

Dieppe

It is sometimes said that more is learned from mistakes than from successes. This could easily be applied to the Germans who had enjoyed continuous success throughout 1939 and 1940, and on into 1941, and perhaps did not fully realise just what a full-scale amphibious assault against an enemy that was determined and prepared would mean. The British were still recovering and rebuilding their armed forces even as 1942 dawned, but much had been achieved.

That year, the Allies decided to test the defences of a major French Channel port, Dieppe. Landings were mainly carried out by Canadian troops after their government and their commanding officers had pressed for them to see some action rather than remaining in barracks and on exercises in southern England. The raid, originally known as Operation Rutter but later renamed Operation Jubilee, was to be launched from five ports in the south of England with Southampton as the most westerly and Newhaven the most easterly. There would be 5,000 Canadian troops, 1,000 British and 50 US Rangers, supported by 237 ships and aircraft from 74 air squadrons, of which 66 would be fighter squadrons.

This was a reasonably substantial force for an operation with limited aims, but the preparations were also to be limited. There was no beach reconnaissance, and no preliminary aerial bombardment as the RAF did not want to be distracted from its planned bombing operations over the industrial areas of Germany and occupied Europe. Despite Royal Navy involvement, there was to be no covering fire from battleships or cruisers as the Admiralty felt that these would be at excessive risk in the confined waters of the English Channel. There was also the consideration that bombardment from the air or from the sea could cost French lives. The most the landing force could expect was fire support from destroyers, whose guns, usually just 4-inch, did not have the range or the impact of the 6 or 8-inch guns of a cruiser, still less the 14, 15 or 16-inch guns of a battleship.

Given the complexity of the exercise and the lack of experience amongst the men and their commanders as the first of the Mediterranean landings was still some months away, an exercise was conducted to provide training and also to ensure that the arrangements were workable. This was just as well as the first exercise was a complete disaster, but ten days later all went well with a second exercise. A date still had to be fixed, and it was not until 1 July 1942 that the date for the Dieppe operation was set as 4 July or the first day after that date with favourable weather conditions.

The weather was bad and continued to be so until 7 July, when the operation was postponed. General Montgomery in command of forces in the south of England wanted it cancelled as the troops involved had been briefed and he feared that security would be compromised. His objections were ignored and planning continued, while he was then removed from the operation and posted to Egypt to command the British Eighth Army, where he proved a successful and inspirational commander.

One of the changes made after his departure was that of the name to Operation Jubilee, but more serious was the decision to cancel the planned aerial bombardment which, as already mentioned, was feared could cost heavy French casualties. Instead, eight British destroyers would bombard the port, but there was no change to allow battleships to be present as they would be vulnerable to German shore-based artillery once they were in coastal waters. This was being overly cautious as the guns of these ships could easily fire over ranges of twenty miles, which was outside the range of most German coastal artillery. Meanwhile, Montgomery's concerns about security were soon justified as French double agents warned the Germans about British interest in Dieppe, while the commanding officer of the 1st Parachute Battalion was later to comment that from the start, 'security was abysmal'. Increased radio traffic and the growing concentration of landing craft in the south coast ports were also detected by the Germans. The next change, as the weather continued to be poor, was that the planned paratroop landings were cancelled as the use of airborne forces was even more vulnerable to bad weather, with the risk of being blown away from the landing area. This decision was reversed before the operation went ahead.

In command of combined operations, Admiral Louis Mountbatten was anxious to see action and impatient for a landing on enemy territory, although this would be just another 'hit and run' raid. In this he was not alone. Churchill felt that there was much to be gained both in raising morale amongst the Allies, and in showing Stalin that the British were taking the war to the enemy. In fact, by this time Stalin was already on the offensive in northern Russia, and his main concern was that the German thrust had turned southwards towards Stalingrad.

Churchill later recalled:

> I thought it most important that a large-scale operation should take place this summer, and military opinion seemed unanimous that until an operation on that scale was undertaken, no responsible general would take the responsibility of planning the main invasion.
>
> In discussion with Admiral Mountbatten it became clear that time did not permit a new large-scale operation to be mounted during the summer, but that Dieppe could be remounted (the new code-name was "Jubilee") within a month, provided extraordinary steps were taken to ensure secrecy.
>
> For this reason no records were kept, but after the Canadian authorities and the Chiefs of Staff had given their approval, I personally went through the plans with the C.I.G.S.[1], Admiral Mountbatten, and the Naval Force Commander, Captain J. Hughes-Hallett.

The initial plan for the attack was an unimaginative frontal assault, but this was developed after the decision not to use British paratroops was reversed so that they could attack the German artillery positions mounted on the headlands either side of the town and the port. As already mentioned, the plans for an aerial bombardment before the raid to soften up the target were abandoned.

The special troops who were still assigned to the operation were Royal Marine and Royal Navy commandos, although the idea was not that they should lead the operation but instead they would follow the main force ashore from motor gunboats and destroy the harbour installations. There was even an ex-burglar on their strength who was supposed to break into a port office and burgle the safe, hoping to find important documents.

If security was poor before the raid, so too was intelligence about the target area. Allied air reconnaissance missed the German gun positions embedded in the cliff faces, while the suitability of the beach for tanks was assessed, not by landing reconnaissance parties under cover of darkness, but instead using holiday postcards and amateur photographs. In addition to poor knowledge of the terrain and the defences, there was little knowledge of enemy strength.

Although Mountbatten was in command of special operations, he was not going on the raid, which had the assault force led by Major General Roberts

The Lessons of Normandy

and the naval force by Captain Hughes-Hallett. Mountbatten did, nevertheless, address at least some of the troops before they embarked, as Sergeant George Cook of No.4 Commando, which was to attack the artillery batteries at Varangéville, recalled:

> Mountbatten gave us a lecture – said he wished he was coming with us. Once we realised where we were going, I think 200 blokes thought, 'I wish he were going instead of us.' But yes, very nice talk. We cheered him – off he went. Then we started priming grenades, drawing ammunition. Our troop were doing the demolitions, so we drew explosives and we'd a fair amount of stuff which we packed up… Then we had a meal and we sailed – a beautiful evening, as we went down the Solent and past the Isle of Wight.
>
> Suddenly an officer said, 'Oh – they've got all the harbour lights lit.' I looked over the prow of the boat and you could see lights on the shore. The lighthouse at Varangéville was flashing, so I thought, Cor blimey – everybody awake. We're going to have a pretty bad welcome here.
>
> When we landed, there was some barbed wire. We'd a roll of wire netting which we threw over the barbed wire so we could run over it. The Germans were firing tracers from their pill-boxes, and Lord Lovat said, quite casually, 'They're firing too high.' He was about six foot – I'm five foot four – so I thought, 'If they're firing over his head, there's no danger they're going to hit me' – but they did fire their mortars and four or five blokes were killed on the beach.[2]

Cook and his comrades advanced firing. One of them shot a man out of an ack-ack tower, who 'did a lovely swallow dive off the top', before they reached an orchard accompanied by one of Cook's friends, another sergeant, Geordie Horne, who was almost immediately shot dead, before Cook himself was hit in the face and the shoulder.

Even before the raid began, at 04.50 on 19 August, the cover was blown completely as a number of the escorting warships had already engaged warships accompanying a German convoy off Puys and Berneval at 0348.

To avoid confusion, the landings were at four beaches each given a colour designation for the operation. One of these, the most easterly, was Blue Beach, where the assault started badly. After leaving the converted Belgian cross-Channel ferry *Princess Astrid*, the 10th Landing Craft Assault Flotilla started off in the wrong direction, and eventually reached the beach sixteen minutes late, as dawn was breaking and the element of surprise had been lost.

The initial attacks were on the coastal batteries. The attack at Varangéville by No.4 Commando was successful, but this was the only unit to meet all of its objectives during the operation. The Royal Regiment of Canada landed at Puys, where they were virtually wiped out with just 60 of the regiment's 543 men being evacuated from the beach. Many were cut down on the ramp, where the bodies piled up, while others were mown down by machine gun fire as they attempted to cross the pebbled beach to the shelter of the sea wall forty feet away.

Those offshore could not see what was happening ashore because the ships covering the landings had laid a dense smokescreen. This did nothing at all to protect those involved in the landings, but made command and control difficult.

In the ensuing chaos, most of the landing craft carrying the marines were hit by gunfire on the run-in and the few men who reached the shore were killed or taken prisoner. In an attempt to regain control and end the suicidal mission, their CO stood up in the stern of his craft and signalled to those behind that they should turn back, before he was killed by German gunfire.

The RAF had allocated aircraft, including many fighters, to the operation, but Squadron Leader 'Johnnie' Johnson, leading No.616 Squadron, recalled that there was supposed to be a headquarters ship, HMS *Calypso*, with radar and RAF controllers aboard to control air operations, but on four sorties over Dieppe that day, he could never establish communications:

> We could see very little except for a bloody great pall of smoke over the town, and lots of shelling going on down below. But we could do nothing about it because the attackers and defenders were all within a hundred yards of each other. We couldn't help the army. When we got home after the first patrol, we knew that the whole thing had been a disaster, but there was nothing we could do to help them.[3]

Withdrawal began at 1100 as the heavy fire continued. It took until 1400. When it left, the assault force left behind 3,367 Canadians who had been killed, wounded or taken prisoner, as well as 275 Royal Marine commandos. The Royal Navy lost a destroyer and 33 landing craft, with 550 men killed or wounded. The RAF lost 106 aircraft. Compared to this, the Germans lost 591 men killed or wounded, and 48 aircraft.

The surviving landing craft had been ordered to the main beach at Dieppe at 1030. When the first landing craft arrived there, it was met by a solitary soldier, and it was only after he had been handed a Lewis gun with which to defend himself that someone realised that he was a German soldier attempting to desert. Once the withdrawal started in earnest, the few landing craft were overcrowded and in danger of being swamped. One of them was hit by a shell and capsized, but the crew managed to get their passengers aboard another landing craft.

In the inevitable enquiry into what went wrong, many tried to blame Mountbatten, but as there was no reprimand and he remained in post, it seems that it was not his fault, and he did not act alone, although there is no written record of the operation being given the go-ahead. General Sir Alan Brooke, C.I.G.S., was abroad at the time and many believe that had he been at home in the War Cabinet, he might have persuaded Churchill to cancel the operation, but this is conjecture.

Some believe that the disaster at Dieppe was necessary so that lessons could be learned in time for the Normandy landings, but even so, there were many avoidable failings. There either had to be a heavy aerial bombardment before the operation, or it should have been called off. Some form of reconnaissance from the sea was necessary and it would have noticed the gun positions in the cliff face. The preparations also needed to include an assessment of the shingle on the beach to discover whether it would have damaged tank tracks. This would have required reconnaissance parties to land on the beach and take samples, without being noticed. Much heavier naval firepower was needed and it had to continue right up to the moment when the landing craft hit the shore.

Operation Overlord

The Allied invasion of Normandy in 1944 gives a good idea of the resources the Germans would have needed for a successful invasion of the south of England. Operation Overlord was the code-name given to the Allied landings in Normandy by air and by sea, but the naval aspect of the landings was so important that it was given its own code-name, Operation Neptune. This was the largest operation ever undertaken by the Royal Navy, which provided the majority of the warships involved on D-Day. The largest maritime invasion in history required almost 7,000 ships of all kinds to land 75,215 British and Canadian troops and 57,500 US troops, a total of 132,715 men, plus armoured vehicles, artillery, motor vehicles and supplies, on the first day alone. The German assault on the south coast of England would have had far fewer personnel than this, and the number of ships would also have been less, and much less capable.

Some say that to those aboard the ships in this massive armada, it *seemed* to stretch to the horizon, but the truth is that it almost certainly did, as once assembled at the rendezvous point, code-named 'Piccadilly Circus', actually some miles to the south of the Isle of Wight rather than the centre of London, the assembled fleet covered five square miles of sea. There were more than 4,000 landing ships and landing craft, preceded by 287 minesweepers in line abreast, clearing the English Channel ahead of the invasion fleet. Escorting the convoys, but not the landing ships and craft, were 6 battleships; 4 monitors, shallow draft ships with a heavy armament who would join the battleships in giving naval gunnery cover; 22 cruisers; 104 destroyers and another 152 escort vessels such as corvettes and frigates; 80 patrol craft, including anti-submarine trawlers and gunboats, and 360 motor launches. No less than 79 per cent of the warships were British or Canadian, while 16.5 per cent were American, with the remaining 4.5 per cent manned by crews from France, Greece, the Netherlands, Norway and Poland. The US contribution consisted not just of United States Navy warships, but also those of the United States Coast Guard, which in wartime passed from the US Department of Transportation (sic) to the USN, although today its peacetime home is the Department of Homeland Security.

Missing from the vast armada of ships was the aircraft carrier. There was no need for aircraft carriers with the landing zones around eighty miles from the south coast of England. Equally important, there was no room, as with so many ships in a relatively small area of water, aircraft carriers would not have been able to charge around at full speed, heading into the wind ready to launch aircraft for a sortie or recover them afterwards.

Even though the strength of the Royal Navy, Royal Canadian Navy and the United States Navy had increased massively since the outbreak of war, assembling such a vast armada was no easy task, and operations elsewhere were seriously affected. The most obvious change was the decision to postpone the invasion of the South of France until August, but less obvious was the suspension of a number of convoys for the Soviet Union. The navies concerned were stretched to the limit, especially as the war in the Pacific moved steadily towards Japan. Perhaps Stalin did not appreciate that this would happen when he insisted on a 'second front', but, like Hitler, naval operations were never his strongpoint.

An indication of how the Normandy landings differed from any invasion before or since, was the fact that they required more than just shipping.

First, two harbours, known as Mulberry harbours, built from prefabricated parts, had to be towed across the Channel and assembled, one for the British zone and one in the American zone. A bad storm hit the area before the harbours could be completed and the American Mulberry was so badly damaged that it had to be abandoned. This left the British harbour as the main supply point. Such harbours were important because landing ships had a much lower cargo space than conventional cargo ships, which could carry supplies all the way from the United States and Canada without the need for transhipment. While strenuous efforts were made to capture ports in France, these were not immediately available for use as the Germans took care to damage and sabotage as many of the facilities as possible.

Fuel was another problem for the heavily mechanised Allied armies and for the intense air support they needed. There were two tactical air forces, one American and the other, the Second Allied Tactical Air Force, or '2nd TAF', with aircraft and personnel drawn from the Royal Air Force and British Empire air forces. A pipeline, known as PLUTO for 'pipeline under the ocean', was laid from Shanklin on the east coast of the Isle of Wight, with the initial single line being joined by others. It met the fuel needs of the Allied armies.

The 2nd TAF, which landed their first aircraft in France late on D-Day, had developed from the lessons learned in North Africa by the Desert Air Force, from which effective army and air force coordination developed, in effect enabling the Allies to emulate the Blitzkrieg tactics of the Luftwaffe and the Panzer divisions.

Many of the minesweepers used to prepare the way for the landing fleet were of the Royal Navy's Bangor-class, with a displacement of 672 tons and a complement of 60 men. They were capable of 16 knots. Armaments consisted of a 3-inch gun and one 40-mm cannon, as well as four .303 machine guns. Clearly such ships had little chance of standing up to a German destroyer had they come up against them, but the Allies had never lost naval supremacy in the war against Germany.

The navies of the day knew how to sweep contact mines, and the Royal Navy had discovered a means – degaussing – of protecting ships from magnetic mines. Acoustic mines that reacted to the sound of ships' propellers or machinery were more difficult. Worst of all were the new pressure mines, known as 'oysters', triggered by an increase in water pressure, which responded when a ship passed over the mine. Acoustic mines had the unpleasant characteristic of being able to be set not to explode the first time a ship passed over them, but instead waiting for the second or third ship, which made mine clearance more difficult.

There were many American minesweepers, as well as British, and on the afternoon before the landings, at 17.57, one of these ships, the USS *Osprey*, was to discover just how necessary minesweeping was to be to the landing force. The *War Diary* of Mine Squadron 7, part of Force U covering Utah beach, tells the tale:

> USS *Osprey* (Lt Charles Swimm, captain) was struck by an underwater explosion, under forward engine room; explosion is believed to be from a moored contact mine. Position 50 degrees 12.9N, 01 degrees, 20.4W – about 35 miles south of the Isle of Wight. USS *Chickadee* came alongside *Osprey* to assist. Fire that broke out onboard *Osprey* was under control in 3 to 5 minutes and extinguished in 10 minutes... In view of the list and irreparable damage and lack of watertight integrity, as a result of the blast, the order to abandon ship was given at 1815. *Chickadee* took all survivors onboard. (Casualties were six dead, twenty-nine wounded).

Such a loss in broad daylight and twenty miles north of where the nearest enemy minefield was charted was a sobering warning of what might lie ahead.

Potentially the most serious casualty from hitting a mine was the Royal Navy's Queen Elizabeth-class battleship HMS *Warspite*, a veteran of the First World War that had seen action at Narvik during the Norwegian campaign in 1940, and later at the Battle of Cape Matapan. This mighty warship, with a full load displacement of 36,450 tons and eight 15-inch guns, had been repaired in the United States after being damaged at Matapan, and then operated in the Far East before returning to Europe for the Mediterranean landings, but was not fully repaired after being struck by a glider bomb off Salerno. Playing an important part in the Normandy bombardment, she hit a mine and damaged her propulsive system to the extent that when needed for further bombardment duties, at Brest, Le Havre and later at Walcheren, she had to suffer the indignity of being towed into position by tug. Even then her 'X' turret, one of her two aft turrets, remained inoperable.

The most the Germans would have had available had Sea Lion gone ahead would have been two battlecruisers, two *Panzerschiffe*, and a small number of destroyers, never in abundance in the Kriegsmarine, but their numbers depleted even further in the two naval battles at Narvik during the Norwegian campaign.

Combined, naval personnel and men from the Allied merchant navies, 195,701 seafarers took part, actually outnumbering the numbers landed ashore.

Overall command of this vast armada was given to a British naval officer, Admiral Sir Bertram Ramsay. His signal on 31 May to all the ships under his command summed up the situation, and the task, perfectly:

Our task in conjunction with the Merchant Navies of the United Nations,[4] and supported by the Allied Air Forces, is to carry the Allied Expeditionary Force to the Continent, to establish it there in a secure bridgehead and to build it up and maintain it at a rate which will outmatch that of the enemy. Let no one underestimate the magnitude of this task.

The absence of aircraft carriers did not mean that naval aviation did not play a part. At any one time, a number of the Royal Navy's Fleet Air Arm squadrons would be based ashore, often under the control of RAF Coastal Command, and in 1944, squadrons such as No.811 NAS, equipped with Fairey Swordfish, played a part in protecting the Normandy convoys from being attacked by German U-boats.

Several years into the war, the standard of aircraft recognition was still so poor that to protect British and American aircraft over the Normandy area from being shot at by Allied anti-aircraft gunners, aircraft were painted in 'invasion stripes', that is the wings and rear fuselage had black and white stripes painted to show clearly that they were Allied aircraft.

By 1944, the Royal Navy was well on its way to its war-end strength of 61 battleships and cruisers; 59 aircraft carriers; its capital ships, as well as 846 destroyers, frigates and corvettes, which could be covered by the catch-all phrase of 'escort vessels'; 729 minesweepers; 131 submarines; 1,000 minor naval vessels, including trawlers and drifters adapted for patrols; and 3,700 aircraft. Many of the aircraft carriers were the small auxiliary or escort carriers, most of which were supplied by the United States under Lend-Lease, although there were a handful of British-converted escort carriers.

The service included a number of types of vessel no longer in service today. The large battleships with their 14, 15 or 16-inch guns, so useful for bombarding targets ashore, were augmented by the much smaller monitors, again with 15-inch guns but being smaller they also had a shallow draft allowing them to operate closer inshore. Two of these were of wartime construction, HMS *Roberts* and *Abercrombie*, of 8,123 tons displacement and each with two 15-inch guns, as opposed to up to eight on a battleship, and eight 4-inch guns, which could also be used as anti-aircraft weapons, as well as multi-barrelled anti-aircraft pom-poms, known as 'Chicago pianos' to the men of the fleet. Another two, HMS *Terror* and *Erebus*, dated from 1916 and were slightly smaller but still had two 15-inch and eight 4-inch guns. *Roberts* and *Abercrombie* were off the British beaches while *Erebus* was off Utah beach, one of the two landing beaches assigned to American forces.

The bombardment group consisted of the elderly battleships HMS *Warspite* and *Ramillies*, as well as twelve cruisers and thirty-seven destroyers. In reserve were the battleships *Rodney* and *Nelson*, with their 16-inch guns, and three cruisers. An indication of the lack of realism on defence amongst British governments of the interwar period was that the last British battleship class introduced before the war was the King George V-class, with just 14-inch guns. This had been part of a general attempt to enforce even tighter restrictions on British warships than laid down under the Washington Naval Treaty of 1922.

A shell from a 15-inch gun weighed more than a ton and had a range of more than twenty miles. A shell from a 16-inch gun was even more effective, and that of a 14-inch gun less so.

It was important that the landing ships and landing craft should reach the part of the Normandy coast where they were to land. Matters of command and control were simplified by the establishment of British and American sectors, with the British eastern sector having the beaches designated Gold, Juno and Sword, and the American western sector having the beaches Omaha and Utah. The American sector was west of the British, which also included a substantial Canadian force destined for Juno beach. The disposition of the British and American sectors was dictated by the basing of the troops in England. Some argue that the Americans would have been better equipped to take the eastern sector and the British the western, but that would have complicated an already difficult and demanding convoy system for the landings. Swapping the troops around before embarkation would have avoided this, but then created problems of a different kind, stretching transport and logistics resources at a time when everyone was preparing for the cross-Channel assault, and certainly creating enough of a commotion to have put security at risk.

Not everyone could wait until the night of 5/6 June before crossing the Channel. Getting the mass of landing ships and landing craft to the right beach was no easy task. Once clear of the rendezvous the ships headed for the five invasion beaches, but guidance was necessary, and this came from the crews of midget submarines, the 'X' boats. These craft usually had a crew of four, two officers and two ratings, and when used offensively they would all be divers, capable of fixing mines to the hulls of enemy warships. For Neptune, the officers were drawn from amongst the best of the Royal Navy's navigators.

These small craft left what was then the Royal Navy's main submarine base at Gosport, HMS *Dolphin*, just across the harbour from the major naval base of Portsmouth, late on Friday, 2 June. They cleared the Isle of Wight, towed most of the way by converted trawlers, and crossed the eighty miles to the coast of Normandy, and once in position submerged and spent the daylight hours sitting on the sea bed, just off shore. On Sunday night, once on their marking position, the midget submarines surfaced and dropped anchor. Those aboard *X23* watched as a lorry dropped a crowd of German soldiers on the shore who then played a game of volleyball, unaware that they were being watched, or of what the future held for them. Lieutenant George Honour was aboard *X23*:

> We hoisted our radio mast and got a signal that the invasion had been postponed, so then we had to retreat to the bottom again and wait until Monday night. That night we surfaced and received a message that the invasion was on. So we went back to sit on the bottom and at about 0430 on Tuesday, 6 June, we surfaced again, put up all our navigational aids: 18-foot telescopic mast with a light shining seaward, a radio beacon and an echo sounder tapping out a message below the surface. This was for the navigational mine-layers used to guide the fleet to pick up as they brought the invasion in.
>
> Our particular operation for D-Day was called 'Gambit'. When we looked it up in the dictionary, much to our horror it said the pawn you throw away before the big move in chess, which didn't encourage us too much.[5]

Not everyone could wait until H-hour before landing on the beaches. The troops arriving aboard the landing craft would need to be shown the way off the beach and not spend time exposed to German fire on the beach. The Royal Navy Commandos were given the task of landing to set up signs and indicators for the main assault force. One of their landing craft was hit before it reached the beach, with the ramp blown down so that it dropped below the bows, leaving those aboard unable to use it and having to leave the landing craft by the stern, dropping to the rough seas. None of them were too pleased as they had spent weeks training for the landing on windswept beaches in Scotland.

On coming ashore, they were met by the discouraging sight of bodies being swept in and out with the waves, and hastened to seek shelter in the sand dunes.

Reaching the beaches was an ordeal in itself. The Germans had placed obstacles along the coast, tetrahedral steel posts with shells and mines attached. A number of landing craft had been modified with twenty-four 60lb spigot bombs so that they could blow up the beach obstacles at half-tide. Immediately behind them came the 'landing craft tank', carrying tanks with flails which would clear the beaches of any mines to allow infantry to follow them ashore. The landing craft heading for the beach obstacles sailed in under a heavy destroyer bombardment, but at H-hour minus one minute the bombardment lifted, the landing craft let go their spigot bombs, and within seconds the air was rent with massive explosions.

It seems that not all of the beach obstacles could be cleared in time for the landing force. Able Seaman Ken Oakley was a Royal Navy Commando, preparing to go ashore with the beach master, a naval officer who would take charge of operations ashore and ensure that the beaches were cleared quickly, the priority being to dismantle 'Rommel's asparagus', each of which had an unhealthy 88-mm shell on the end:

> All around the sea was one mass of craft, landing craft of all kinds, shapes and sizes. A lot in our immediate area were LCAs because we were going for the initial assault. There was a good feeling as we went forward, except that most of the army was seasick. I wasn't very happy myself. However, when we got within sight of the shore we were getting splattered with light gunfire, nothing very heavy at this moment. Finally, we got within sight of the stakes, the dreaded stakes, with the shells and mines on, which protected the beaches. Our coxswain did a marvellous job. We were headed straight for this stake and I could see the 56lb shell lashed to it. In just the last second, he missed it. He got it just right. He steered us in between the stakes and got ashore without touching one of those shells. At the order 'Down ramp', we were all surging ashore. We were in a few inches of water. All around were craft beaching and chaos and more gunfire was pouring down on us. We ran, under fire, up to the top of the beach where we went to ground, about a hundred yards from high water. People were going down and screaming and crying all around us. As we hit the sand at the top of the beach we took stock of our bearings and realised that we had landed almost exactly in our correct positions.[6]

The landing craft infantry, LCI, sailed towards the beach in tight circles, and when they closed on the beach, they peeled off one at a time and rammed their bows onto the beach, with the next LCI coming alongside the previous one. After the rough seas, many must have been longing to reach the shore. Some of the landing craft were hit by German artillery fire and were ablaze, often with many casualties aboard.

Other ships, including converted merchant vessels as well as landing craft, were fitted with artillery rockets to clear the beaches and also put the defences under pressure. This was in addition to gunnery. Destroyers at the time were generally fitted with a main armament of 4-inch guns, although a few of the more modern ships had 4.5-inch. Cruisers had 6-inch guns with 4-inch as a secondary armament. One of these was HMS *Danae*, and on her bridge was Captain J.H.B. Hughes, a Royal Marine:

> Just before dawn, those of us on the bridge of HMS *Danae* had a tot of the most superb 1812 brandy from a bottle laid down by my great-grandfather in 1821, sent to me by my father with the comment, 'You may find this of some use in the near future.' We then commenced the operations for which we had been trained, namely engaging and knocking out three enemy batteries. At about 1000 we closed the beaches to knock out the opposition to the landing forces in the Ouistreham area. Our open 6-inch and twin 4-inch guns went into independent fire, the guns being laid, trained and fired by the crews stripped to the waist. This was real 'Nelson stuff'. We knocked up a fantastic rate of fire. X and Y[7] guns[8] were firing at least 19 rounds per minute on occasion. We all joined in, jumping in to relieve the exhausted crew members where we could. It was exhilarating beyond description and even my thirteen-year old boy bugler fired Y gun with the lanyard while the captain of the gun, a corporal, leapt to get more charges into the breach.
>
> Then it all came to a halt and we sailed to Portsmouth for re-ammunition.[9]

HMS *Danae* had been in Greenock when the plans for the landings had been finalised. Her commanding officer assembled her ship's company in their respective divisions on the quarterdeck in freezing cold weather to tell them of her role. He commented that they had 'the honour to be expendable', to which someone in the ranks of the stokers' division promptly commented, 'Fuck that for a lark!'

Another rating aboard one of the ships in the bombardment force commented, 'Cor! I'm sorry for those poor bastards on the other side.' The Germans might not have seen the invasion fleet coming, but they certainly heard it when it arrived. The bombardment started before the landing craft went in and crept ahead of the troops once they were ashore. There seem to have been no reports of 'friendly fire' casualties once on the beaches.

The naval bombardment started at 0530 and the landings commenced at 0630 by which time the bombardment moved away from coastal targets and headed inland.

There was a sense of improvisation even in this, the largest amphibious assault in history and with first call upon the resources of the British. While the Americans had much to do in the Pacific, there was no doubt that this was their biggest effort in the Atlantic. The naval commander in the eastern sector was Admiral Philip Vian, whose flagship was the light cruiser HMS *Scylla*. Aboard the ship, the volume of messages to be decoded and encoded meant that extra officers were required, but there was no space to accommodate them. The result was that they were sent every other day from Portsmouth aboard MTBs and stayed working aboard for forty-eight hours before being returned to Portsmouth.

To stiffen the bombardment, a large number of landing craft were fitted to fire rocket projectiles, laying down a curtain of lethal fire on the beaches and the area immediately behind them.

Despite the best efforts of the minesweepers, by the time Operation Neptune officially ceased on 30 June, 59 ships had been sunk and another 110 damaged, many by pressure mines.

The one remaining Mulberry harbour landed 850,279 men, 148,803 vehicles of all kinds and 570,505 tons of supplies.

Once the initial landings had been made, the major warships were back to continue bombarding enemy-held territory. Ships were routinely rotated out of the Normandy coastal waters and back to Portsmouth or even Plymouth to re-ammunition and if necessary refuel. The fire could be so devastating that on one occasion Rommel authorised the movement of a Panzer division away from the coast to a safer location further inland. Even the armour of a tank was not proof against a 15-inch shell.

Throughout June 1944, more than 70,000 shells were fired by the Royal Navy at German shore targets. Naval shellfire is more constant and wearing than that of land-based guns as the mechanised handling equipment means that a warship gun can fire six times as many shells in a given period as a land-based artillery piece, and often the shells are much heavier.

The German Commander-in-Chief, Army, West, Gert von Rundstedt, reported later,

> The enemy had deployed very strong naval forces off the shores of the bridgehead. These can be used as quickly mobile, constantly available

artillery, at points where they are necessary as defence against our attacks or as support for enemy attacks. During the day their fire is skilfully directed by … plane observers, and by advanced ground fire spotters. Because of the high rapid-fire capacity of naval guns they play an important part in the battle within their range. The movement of tanks by day, in open country, within the range of these naval guns is hardly possible.[10]

Another German report discovered later noted, 'Even more disastrous than the material effect was the morale effect of the rapidly and precisely firing naval guns. Even when not reinforced by simultaneous air bombing, the drum fire inspired in the defenders a feeling of utter helplessness, which in inexperienced recruits caused fainting or indeed complete paralysis. The supporting fire of warships was extremely accurate and made the movement of strategic reserves impossible within the 20 mile range of their guns.'

So that was it. The constant hammering of exploding shells all around them kept many Germans imprisoned within their shelters and concrete gun emplacements.

The Germans weren't the only ones to suffer. Those aboard the ships got no rest until they withdrew to refuel and re-ammunition. The firing and recoil of a heavy gun aboard a warship sends sound and shock waves right through the ship. The battleship *Nelson* had nine 16-inch guns spread over three turrets, the heaviest calibre in the Royal Navy at the time, and these fired a round once every minute on the night of 12/13 June, bombarding Caen. Those aboard the bombarding ships showed great endurance. They also had to be ready for action at a moment's notice at any time of day or night. Some of the officers did not take off their clothes for several days, some reports suggest for as long as seventeen days. It was tiring, but it says much about the poor state of the defenders and of the weakness of the Kriegsmarine that the Germans never tried to take advantage of their weariness. Hitler had, of course, brought home his battlecruisers *Scharnhorst* and *Gneisenau*, with the heavy cruiser *Prinz Eugen*, earlier in the celebrated 'Channel Dash' of February 1942.

The Allied navies continued to shell for as long as it was needed and there were enemy targets within range. On 30 June, US troops seized the port and city of Cherbourg, one of the great Channel ports. Elsewhere, the Allied armies took Caen on 9 July, followed by St Lô on 18 July, in turn followed by Avranches on 25 July, which finally allowed the bombardment fleet to leave the Normandy coast, their work done. Seizing ports helped, and was necessary, but capture often marked the start of considerable work to clear a port and its approaches of mines, and the Germans had usually been careful to sabotage many of the port installations.

Friendly Fire

While Neptune ended on 30 June, the Royal Navy's involvement did not, and the service continued to patrol the waters off the coast of Normandy looking for mines, while E-boats and U-boats were not forgotten. The campaign had seen relatively few naval casualties, a tribute to the use of overwhelming force and a reflection of the weak state of the German Kriegsmarine and Luftwaffe. The Germans were by this time on the defensive in both Italy and the South of France as well as in Normandy and on the Eastern Front.

What happened next was all the more distressing because it did not come as a result of an engagement with the enemy but was a clear case of 'blue on blue' or 'friendly fire'. On 27 August, two of the Royal navy's minesweepers were sunk and a third had its stern torn off after an attack by rocket-firing Hawker Typhoon fighter-bombers from the Royal Air Force's 263 and 266 squadrons.

The Royal Navy's First Minesweeping Flotilla was operating off the French coast in the region of Cap d'Antifer when it was decided to move it to a new area, and details of the change were sent by signal to all interested parties. Later that day, another naval officer came on duty and decided to send the flotilla back to its original area of operations, and again a signal was sent, but somehow the area naval headquarters was not included in the recipients and therefore could not notify the Royal Air Force. As a result, when Allied radar spotted five ships sweeping in line abreast at noon on 27 August, it was immediately assumed to be a German formation. Not having received the signal detailing the change, the Flag Officer, British Assault Area, FOBAA, agreed that any ships must be German. Two of the ships, HMS *Hussar* and *Britomart*, were larger than most minesweepers and had served as sloops on convoy escort duties. From the air they seemed large enough to be small German destroyers. A Polish airman flew over the ships in a Spitfire and reported that they seemed to be Allied vessels, but gave the wrong position. FOBAA attempted to contact the officers controlling minesweeping, but couldn't get through as the lines were down. FOBAA then called for an anti-shipping strike, and sixteen Typhoons of the RAF's 263 and 266 squadrons were ordered into the air. As he approached the flotilla, the strike leader thought that he could see Allied ships, so he radioed questioning his orders, only to be told to attack. He subsequently queried his orders twice.

At 1330, the attack began. Sweeping out of the sun towards the first ship, *Britomart*, the Typhoons started strafing and firing anti-tank rockets, deadly against the thin-plated hulls of minor warships. In less than two minutes, the ship had lost its bridge and was listing heavily, while another, *Hussar*, was on fire. Those aboard the ships immediately assumed that the aircraft must be those of the Luftwaffe and *Jason* signalled that she was under attack by enemy aircraft, but as the aircraft raced away, the distinctive D-Day black and white 'invasion stripes' could be seen and another ship, *Salamander*, fired recognition flares, forcing the hapless leader of the strike to query his orders yet again. Yet he was again ordered back into the attack, and at 1335 dived down again towards the warships, hitting *Britomart* once again and strafing *Jason* while rockets went into both *Salamander* and *Colsay*. Despite a large white ensign and a Union flag being draped over the stern of *Jason* as she fired further recognition flares, a third attack followed at 1340, hitting *Hussar*, which exploded, and *Salamander*, whose stern was blown off by rocket strikes. As the crippled *Salamander* drifted shoreward, a no doubt bemused German artillery battery with 9.2-inch coastal guns opened fire, forcing *Jason* to launch her small boats to tow *Salamander* out of danger.

This was the Royal Navy's worst friendly fire incident of the Second World War, with 117 officers and ratings killed and another 153 wounded. The whole incident was covered up and those involved sworn to secrecy on threat of prosecution. It only came to light in 1994 when the then Public Record Office, now the National Archives, released the papers.

The three officers who were responsible for this appalling and unnecessary loss of life and valuable ships were court marshalled. Two were acquitted and another severely reprimanded. No doubt had the strike leader disobeyed his orders he would have been dealt with far more severely.

Beyond Normandy

The Normandy landings did not mean that the war in Europe against Germany was over, not even for the Royal Navy. The Russian convoys had to be run, and there was much to do even as the Allied armies moved across Europe. Seizure of the port of Antwerp was vital as the supply lines from the French Channel ports became extended. This was initially hampered by the need to capture the Dutch island of Walcheren, which blocked access to the port. After valiant attempts by Canadian troops to take Walcheren across a causeway linking the island to the land, it was taken by a seaborne assault, with covering fire from the battleship *Warspite* which, as mentioned before, had to be towed into position by a tug.

On 1 November at 0554, the three Royal Marine Commando units of the British 4th Special Service Brigade attacked from seaward at Westkapelle, in Operation Infatuate I, accompanied by troops of the No.4 (Belgian) and No.5 (Norwegian) Commandos from Brigadier Peter Laycock's No.10 (IA) Commando. No.4 Commando with French troops in support then crossed from Breskens to attack Flushing with support from No.155 Infantry Brigade in Operation Infatuate II, aided by a heavy naval bombardment from the crippled *Warspite*, two monitors, including HMS *Roberts*, and other naval vessels, despite many of their landing craft being sunk by fire from German coastal batteries. The crossing was made mainly in Buffalos, which one Royal Marine present described as being 'like tanks with no tops'.

The run ashore was not easy, as Captain J. Linzel of No.10 Commando recalled:

> This operation had more impact on me. The objective was to clear the seaway to Antwerp. We went to Belgium, where the No.4 Troops Brigade and the No.10 Commando were billeted. We were an attached unit of 14 men. We entered our Buffalo amphibious vehicles to go to Walcheren where we experienced heavy German artillery. Our vehicle got hit direct by a grenade, setting our flamethrowers and ammunition on fire. This was a chaos. Our burning Buffalo was pushed into the sea and I can remember that together with 10 other men I ended up in another Buffalo and landed at Westkapelle. We experienced some serious fighting there and a lot of the brigade were killed. It took us 3 days to capture the German dyke at Vlissingen, there were about 300 casements.[11]

Frederick Weston was a sergeant in No.41 Royal Marine Commando:

> We were in the open, unlike D-Day, so we saw everything as we went in. It was very heavily defended, we manned gunboats to take these on and we also had rocket ships that shot off scores of shots at a time. We'd also been told that there could be fixed flame-throwers on this part of the beach, so that was something to look forward to. We managed to get on all right and got into the village there, and saw their strongpoint at the base of a lighthouse. We got cover in an old house and found the old hands in

there getting a brew of tea going. As we were pretty wet and miserable at the time, we had a quick cup of tea.

Unfortunately our troop commander was killed when we reached their strongpoint. It was a very sad occasion for us, it seemed like they were giving themselves up and then one man decided not to, and that was the end of our troop commander. It made us all very angry.[12]

This was the one thing that most fighting men could not accept: enemy troops surrendering and when approached to be taken prisoner, shooting their exposed would-be captors. It says much for the discipline of the Royal Marines that they did not shoot the Germans, or at least the man who betrayed their trust.

Two days of street fighting followed before the regional capital Middleburg could be seized and the Germans surrendered there on 5 November. Nevertheless, some resistance continued in the north of Walcheren and it was not until 8 November that this ended.

Tragedy awaited the Allied navies at Ostend.

Even by spring of the following year, most of the Netherlands was under German control, including the major naval bases of Ijmuiden and Den Helder, acting as bases for E-boats. The E-boats posed a major threat to the steady stream of shipping crossing the southern North Sea and, as always, the best defence against E-boat attacks on the northern flank of the Allied convoys was to provide motor gunboats or motor torpedo boats as escorts or on patrol to ward off E-boat attacks before they could get within reach of a convoy. Two MTB flotillas were based at Ostend, the Royal Navy's 55th and the Canadian-manned 29th, with a mobile base unit to service the motor torpedo boats. These two units had been fighting alongside each other since June 1944. The 29th had eleven 72 ft 6 in MTBs while the 55th had the larger Fairmile 'D' boats, more usually known as 'Dog Boats'. Most British MTBs and MGBs had petrol engines rather than the safer diesel engines, which meant that accidents involving fuel vapour-induced explosions and fires were relatively common.

On 14 February 1945, there were no less than thirty-one MTBs of all kinds as well as other small craft gathered in the harbour at Ostend, with many of the MTBs moored alongside one another. Many of the crew members had been granted shore leave, but others were busy preparing for that night's patrols.

Amongst those preparing for that night's patrols were four of the Canadian boats of the 29th MTB Flotilla. Of these, *MTB464* was carrying out an armament check at sea when one of its engines cut out due to water in the fuel system. This was a common problem as one of the tankers supporting the MTBs had pumped water-contaminated fuel ashore, which was then used to refuel the MTBs.. The base maintenance staff were too busy to provide assistance, and simply suggested that the MTB's crew pumped water from their fuel tanks into buckets and then disposed of the contents over the side. Before long, a strong smell of petrol spread throughout the harbour. Many noticed this, but no one reported it or took any action.

What happened next was a major fire, but what ignited it remains unknown. One witness was Ken Forrester, serving aboard one of the Royal Navy's MTBs, *MTB771*, in the 55th Flotilla:

> It was a rest day, and half the crew had been taken on a sightseeing trip to Brugge for the afternoon. It was around 3 o'clock in the afternoon. I had volunteered to make the tea and went up on deck to go to the potato locker which was just below the bridge. Before I got there I saw flames and smoke rising from the middle of a group of MTBs that were berthed in a large lock entrance some 30 yards away. Our boat was tied up to the wall with two others of our flotilla tied alongside us. The tide was low which meant that our torpedoes were below the level of the seawall. There was a raised gangway over the torpedoes bypassing the 0.5in turret. This gangway was level with the top of the wall. On seeing the fire I ran to the forward hatch—the crew's quarters—and yelled out *Fire!* Ran to the stern of the boat, took hold of a fire hose that was permanently rigged and ran unreeling it as I went. I was just passing over the gangway that was level with the wall when the boat that was on fire blew up with a huge *Woomph* noise. There was a rush of seething hot air which blew me over. The next thing I remember was picking myself up on the dockside with burning debris everywhere covering the quayside and all of our boats. Our own boat had been protected somewhat with being shielded by the dockside. I was still dazed, realised I'd lost my shoes and beard mostly singed off. I had blood running down my face by that time. Someone was running past me, so I ran while pandemonium was going on. Ammunition was exploding, torpedoes going off, pieces of flaming boats everywhere.[13]

It seemed as if the entire harbour was ablaze, with torpedoes and other ammunition exploding, fuel tanks rupturing an exploding, adding their contents to the fire.

Thirty-six members of the Royal Navy were killed, with the loss of seven boats, while the Royal Canadian Navy lost twenty-six personnel and five boats.

Taking the South of France

It had originally been intended that the Normandy landings would coincide with landings in the South of France, forcing the Germans to divide their forces. Another advantage of this two-pronged attack was that it would put pressure on German forces still fighting in Italy who risked being cut off should the Allied landings result in an advance eastwards into northern Italy. No matter what the advantages of such a coordinated assault, it soon became plain that insufficient resources were available to land in two places at once. The original plans for the Normandy landings had been on a much smaller front with fewer landing beaches than were eventually used, with a broader front seen as being less vulnerable to a German counter-attack. This was not all. The Normandy landings were not happening in isolation. American forces were moving across the Pacific and the demand for landing craft and landing ships, and supporting fire from battleships and cruisers, was such that the south of France would have to wait.

It could be argued that, even if Stalin only saw land battles as constituting a 'front', then the Normandy landings provided a second front, but in the Pacific there was a 'third front' and a 'fourth front' as the United States Army conducted landings in the southern zone and the United States Marine Corps in the north, steadily advancing towards Japan, and even this was to ignore the fighting in Burma.

This global demand for resources also explains why so many of the warships engaged in supporting the Normandy landings came from the Royal Navy. The United States Navy was otherwise engaged, and did well to provide the support it did off Normandy.

Operation Dragoon

The landings in the South of France were originally code-named 'Anvil', possibly because the planners saw the landings in Normandy and in the South of France hammering the German occupiers into shape!

The South of France did not compare with Normandy. The Germans had left a substantial part of France unoccupied and under Vichy control partly to avoid overstretching their occupation forces. Even after they occupied Vichy territory after the Allied landings in North Africa in late 1942, the resources were not available to build a 'Mediterranean Wall', and indeed the 'Atlantic Wall' itself was far from complete.

Allied landings in the South of France had been delayed by the need to devote further resources to the campaign in Italy. The landings at Salerno had not produced a fast enough advance, and those at Anzio had been even more disappointing. These problems and the strong German resistance at Monte Cassino had delayed the entry into Rome until just before the Normandy landings.

The scale of the landings in the South of France almost make it seem like a sideshow compared to North Africa, Sicily and Normandy, but even so the resources expended were considerable. The seaborne operation was under the command of Vice Admiral Henry Hewitt, USN. He led a fleet of 500 landing and 200 escort vessels to put ashore Lieutenant General Alexander Patch's US Seventh Army between Cannes and Toulon on 15 August 1944. Hewitt had three American battleships as well as one each from the Royal Navy and the French *Marine Nationale*. There were also 9 escort carriers, 25 cruisers and 45 destroyers.

Little resistance was met, and within a few days both the major naval base at Toulon and the important port of Marseilles were in Allied hands. The Luftwaffe mounted little resistance and before long the Supermarine Seafires from the British escort carriers and the Grumman Hellcats from the American escort carriers found themselves providing ground-attack missions in support of ground forces. This had not been entirely unexpected and to ensure that the Fleet Air Arm was ready for what was to be a new role, some naval air squadron commanders had been granted time to fly with RAF squadrons flying ground-attack sorties in Italy.

Operations were helped by the fact that there were more escort carriers than at Salerno, and there was plenty of room to manoeuvre, while the escort carriers could be rotated out of operations for refuelling off Corsica, avoiding the dramas caused by the shortage of fuel off Salerno. After 24 August, the Germans were clearly withdrawing and being out-of-range for the carriers; air-to-ground operations were taken over by the USAAF.

Chapter Thirteen

Was a Negotiated Peace an Option?

Whether a negotiated peace is an option in any conflict really depends at what stage it occurs. The same applies to those who argue that the Second World War might have been avoided. Could it have been avoided by giving in and allowing Germany to seize Poland? Or could Hitler have been stopped at an earlier stage before too much damage was done? Many believe that the last chance to stop Hitler was when he invaded the Rhineland on 7 March 1936, with German troops entering what was supposed to be a demilitarized zone. As the Allies had vacated the area, responding rapidly to this move by the Germans would have been difficult, but the French should have been able to intervene with superior force and the British able to follow up with reinforcements within days.

The belief still exists that Hitler would have been happy to allow the British Empire to remain intact if, after the fall of France, Germany had been allowed to retain its territorial gains in Europe and Scandinavia. Certainly Hitler could not understand why the British continued to fight after their withdrawal from France, just as he had failed to realise that the two countries would honour their commitments to Poland.

There can be no doubt that the credibility of both the United Kingdom and France was seriously damaged by the Munich Agreement of October 1938. Yet it encouraged Hitler and his senior officers to believe that the ultimatum of September 1939 was yet another case of Anglo-French sabre-rattling, and that the Führer would get away with it once more. They were encouraged in this view by the fact that neither of the two allies had seemed unduly concerned when, earlier that year, the Germans completed their conquest of Czechoslovakia. Interestingly, the British government-sponsored research organisation, Mass Observation, found that the desire for peace by Chamberlain's government was welcome to a population anxious to avoid war, with the horrors and losses of the First World War still very much in mind.

The problem was that none of the three nations involved was really ready for a major conflict in 1938. The British in fact made better use of the period of almost a year gained by the Munich Agreement than did the Germans, who were already running short of money, and especially foreign exchange, or the French, who had created confusion and uncertainty by nationalising their aircraft industry. The French were preoccupied with internal politics and neglected the international situation. The British continued to re-arm and expand their armed forces.

Yet, could the Germans have been stopped earlier?

Two opportunities were missed in the years before the outbreak of the Second World War.

As mentioned above, the first was the failure to stop the Germans marching into the Rhineland on 7 March 1936. The force deployed by the Germans was not large, just 22,000 troops, of which only 3,000 entered the Rhineland proper rather than just the demilitarised zone. There was no military confrontation, only diplomatic protests afterwards. This event added immensely to Hitler's prestige, and his image, at home and abroad, of a man who got things done.

It would have been relatively easy for the French to have stopped this breach of the terms of the Treaty of Versailles.

It is certainly the case that the victorious First World War allies could not have kept German forces out of the Rhineland forever. Diplomacy would have been used to negotiate an end to the demilitarised zone, although the French would have objected as the zone offered a barrier between Germany and France. The comparison with more recent years lies in the reunification of Germany after the fall of the Soviet Union. This would have been impossible to stop, although many senior officers in the North Atlantic Treaty Organisation and the then British prime minister, Margaret Thatcher, were opposed to German reunification seeing this as a threat to the balance of power in Europe.

After the rise of Hitler, the other major chance of signalling to Germany that the United Kingdom and France were prepared to stand and if necessary fight for their beliefs had come the previous year when the Italians invaded Abyssinia, present day Ethiopia, in 1935.

There were protests, but the League of Nations was impotent as the French refused to countenance military action against the Italians. Discord between the two nations had existed already, with an arms race, and especially a naval arms race, between them throughout the 1920s and '30s. The power and influence of the League of Nations was not helped by the absence of the United States from its membership, even though it was in part the brainchild of an American president.

The Royal Navy had already drawn up plans to use the British Mediterranean Fleet's aircraft carrier, HMS *Glorious*, for an attack on the major Italian naval base at Taranto. Planning was sufficiently detailed that it included the immediate withdrawal of the ship after the attack, recognising that she would be vulnerable to heavy Italian aerial attack afterwards. This was to prove realistic after the successful attack by HMS *Illustrious* on the night of 11/12 November 1940, when the ship faced a massive and crippling onslaught by German and Italian bombers early in January 1941.

At the time of the Italian invasion of Abyssinia, there were British forces in Egypt. The British Mediterranean Fleet used Alexandria as a base, so closing the Suez Canal to Italian shipping would have hampered Italian efforts to expand their colonial empire without too much difficulty. True, the canal was supposed to be an international waterway, but the Italians were engaged in an act of aggression, and the United Kingdom and France had League of Nations support.

Perhaps the French government was concerned about a land war with Italy, with both countries sharing a border, but the British were also vulnerable to Italian attack on their island colony and major naval base at Malta. The point is that both countries acting together could have curbed Axis ambitions and forced Germany and Italy not to presume that they could invade without retribution.

The big problem about Czechoslovakia, and Neville Chamberlain's description of it as a 'far away country of which we known nothing', was that in reality there was little that the UK and France could do as Czechoslovakia was not well placed for intervention with Germany lying between France and Czechoslovakia. But the same applied to Poland, which was provided with guarantees by the UK in 1939. Not for the first time or even the last time, the British Foreign Office handed out guarantees for another nation's security without considering the military implications, or even whether defensive aid would be possible.

Surrender once the Germans started moving into Scandinavia, and even more so once they advanced westwards, would have meant the end of the British Empire and a complete loss of credibility and international influence. Resistance movements, already strong and troublesome in India, would have flourished, and even colonial governments and those in the dominions would have come to see that the United Kingdom no longer could provide the guarantees of protection and intervention that they required. As with the promises made to Poland, some of these had been recklessly made, with Australia and New Zealand assured that if Japan should start a war in the Far East, the UK would send a 'strong fleet'. By December 1941, when war finally spread to the Far East, sending a fleet of any kind, let alone a strong one, was beyond the mother country's capabilities.

By 1940, even the United States had grave doubts about the UK's ability to survive. Probably encouraged by the defeatism of the US ambassador in London,

Joseph Kennedy, the United States even developed a bomber that could be used to attack Germany after the defeat of the UK, the Convair B-36. Just how successful this massive aircraft would have been is doubtful. It was piston-engined, as were all aircraft at the time, and piston-engine reliability was so poor that post-war, some transatlantic airlines changed an engine after every two return trips, or 'rotations' in airline terms, in a bid to enhance reliability and avoid in-flight engine shutdowns.

One thing is certain, without bases in the east of England for the Americans to use, Germany would have been spared the hardships of what often amounted to round-the-clock heavy bombing, with the United States Army Air Force attacking by day and the Royal Air Force by night. The best the USAAF could have hoped for would have been to use bases in Iceland and perhaps the Azores.

A negotiated peace would have been very difficult and the United Kingdom would have been negotiating from a position of weakness with a strong and successful Germany that had been victorious and achieved everything it had planned since the occupation of the Rhineland in 1936. It was this realisation that spurred Churchill and others on to continue the fight. 'Peace in our time' was one thing, but peace on German terms was no different from surrender and could well have resulted in, if not outright occupation, Germany dictating what the British would and could not do, as in Vichy France, where political appointments not to the liking of the Germans had to be reversed.

Chapter Fourteen

Could The Germans Have Invaded?

By the time the Allies landed in Normandy, they had had extensive experience in making opposed amphibious landings. Apart from the lessons learnt in the disastrous Dieppe raid, there had been the successful landings in North Africa, followed by Sicily, then Salerno on the Italian mainland, and when the post-Salerno advance up the leg of Italy proved to be more difficult than planned, there was a further landing, again less successful in the aftermath, at Anzio.

The demands of the Normandy landings were so great that landings in the south of France, originally planned to coincide with Normandy, were postponed, and the convoys to northern Russia had to be interrupted while the landings took place. This indicates the scale of the Normandy landings and the resources required, even with the combined efforts of the British, the Canadians and the Americans, as well as forces from the 'free' armies and navies of the European countries occupied by the Germans.

The Germans, who were the most experienced armed forces in the world in 1940, and the most successful, were still not accustomed to making a strongly opposed landing on a hostile shore in 1940, and even later in the war failed to gain such experience. There were river crossings, but a river crossing, even if opposed, is different from landing an army on a strange shore, and then reinforcing and supporting it.

Hitler wanted aerial supremacy before launching an invasion, but the Luftwaffe failed to ensure this. There has been speculation that aerial supremacy might have prevailed had Goering not moved the Luftwaffe away to begin the 'blitz' on British towns and cities. It is impossible to be certain whether or not the RAF might have been crippled had the Battle of Britain continued, but a substantial part of the UK was at the very end of endurance for the Luftwaffe's bombers and beyond fighter escort cover. This is why there were so few heavy air raids on Scotland and Northern Ireland. The RAF's squadrons could have re-equipped and regrouped in these areas.

Even if the Luftwaffe had achieved the objectives set for it, it is far from certain that the invasion could have proceeded. *Vizeadmiral* (Vice Admiral) Kurt Assmann of the German Naval Staff made it clear after the war that 'air supremacy alone could not provide permanent security against vastly superior naval forces in the crossing area'.

The fact was that the Royal Navy *was* vastly superior to the Kriegsmarine at the time. As the loss of Crete was to show later, losing aerial superiority did not guarantee victory to the enemy, although it did increase the losses and serious damage to warships, with the aircraft carrier HMS *Formidable* having to be withdrawn from the Mediterranean for major repairs.

At the time, effective landing equipment was not available and the Germans would have had great difficulty in landing, especially tanks and heavy artillery. While the Germans were adept at airborne assault, at the time aircraft capable of handling main battle tanks were not available and, as mentioned before, their transport effort was hampered by having to use aircrew from the bomber schools to man their transport aircraft, and the backbone of their air transport effort, the famous Junkers Ju52/3m transport, was already obsolete in 1940.

The Germans also lacked other important equipment. There were no real battleships in the Kriegsmarine in 1940 – the first, *Bismarck*, was not due to make her maiden voyage until 1941 and the other, *Tirpitz*, was even further behind. The battlecruisers *Scharnhorst* and *Gneisenau* were supposed to have been retrofitted with 15-inch guns, but this never happened and they only had 12-inch guns, as did the two surviving *Panzerschiffe*, each of which had just four guns in two turrets. There were no monitors, no mini-submarines for guidance and beach reconnaissance, and too few destroyers for anti-submarine work on either side of the assault fleet or the resupply convoys.

The Allies were to find in 1944 that fighting their way out of the Normandy landing zones was difficult because of the terrain – the *bocage* with its high hedges and sunken country lanes, which favoured the defenders – but they could at least dominate the area up to twenty miles from the coast because of the weight of fire and range of the battleship guns. Had Operation Sea Lion gone ahead, the Germans would have found that the downland behind the south coast of England would have also favoured the defenders.

The Germans had no plans to build temporary ports on the style of the Mulberry harbours used by the Allies, and no plans for an undersea fuel pipeline such as Pluto. They would have been heavily dependent on seizing a port. They were to show after the Allied landings in Normandy that they knew how to render a port inoperable so that it took time for an advancing army to get any benefits from it, but how much consideration was given to the British doing the same at their major Channel ports?

The two entrances to Dover would have been easy to block, sinking a large ship across each of them. The main railway line from Dover ran through a tunnel cut in the chalk cliff face, and this would have been destroyed. Dover had yet to be equipped with heavy artillery to use against German shipping in the Channel because of the heavy losses of equipment incurred in the evacuation from France. What was available was sufficient to defend the port from an attack by fast E-boats, possibly landing small parties of commandos for sabotage of the port facilities. This never happened and many believe that such a raid would have been suicidal, but another reason was that the port facilities were little used in wartime as the cross-Channel traffic for which they were intended had ended for the duration of the war. There was no point in making a raid, especially as Dover was under heavy and almost constant heavy artillery fire from across the Channel.

The garrison at Dover was responsible for the protection of some ten miles of coastline rather than just the port itself. A 'Dover Defence Scheme' was finalised on 24 September 1940; a copy of this was appended to the War Diary of the Dover Garrison.[1] In all, it has been estimated that around 8,000 men drawn from a wide spread of British Army units were based on or near Dover, augmented by locally raised Home Guard units, with that of C Company (Dover) of the 8th Kent (Cinque Ports) Battalion having eight platoons. The British after Dunkirk had plenty of men and plenty of rifles, but coastal artillery was in short supply. The most potent artillery weapons were just two twin six-pounders, capable of firing thirty-six rounds per minute per barrel, which would have been lethal against landing craft. There were also some 9.2-inch coastal artillery pieces. Also, the big problem with any frontal assault on Dover was that the town was dominated by the castle and high ground, which would have given the defenders a dominant position.

Beach landings, as at Normandy, would have required the Germans to plan their invasion further west or further north, in each case extending the Channel crossing during which the invasion force would have been exposed to attack by the Royal Navy and the Royal Air Force.

Whether an attempt was made to seize Dover itself or beach landings were made, the defensive plan extended well inland, with strong defensive positions identified in areas where the advancing enemy could be brought to a halt and bombed.

As mentioned earlier, the German Army High Command had proposed landings on a 200-mile front that would have stretched as far west as Lyme Regis, in Dorset, and east to Ramsgate, on the north coast of Kent. This plan was opposed by the German navy, which knew it could not protect or supply and then resupply such a wide front, especially with the major naval base of Portsmouth in the middle of it. A compromise was agreed, with landings between Brighton in the west to Hythe in the east. Another army scheme, to land in East Anglia, had been opposed by the air force because of the changeable weather conditions over the North Sea, while again the navy was concerned about intervention from the Royal Navy. A first wave of 67,000 men would seize and hold the beaches, while an airborne division would land inland. These advance forces would be joined by a second wave consisting largely of armoured units that would break out from the beachheads. Overall, 160,000 men were to be landed and a force of 2,000 barges assembled for the operation.

Contrast this plan with the Normandy landings which were to take 7,000 ships of all kinds to land 75,215 British and Canadian troops and 57,500 US troops, a total of 132,715 men, plus armoured vehicles, artillery and motor vehicles.

The Kriegsmarine wanted it to be even more concentrated and confined, between Dover and Eastbourne. The naval general staff maintained that the area between Le Havre or Cherbourg and the Dorset coast would be highly exposed to ships operating from the Royal Navy's bases at Portsmouth and Devonport. It was not just that the strength of the Royal Navy and its control of the seas was a problem, covering too wide a front also meant that the various ports and landing beaches had high tides at different times. This would be less of a problem with purpose-designed landing craft, but even so, it ruined any chance of a surprise attack.

But, of course, the Germans did not have purpose-designed landing craft, just modified barges and coasters. The large landing ships used by the Allies at Normandy were some years away and, needless to say, the Germans did not have them. They did have amphibious tanks, but these had their limitations and needed to be launched into fairly calm waters.

In short, the Germans could project their armies across rivers and even lakes, but not across the open seas.

The problem with the revised landing zones was that between Dover and Eastbourne good landing beaches were few and far between, with many high cliffs. The countryside inland was, and remains, downland, offering good defensive positions. Nearer the coast, the areas around Romney and Dungeness included marshland and beaches over which movement could be difficult due to shingle, so much so that when railway lines were extended into the area, it had to be by building a narrow gauge railway. The intense competition between railway companies in the nineteenth century, so despised by economic historians, with many lines built that would never be viable, meant that even at the height of the 'blitz' it remained possible for trains to travel between London and the southeast coast. During Operation Dynamo, the evacuation from Dunkirk, the four British railway companies had managed to get trains through to the ports where the rescued troops were being landed and then moved them inland quickly and efficiently, and no doubt they could have done the same in reverse so that the Germans could expect reinforcements to reach the area quickly, while the lines and bridges as well as tunnels would be sabotaged by retreating British troops.

The Allies had also allowed themselves more than a year to plan the Normandy landings. They had experience in North Africa, Sicily and Italy. Hitler had not allowed his forces the time to plan. Even if he had, as we have seen, German planning and preparation was not as good as many have come to believe. The advance into the Soviet Union, for example, was without adequate preparations for the harsh Russian winter. Added to this was Hitler's meddling with the running of the war, changing priorities and objectives. Churchill and Stalin also attempted this. Churchill's 'midnight follies', a reference to ideas that emerged after an evening's heavy drinking, were well known, but most of the time he was capable of listening as well as ordering. Stalin used the threat of the *Gulag* against his close inner circle and his senior commanders to force decisions through, and the firing squad was an everyday reality. The families of his advisers and commanders were not immune from Stalin's displeasure, something that Hitler could not be accused of doing.

Another problem was that there was no unity or unifying force for the German armed forces. There was no equivalent of a war cabinet or a joint chiefs of staff committee. The heads of the armed forces were allowed to compete with one another and that also meant competing for Hitler's ear. Goering was the most effective at this. He persuaded Hitler that the Luftwaffe could eliminate the British Expeditionary Force at Dunkirk, leaving the army to stand back, but the Luftwaffe failed. The Luftwaffe was going to destroy the Royal Air Force, but it didn't. He persuaded Hitler to allow paratroops and air-landed troops to seize Crete; they did but at an unbearable cost. At one stage, steel intended for the Kriegsmarine was taken by the Luftwaffe to construct tropical barracks, which were not needed.

Rivalries in the British and American armed forces were not unknown, but they were controlled and managed much better than under Hitler. An example of this was in the Pacific war, where the United States Navy and US Marines were given different zones in order to avoid personality problems, mainly because of the self-seeking ambition and difficult personality of the army chief, General Douglas MacArthur.

The Germans could not have managed a successful invasion of southern England, and if they had done so, they would not have been able to embark on Operation Barbarossa, the invasion of the Soviet Union. Just as that invasion was the final act that made the invasion of the UK impossible, the opposite also held true. Yet it was the invasion of the Soviet Union that was more important to Hitler. He had planned this for much of his life, and saw it as having the dual outcome of defeating Bolshevism and securing the elimination of the Jews.

Hitler had to hand over the reins of power. He nominated the head of the Kriegsmarine, Dönitz, as his president and Goebbels as chancellor, while denouncing Goering and Himmler as traitors, Goering for his failure to protect the Reich, and Himmler for his contacts with the Allies (ostensibly as peace feelers and to ensure the safety of the surviving Jews, although in reality a desperate bid to distance himself from the mass murder and genocide).

Hitler held to his beliefs to the bitter end, which was to mean suicide rather than face capture by Soviet troops. As they closed in on the Reich Chancellery, where he was a virtual prisoner, he dictated his last will and testament to his secretary, Traudl Junge, which was accompanied by what he called a 'political testament'. He blamed the Jews for the outbreak of war in 1939 and forecast that in the future mankind would turn against 'international Jewry and its henchmen'. He continued: 'Above all, I charge the leadership of the nation and their subjects with meticulous observance of the race-laws and merciless resistance to the universal poisoner of all peoples, international Jewry.'[2]

Appendix A

The Invasion Barges

European canal and river traffic operated on a far larger scale than in the British Isles. The canals were much wider and deeper and the distances that could be travelled by canal or river were much longer than in the British Isles. River and canal traffic was carried by ships or barges that were more like a British coaster than a British canal barge, appropriately known as a narrow boat.

As mentioned earlier in Chapter 5, two main types of inland river barge were available in Europe: the *Peniche*, which was 126 feet long and carried 360 tons of cargo, and the *Kampine*, which was 164 feet long and carried 620 tons of cargo. Of the barges collected for the invasion, just over 1,300 were classified as *Peniches* and almost a thousand as *Kampinen*. The Germans designated any barge up to the size of a standard *Peniche* as Type A1 and anything larger as Type A2. This sounds neat and standardised, but the Germans had to make extensive modifications to the barges, as shown below.

Type A

The Germans converted the Type A barges into primitive landing craft by cutting an opening in the bow and installing a wooden ramp for offloading troops and vehicles. To improve seaworthiness they welded longitudinal I-beams and transverse braces to the hull and poured a concrete floor into the hold to strengthen it for carrying tanks. These changes enabled the Type A1 to carry three medium tanks while the Type A2 could carry four.

Type AS

A modification of the Type created because it was realised that it would be necessary to provide the advanced infantry detachments making the initial landings with greater protection from small-arms and light artillery fire, so the sides of Type A barges were lined with concrete. Wooden slides were also installed along the barge's hull to accommodate ten *Sturmboote*, assault boats, each capable of carrying six infantrymen and powered by a 30 hp outboard motor. The extra weight of this additional armour and equipment reduced the barge's load capacity to 40 tons. By mid-August, 18 of these craft, designated Type AS, had been converted, and another five were ordered on 30 September.

Type AF

Another variant was the Type D, this time devised by the *Luftwaffe*, which for some reason had formed its own special command under Major Fritz Siebel to investigate the production of landing craft for the invasion in another example of the Luftwaffe using what had become a privileged position to interfere with the plans best left to other branches of the German armed forces. Siebel proposed giving the unpowered Type A barges their own motive power by installing a pair of 600 hp surplus BMW aircraft engines on them driving aircraft propellers. The Kriegsmarine was highly sceptical of this venture, but the Army high command took to the idea and Siebel proceeded with the conversions.

The aircraft engines were mounted on a platform supported by iron scaffolding at the stern. Cooling water was stored in tanks mounted above-deck. The Type AF had a speed of six knots, and a range of 60 nautical miles. The big drawback was that the Type AF barge could not move astern and had limited manoeuvrability. The deafening noise of the engines would also have made a night assault vulnerable while voice commands would have been inaudible. Nevertheless by the beginning of October, more than 120 Type A barges had been converted to airscrew propulsion and this number almost doubled by the end of the month, after the invasion had been called off.

Type B

This barge was a Type A altered to carry and rapidly offload the *Tauchpanzer*, submersible tanks, which the army had developed for the invasion. Compared to the Type A barges, the Type B could unload their tanks directly into water up to 15 metres deep several hundred yards from shore, whereas the unmodified Type A had to be firmly grounded on the beach, making it more vulnerable to enemy fire. The Type B required a longer ramp, some 36 feet long with a float attached to the front of it. The ramp did not fall down easily: the crew had to deploy it with block and tackle sets until it was resting on the water's surface. As the first tank rolled forward onto the ramp, its weight would tilt the forward end of the ramp into the water and push it down onto the seabed. Once the tank rolled off, the ramp would bob back up to a horizontal position, ready for the next one to exit. Initially the Kriegsmarine ordered 60 of these vessels, but this was increased to 70 to allow for losses, and five more were ordered at the end of September as a further attrition reserve.

Type C

The Type C barge was specifically converted to carry up to four *Schwimmpanzer*, Panzer II, amphibious tanks (see Appendix B below). The Panzer II was fitted with floats attached to its sides, increasing its width to such a degree that it was decided that bow doors and a ramp would have to be so wide that seaworthiness would be adversely affected. The solution was to cut a large hatch in the stern, so that the tanks could drive directly into deep water before turning under their own motive power and heading towards shore. Fourteen Type C barges were ready by late September 1940.

Conclusion

German resources were finite, and hugely stretched under wartime conditions, so the Luftwaffe's interference in the barge modification programme was reckless and unwanted, wasting resources, as well as being impractical. Nevertheless, all was not lost, with the *Kriegsmarine* later being able to use some of the motorised invasion barges for landings on the Russian-held Baltic islands in 1941 and, though most of them were eventually returned to the canals and rivers from which they had been taken, a number were kept for military transport duties.

Appendix B

Specialised Equipment

Fast-moving armoured formations were an integral part of German warfare. Tanks were heavy and cumbersome beasts, difficult to put ashore without good port facilities, but the initial wave of invading troops would be highly vulnerable, and much effort was devoted to ensuring that they had armour once they were on the beaches.

Tanks

The first of these was the amphibious or 'swimming' tank, the *Schwimmpanzer*, a variant of the Panzer II, a light tank of just under 9 tons, which could be made amphibious by adding long buoyancy boxes to each side of the hull. The aluminium boxes were filled with Kapok sacks to improve buoyancy. The tank tracks were connected by rods to propeller shafts which ran through the floats. To make the tank watertight, an inflated rubber hose was installed around the turret to provide a seal between the turret and the hull. The tank could move at around 3 knots in the water, and the 2-cm gun and the machine gun could be used as the tank travelled towards the shore.

As mentioned in Appendix A, the increased width of the tank meant that a basic modified barge with bow doors and a ramp was regarded as being unsuitable and vulnerable because of the size, so the stern ramp Type C barge was necessary for these tanks. More than 50 of these tanks were produced before the invasion was cancelled.

Light tanks were, of course, more vulnerable to anti-tank measures than larger tanks. The next stage was to convert a medium tank, such as a Panzer III or Panzer IV, to create the *Tauchpanzer*, or 'deep-wading tank', which effectively moved under the water. These tanks were waterproofed by being sealed completely. As with the *Schwimmpanzer*, an inflated rubber hose was installed around the turret to provide a seal between the turret and the hull, but in addition, all sighting ports, hatches and air intakes were sealed, while the gun, radio operator's machine gun and other openings were sealed with rubber. On reaching the beach, all of these rubbers and seals could be blown off quickly by using explosive charges so that the tank was ready for combat almost as soon as it emerged on dry land.

Of course, the tank and its crew still needed air. This was drawn into the tank using a long rubber hose, almost 60 feet long with a float attached to one end to keep it above the surface. A radio antenna was attached to the float so that the crew could still communicate. The engine also had to be modified to be cooled using sea water and the exhaust fitted with valves to allow exhaust to escape while keeping sea water out. In case any of these measures failed and water did enter the tank, a bilge pump was fitted.

Navigation was by gyrocompass or by communication with an accompanying vessel.

By late June a prototype was available for testing near Wilhelmshaven. This proved that the tank had to be kept moving, as once stopped they started to sink into the sand or mud. Rocks or other obstacles on the sea bed stopped the tank, and it was decided that they should only be launched at high tide so that any tank that failed, and its crew, could be rescued at low tide.

A sizeable number of tanks were available by late August, including 160 Panzer IIIs, 42 Panzer IVs and 52 Panzer IIs. They were split into four units, *Panzer-Abteilung* A, B, C and D. Fuel for an initial operation of 125 miles was carried.

Landing Equipment

Realising the problems of landing reinforcements and supplies without harbour facilities, the Kriegsmarine commissioned Krupp and Dortmunder Union to design and build competing prototype jetties. These were not ready in time for Hitler's September 1940 deadline, and did not appear until late 1941. Both prototypes were tested in the North Sea during the winter of 1941-42 and withstood the poor weather and high seas well. The Krupp design was regarded as the winner because it took just a day to assemble, as opposed to four weeks for the Dortmunder Union jetty.

The Krupp design was built up using 32-metre-long platforms, with each supported by four steel columns that stood on the seabed. The platforms could be raised or lowered depending on the state of the tide. Eight jetties each of six platforms were ordered by the Germans, but this was cut to six jetties and then cancelled once it became clear that the invasion was cancelled and would not be reinstated. The two prototypes survived, however, and were taken to Alderney, the third largest of the Channel Islands, in mid-1942 where they were both assembled and used to unload materials needed to fortify the island. They survived until 1978 when demolition of the 'German jetty' started.

Despite the shortage of raw materials, the German army also decided to build a landing jetty of its own, the *Seeschlange* or Sea Snake. This doubled up as a floating road and like the Krupp jetty was assembled from floating platforms which could be transported by railway or towed at sea. Successful trials at Le Havre in northern France in autumn 1941 proved the concept would work, but it was too late for Operation Sea Lion. Instead it was decided to use it on a planned invasion of Malta, Operation Herkules, which did not go ahead.

One piece of equipment which was ready in time was the *Landwasserschlepper*, LWS, which was an amphibious tractor on which work had started well before the war, in 1935. It was not designed for an invasion but to enable army engineers to make crossings of rivers or other inland waterways. Nevertheless, in an invasion they would have been used to pull barges further up the beaches or to move vehicles across the beaches. By towing an amphibious trailer with a payload of up to 20 tons, they would also have been used to ferry supplies from a ship or barge moored offshore. Halder, the chief of the army general staff, thought that its profile was far too high, making it an easy target, although he did appreciate that it would be useful in supporting an amphibious operation.

The plan was that each invasion barge should have two tractors, but the industrial capacity did not exist for such lavish provision.

It had been planned that the invasion force would require around 45,000 horses, but Germany's own resources were augmented by captured equipment, which included French armoured tractors. These provided a significant advance for the Germans who were still so heavily dependent on horses for haulage. The Germans planned to use the tractors initially to get their equipment off the beaches, but later, once the landings were established, they would be the haulage of choice for anti-tank weapons and munitions trailers.

Around 3,000 Renault UE Chenillette light tracked armoured carriers were captured intact and became known to the Germans as the *Infanterie Schlepper UE630*. In addition to the internal storage, this vehicle could pull a trailer with a three-quarter ton load and manage a gradient of 1 in 2. The armour varied between 5 and 9mm, enough to stop shrapnel and bullets.

Better still was the Lorraine 37L, but the Germans captured just 360. It could move a total of almost 1½ tons split between the vehicle and its trailer.

Appendix C

New Equipment

So significant was Sea Lion that the Germans planned to introduce new equipment and also upgrade existing equipment, incorporating the hard-won experience of the first twelve months of war.

The Germans are often credited with having superior armoured vehicles to the British, but the standard German anti-tank gun, the Pak 36, fired 37mm rounds which could not penetrate the armour of the new British Matilda and Valentine tanks. Fortunately for the Germans, new armour-piercing tungsten-cored ammunition had been introduced by autumn 1940, but even this was not guaranteed to penetrate the armour of the new Matilda II tank. The units intended to be the first wave of the invasion force were re-equipped with captured Czech and French 47mm anti-tank guns, but these were not much of an improvement. The weapon of choice for anti-tank operations became the Pak 38, which was available from mid-1940 and fired a 50mm round which could deal a knockout blow to a Matilda. This weapon was distributed initially to Hitler's crack unit, the Waffen SS, and to the elite units of the German army, all of which were assigned to Sea Lion.

Current weaponry was also improved, with the Stug III 7.5cm assault gun given some armour protection and improved suspension. A small number of the new and still top secret 75mm *Leichtgeschütz* 40 recoilless guns were to be released to be landed with the paratroops: each one could be easily split into four parts with a parachute landing each part, and assembled once on the ground.

A number of Panzer III tanks were to have their armour reinforced and their 3.7cm guns replaced with 5cm. There were also to be 36 *Flammpanzer II* flamethrower tanks. Flamethrowers were especially effective in dealing with defenders in pillboxes or sheltered artillery positions, rather than in the open.

Glossary

AASF, Advanced Air Striking Force – An RAF formation including fighters and bombers that was sent to France alongside the British Expeditionary Force, and in addition to the BEF's air component.

Allies – A term dating back at least to the early nineteenth century, but used commonly during the First World War to describe the members of the Triple Entente, more properly known as the 'Entente Powers', which were the United Kingdom, France and Imperial Russia. During the Second World War the term was used for just the UK and France initially, later adding the Soviet Union and then the United States.

Asdic – Derived from the initials for the Allied Submarine Detection Investigation Committee, and today known as sonar. Such equipment emits audible pings and then traces submerged objects through their echoes.

Auxiliary cruiser – Merchant vessel taken up from trade and armed with a naval crew. The British used these as convoy escorts, the Germans used them as surface raiders. In neither case could they survive contact with major warships.

Axis Powers – The alliance formed by Germany, Italy and, later, Japan. Unlike the Allies, there was very little coordination at times, especially between Japan and Germany or Italy, or cross-fertilisation of ideas or technical developments.

Barbarossa – Code-name for Germany's invasion of the Soviet Union.

Battlecruiser – A warship usually with battleship calibre armament, but in which armour was sacrificed to give a greater speed. The German battlecruisers *Scharnhorst* and *Gneisenau* had guns of just 12-inch calibre, but were supposed to be replaced by guns of 15-inch calibre, although this never happened.

Battleship – Designation given to large heavily-armed and heavily-armoured ships. Second World War battleships generally had guns of 15-inch calibre, but some British battleships had 14 or 16-inch, and some Japanese ships had 18-inch guns.

BEF, British Expeditionary Force – A substantial formation of the British Army despatched to France the day after war was declared. It also included an RAF air component.

Bomber Command – RAF command responsible for bomber operations from UK bases, but not fighter-bombers which came under Fighter Command. Bomber squadrons based overseas came under local command, and usually lacked heavy bombers, relying on medium and light bombers, often because of a shortage of airfields with good runways.

Capital ship – A major warship such as a battleship or battlecruiser. By the end of the war the aircraft carrier had joined these as a capital ship, and many would say had even usurped their position.

Case White – German code name for the invasion of Poland.

Coastal Command – Royal Air Force command that provided maritime-reconnaissance and anti-submarine patrols, as well as search and rescue, SAR, in the open seas, and was generally meant to be tasked by the Admiralty. SAR in coastal waters was provided by RAF Fighter Command.

Cruiser – Warship smaller than a battleship or battlecruiser, but much larger than a destroyer. The Washington Naval Treaty of 1922 laid down that light cruisers had a main armament of 6-inch guns and heavy cruisers a main armament of 8-inch guns (displacement tonnage was not taken into account). The Royal Navy's Town-class had up to twelve 6-inch guns in four turrets but was classified by the service as 'heavy'. In addition there were auxiliary (see above) or armed merchant cruisers, and anti-aircraft cruisers, which were usually older ships modified to allow continued use.

Cruiser War – A term sometimes used for commerce raiding.

Destroyer – Small fast warship, and by the Second World War much larger than its First World War counterpart. Armament varied between 4 and 4.5-inch on British ships, but some German ships were larger and the French had their *contre-pilleur* destroyers with 5.5-inch armament.

Dynamo – code name for the evacuation of British and French forces from Dunkirk.

E-boat – Enemy fast motor gunboat or motor torpedo boat, known to the Kriegsmarine as *S-Boot*, for *Schnellboot*, or 'fast boat'.

Enigma – Code used by all of the German armed forces, broken once a machine and code-books fell into British hands. The breaking of the Enigma codes was a major factor in the Allied victory and especially in countering the U-boat threat to Atlantic and Arctic convoys.

Fighter Command – RAF command responsible for air defence of the UK and for coastal search and rescue. It was not the only fighter operation in the RAF, as units posted overseas came under local command, but RAF Fighter Command could be regarded as being 'home' to such units.

Fleet Air Arm – Originally that part of the Royal Air Force deployed aboard British warships. It reverted to Admiralty control in May 1939, and naval airmen gradually replaced many of their RAF counterparts, although a large number of RAF personnel transferred to the Royal Navy.

Flight – A sub-unit of an air force, air corps or air arm aircraft squadron. The number of aircraft varied, but in a fighter squadron it would often be four aircraft led in the RAF by a flight lieutenant, and in the Royal Navy's Fleet Air Arm by a lieutenant.

Flotilla – A command of smaller warships such as destroyers, corvettes or submarines. No definition of the number of ships, but usually it would be between six and nine.

Home Guard – A home defence organisation manned by volunteers at first, although later some conscripts were added, intended to augment the regular forces if the UK was invaded. It was also given other tasks such as rounding up downed enemy airmen and guarding important installations as well as, in coastal areas, keeping a lookout along the coastline. Later in the war, used to train young men before conscription. Most of the membership consisted of those too young or too old to be members of the armed forces, and as the latter predominated, it was known affectionately as 'Dad's Army'. When first formed, the Home Guard was known as the Local Defence Volunteers.

Kaiserliche Marine – 'Imperial Navy', the old name for the German Navy.

Kriegsmarine – 'War Navy', the official name given by Adolf Hitler to the German Navy in 1935 to replace the post-First World War name of *Reichsmarine*, or 'State Navy'.

Lend-Lease – A programme under which the United States provided ships, aircraft and other war materiel without payment by the British government and on condition that the equipment be returned to the United States at the end of the war. Naturally, anything that had been lost on war service could not be returned. In return, the United States armed forces were allowed to use bases in British colonies, mainly in the Caribbean. There was also a measure of what has been called 'reverse lend-lease' (see below), with the Royal Navy providing escort vessels fitted with Asdic to the United States Navy which lagged behind in anti-submarine equipment at the outset of the war.

Local Defence Volunteers – predecessor of the Home Guard (above).

Luftwaffe – The German Air Force or Air Arm, which controlled all German service aviation from the early 1930s to the end of the Second World War. Although autonomous, it developed as primarily a tactical air force without long-range heavy bombers until too late in the war for them to make an impact.

NAS – A suffix after the squadron number to denote naval air squadrons.

NKVD – People's Commissariat for Internal Affairs (Narodnyi Komissariat Vnutrennikh Del), predecessor of the Soviet Union's KGB.

Reich – The German state.

Reichsmarine – 'State Navy', official name for the German Navy after the abdication of the Kaiser and following the creation of a republic or 'Reich'.

Reverse Lend-Lease – Equipment provided by the United Kingdom to the United States. While much smaller in quantity than that received by the UK, included some warships equipped with Asdic (sonar), and radar.

RMS – Royal Mail Ship, a designation allowed the fast ocean liner that, as well as conveying passengers in comfort, also carried the mails. Not to be confused with the Royal Mail Line, a shipping company, but ships prefixed as 'RMS' were always owned by ship-owners that were private enterprises.

Sea Lion - Translation of *Seelöwe*, as explained below.

Seelöwe - German code name for the invasion of England, translates as 'Sea Lion'.

Squadron – in air corps, air force or air arm use, a unit for aircraft, the number of which could vary, with later in the war RAF bomber squadrons having up to twenty aircraft. Normally, numbers were much lower, and for fighters could be twelve or sixteen.

Squadron – in naval use, a command of major warships such as battleships, battlecruisers, cruisers or aircraft carriers. A squadron could have as few as two ships. Smaller warships and submarines were grouped in flotillas.

Taken up from trade – A maritime term referring to merchant vessels taken over by a navy, sometimes to provide support but often to be armed for a variety of duties, including minesweeping or convoy escort.

U-boat – In German, *U-boot*, or *Untersee Boot*, a submarine.

Wardroom – RN name for the officers' mess – also used by some merchant shipping lines such as P&O.

Wolf Pack – A group of submarines deployed against a convoy, only used in connection with German U-boats.

Bibliography

Auphin, Mural and Mordal, Jacques, *The French Navy in World War II*, US Naval Institute, Annapolis.

German Invasion Plans for the British Isles 1940, English translation by the Bodleian Library, Oxford, 2007.

Gibson, Wing Commander Guy, *Enemy Coast Ahead*, Michael Joseph, London, 1946.

Holland, James, *War in the West*, Corgi Books, London, 2016.

Johnson, Group Captain J.E. 'Johnnie', *Wing Leader*, Chatto & Windus, London, 1956

Kershaw, Ian, *Hitler 1936-1945*, Allen Lane, London, 2000.

McKinstry, Leo, *Operation Sealion*, John Murray, London, 2014.

Rees, Laurence, *War of the Century*, BBC Publications, London, 1999.

Shirer, William, *Berlin Diary*, Alfred A. Knopf, 1941.

Talbot-Booth, E.C. *All the World's Fighting Fleets*, (second edition), Samson Low, London, 1939.

Wheatley, Ronald, *Operation Sea Lion*, Oxford University Press, Oxford 1958.

Endnotes

Chapter 1: The Unstoppable Hun

1. The day.
2. Gibson, Wing Commander Guy, *Enemy Coast Ahead*.
3. *Panzerschiffe* were armed with 12-inch guns, well below the calibre of Second World War battleships which varied between 14 and 16 in, with some Japanese ships having 18-in guns. The role of the *Graf Spee* and her two sisters was convoy warfare.
4. *The French Navy in World War II*, Auphin and Mordal.

Chapter 2: After Dunkirk

1. The term 'Atlantic Wall' really could only be applied to this sector, but despite strengthening of the defences at many points along the coastline of the newly-occupied territories, there were places where the defences were weak. Nevertheless, these were also the places with a longer sea crossing from the UK. Many in Germany, including senior Nazis, seem actually to have believed that the Atlantic Wall was longer and much stronger than was in fact the case, giving them a false sense of security.

Chapter 3: Lessons of Invasions Past

1. The Highland Line marks the southern and eastern extent of the Scottish Highlands. It does not follow any line of latitude but runs from north of Glasgow to Perth and then curves north-easterly. It lies to the west of Aberdeen, which strictly speaking is not in the Scottish Highlands.

Chapter 4: The Germans Prepare Their Plans

1. It is a point that France might not have fallen had the RAF had a stronger presence in France, but it was clear that the Germans were unstoppable even as they first entered France. Their strength was overwhelming, at least on land and in the air.
2. Coastal monitors were small ships with a shallow draught for close inshore work, armed with heavy guns of 12-inch calibre or higher. These provided the heavy supporting fire that invading troops needed.

3. Gibson, *Enemy Coast Ahead*.
4. Gibson, *Enemy Coast Ahead*.

Chapter 5: Battle of Britain

1. Group Captain 'Johnnie' Johnson, *Wing Leader*.
2. angels 20 = 20,000 feet.
3. Group Captain 'Johnnie' Johnson, *Wing Leader*.
4. Imperial War Museum Sound Archive.
5. Imperial War Museum Sound Archive.
6. Imperial War Museum Sound Archive.

Chapter 10: Barbarossa and Deliverance

1. At one stage in the English Civil War, government moved from London to Oxford.
2. This was a key route between Europe, Russia and the Far East, but much of it was single track.

Chapter 11: What Would German Occupation Have Meant?

1. Ambassadors to the United Kingdom are always strictly speaking 'ambassadors to the Court of St James', in other words to the sovereign, as head of state, rather than the government.

Chapter 12: The Lessons of Normandy

1. Chief of the Imperial General Staff, the professional head of the British Army.
2. Imperial War Museum Sound Archive.
3. Group Captain 'Johnnie' Johnson, *Wing Leader*.
4. 'United Nations' was a term coined to describe the Allies, and not to be confused with the post-war creation which was meant to be a more effective successor to the interwar League of Nations, which had not included the United States and repeatedly proved to be impotent.
5. Imperial War Museum Sound Archive.
6. Imperial War Museum Sound Archive.
7. X and Y turrets, the two turrets closest to the stern, were manned by Royal Marines rather than naval gunners on British warships.
8. By 'guns' he presumably means turrets as this rate of fire would be difficult for a single gun at the time.
9. Imperial War Museum Sound Archive.
10. Imperial War Museum Sound Archive
11. Imperial War Museum Sound Archive.
12. Imperial War Museum Sound Archive.

13. Imperial War Museum Sound Archive.

Chapter 14: Could the Germans have Invaded?
 1. War Office 166/1343.
 2. Ian Kershaw, *Hitler 1936-1945*.

Index

AASF *see* Advance Air Striking Force
Abercrombie, HMS, 185
Abernethy, Treaty of, 38
Abyssinia, Italy's invasion of, 2
Acasta, HMS, 10
Achilles, HMS, 82
Adlertag, 49, 65, 70
Administration, plans for post-invasion, 169
Advance Air Striking Force, 11, 18
Agricola, Governor, 32
Air Defence of Great Britain, 66–67
Air force
    British (*see* Royal Air Force)
    German (*see* Luftwaffe)
Air Raid Wardens' Service, 24–25
Air Servicing Unit (ASU), 77
Air Transport Auxiliary, 71
Aircraft
    comparative numbers, 12–13, 143
Aircraft, British
    Avro Lancaster, 71
    Bolton Paul Defiant, 63–64, 69
    Bristol Beaufighter, 64
    Bristol Blenheim, 11
    Fairey Battle, 11, 18, 75
    Fairey Swordfish, 84, 185
    Gloster Gladiator, 11, 63
    Handley Page Hampden, 17
    Hawker Hurricane, 11, 63–64, 66
    Hawker Typhoon, 192–93
    Supermarine Seafire, 198
    Supermarine Spitfire, 11, 17, 63–64
    Vickers Wellington, 17
    Westland Lysander, 11, 18
    Westland Wyvern, 64
Aircraft, German
    DFS 230 glider, 15, 137
    Dornier Do17Z, 66
    Dornier Do217, 25
    Heinkel He111, 74
    Junkers Ju52/3, 3, 15, 51, 137, 149

    Junkers Ju87, 16–17, 70–71, 86
    Junkers Ju252, 149
    Messerschmidt Bf109, 11, 64–65, 66, 86, 104
    Messerschmidt Me110, 66, 70, 104
Airlift, Leningrad, 163
Ajax, HMS, 82, 140
Albania, 100, 101
Alderney, 29, 128, 214
    see also The Channel Islands
Alexander II, Pope, 36
Alfred the Great, King, 34–35
All the World's Fighting Fleets (E. C. Talbot-Booth), 80
Alsace and Lorraine, 125
Altmark (German supply ship), 82, 112
Andalsnes, 7–8
Anderson shelters, 25
Anschluss, 1
Antonine Wall, 32
Antwerp, 1, 57–59
Anvil, Operation *see* Dragoon, Operation
Anzio, 133
Appeasement, British and French policy of, 2
Ardeatine Caves, 134
Ardennes, 16, 17
Ardent, HMS, 10
Ark Royal, HMS, 80, 88
Armada, Spanish, 39
Armée Secrète, 119
Army, German *see* Heer
Arnhem raid, 123
Arrow Cross (Hungarian political party), 103, 104
Artillerie Kommand 106, 55
Artillery, heavy, 52, 54–55
Ascq, 128
'Asparagus, Rommel's', 188
Assandun, Battle of, 35
Assman, Vice Admiral Kurt, 204
Athena, SS, 82
Atlantic Wall, 24, 175

Augustus, Caesar, 30
Austria, 91
Avalanche, Operation, 133

Bačka, 100
Bader, Wing Commander Douglas, 76
Badoglio, Marshal, 132, 133
Baltic, 1, 97
Banat, 100
Banquet, Operation, 27, 60
Barbarossa, Operation, 2, 62, 97, 102–3, 142–45, 149–53
Barges, 1, 24, 47–48, 52, 209–11
    see also Caigues
Barham, HMS, 140
Batterie Todt naval battery, 55
Batteries, naval, 55
Battle of Britain, 48–49, 63–77
BBC see British Broadcasting Corporation
Bearn (French aircraft carrier), 87
Beaverbrook, Lord, 64
Beetle network, 27
BEF see British Expeditionary Force
Belgium, 116–19
    forces, 12, 14
    Germany invades, 9, 15
    surrenders, 16
Belgrade, 99
Bells, church, 60
Beneš, President Edvard, 92
Berlin, RAF attack on, 75
Berlin Diary (William Shirer), 59
Bernhard, Prince (of The Netherlands), 122
Best, Werner, 111
'Big Wing,' 76
Biggin Hill, RAF, 66, 70, 75, 77
Bismark (German battleship), 86, 167, 204
Bison (French super destroyer), 9
'Black Book,' 51
Blackpool, 173
Blenheim Palace, 169, 173
Blitzkrieg, 3, 13, 124
Blücher (troop ship), 7
Blue, Operation, 159–60
'Blue on blue,' 192–93
Von Bock, Field Marshal, 143, 155
Boelke, Oswald, 72
Bohemia, 92
Bohle, Ernst Wilhelm, 171
Bolsheviks, 141

Bomber Command, RAF see Royal Air Force
Bombing, German, strategy, 25
Bonnet, Georges, 123
Bornholm island, 112
Boudica, 31
Brand, Air Vice Marshal, 67
Von Brauchitsch, Field Marshal, 143, 156, 172
British Broadcasting Corporation, 26, 111
British Expeditionary Force, 11, 18
Britomart, HMS, 192–93
Brooke, General Sir Alan, 181
Brunanburh, Battle of, 34–35
Buffalo tracked vehicle, 194
Bullets, tracer, 69

C-47 Dakota, Douglas, 3
Caesar, Julius, 30
Caigues, 136
Caligula, Caesar, 30
Calypso, HMS, 180
Canaris, Admiral, 5
Canea, 138
    see also Crete
Cannibalism, 158
Cannon, aircraft, 64
Cap d'Antifer, 55
Carlisle, HMS, 140
Carls, Admiral, 86
Casino, Monte, 133–34
Cephalonia, 133
Chain Home network, 10, 25, 68, 70
Chamberlain, Neville, 43, 94
'Channel Dash,' 191
The Channel Islands, 21, 29, 128–31
    see also Alderney
Channel Patrol, 53
Chasseurs Ardennais, 14
Chatfield, Admiral Sir Ernle, 80
Chuikov, Major General Vasili, 161
Churchill, Winston
    favours amphibious assault on Trondheim, 8
    speaks after fall of France, 20
    warns of invasion, 59
    coins term 'Battle of Britain,' 63
    flies to Athens, 1944, 102
    negotiates post-war deal with Stalin, 102
    offers France political union, 124
    on the Duke of Windsor, 170–71
    objects to 1943 Normandy landings, 175–76
Ciano, Count, 132

Civil Repair Organisation (CRO), 77
Claudius, Emperor, 30, 31
Clenshaw, Sergeant Ian, 65–66
Clifton Suspension Bridge, 173
Cnut, King, 35
Coastal Command, RAF, 47
Coasters, 54
Colonial troops, 13, 75
Colsay, HMS, 193
Condor Legion, 64
Conqueror, William the *see* William, Duke of Normandy
Convair B-36, 202
Convoys, 69, 83–84
Cook, Sergeant George, 179
Cossack, HMS, 82, 112
Courageous, HMS, 81, 167
Crete, 101, 135–40
Croatia, 98–100
'Cromwell' codeword, 59–60
Croydon, RAF, 70, 75
Cruelty at Stalingrad, 164
Cruiser U-boat, 85
  see also U-boat
Cunningham, Admiral Andrew Browne, 140
Cyprus, 136
Czechoslovakia, 91–93

D-Day *see* Normandy landings
Dad's Army *see* Home Guard
Daedalus, HMS, 73
Daily life for pilots, 73–74
Dalmati, 100
Danae, HMS, 189
Danegeld, 35, 38
Danelaw, 34
Danish Navy, Royal, 110
Debden, RAF, 75
Deladier, (French) Prime Minister, 123, 124
Denmark, 4–5, 109–12
Derrien, Admiral, 8
DeTeGerät radar, 55
Deutschland panzerschiff, 83
Dido, HMS, 140
Dieppe, 176–81
Digby, RAF, 74
Dockyards, 46
Domesday Book, 38
Dönitz, Admiral Karl, 1, 86
Dordrecht bridge, 15

Dover
  Patrol, 53
  Straits of, 53–54
  Defence Scheme, 204
Dowding, Air Chief Marshal Sir Hugh, 18, 65
Dragoon, Operation, 197–98
Drôle de guerre see 'Phoney War'
Druids, 33
Dunkirk, 1, 18–19
Dunsterville, Major General L. C., 141
Duxford, RAF, 76
Dynamo, Operation, 19, 83–84

E-boats, 83–84, 195
East, German occupation in the, 91–105
East Indies, The Netherlands, 119, 120
Eastchurch, RAF, 75
Eben-Emael, Fort, 14, 15, 116–17
Eden, Anthony, 102, 132
Edgar the Atheling, King, 37, 38
Edgar the Peaceful, King, 35
Edward the Confessor, King, 35
Einsatzgruppen, 145
Eisenhower, General Dwight, 93, 133
Elizabeth, Princess, 27
Elizabeth, Queen, 27
Émile Bertin (French light cruiser), 9
Enemy Coast Ahead (Guy Gibson), 57, 58
Engines, piston, 202
Entente Cordiale, 39
Erebus, HMS, 185
Eremenko, Lieutenant General Andrey, 162
Ethelred the Unready, King, 35
Exeter, HMS, 82

Von Falkenhausen, General Alexander, 118
Fall Gelb, 16–19
Fallschirmjäger, 50
Faroes, 110
FernDeTeGerät radar, 55
Ferry Command, 71
Fighter Command, RAF *see* Royal Air Force
Fiji, HMS, 140
Finland, 147, 150
  Air Force, 72
  Army, 157
Fisher, Admiral Lord, 39
Fitzosbern, William, 37
Flandin, Pierre, 126
Fleet Air Arm, 65, 135, 185

Food production, 84, 126
Forbes, Admiral Sir Charles, 80, 89
Ford, RAF, 73
Foreign Legion, French, 9
Foresters, Company of, 93, 129
Formations
    British (*see* Royal Air Force; Royal Navy)
    German (*see* Heer; Kriegsmarine; Luftwaffe)
Formidable, HMS, 140, 204
Forrester, Ken, 196
'Fortress Holland,' 119
Fowlmere, RAF, 76
France, 123–28
    equipment, 13
    Germany invades, 16–19
    signs armistice, 19
Frank, Hans, 95
Frantisek, Josef, 75
Free Corps, Danish, 111
Free French forces, 127
Freedom Council, Danish, 111
French ships scuttled, 83
Freshman, Operation, 115
Frick, Wilhelm, 93
Friedrich August naval battery, 55
Friendly fire, 192–93
Front de l'Indépendance, 119
'Führer system,' 62, 136

Gajda, General Rudolf, 93
De Gaulle, Charles, 124
George II, King, of Greece, 101
George VI, King, 27, 169
'Germany Calling' (William Joyce), 45
Geta, Hosidius, 31
Gibraltar, 61
Gibson, Wing Commander Guy, 1, 57, 58
Gliders, 15, 117, 137–40
Glorious, HMS, 9–10, 81, 83, 89, 167, 200
Gloucester, HMS, 140
Gneisenau (German battleship), 10, 82, 167, 191, 204
Goering, Reichsmarshall Herman, 49, 86, 125–26, 136, 137
Govorow, General, 159
Graf Spee panzerschiff, 53, 82, 167
Graf Zeppelin (German aircraft carrier), 86
Gravesend, RAF, 75
'Great Patriotic War,' 144
Grebbe line, 119

Greece, 99, 101–2
Greenland, 110
Guderian, General Heinz, 156
Guernsey *see* The Channel Islands
Gunfire, naval, 53

Haakon VII, King, 113, 115
Hacha, Dr Emil, 92
Hadrian's Wall, 32
The Hague, 15
Hairs, Pilot Officer Peter, 68–69
Halder, General Franz, 41–42, 50
Halifax, Lord, 43
Hampden bomber, Handley-Page, 1
Hanneken, Lieutenant General Hermann, 111
Harald, (Norwegian) King, 35
Harold, King, 29, 35–37
Harris, Air Chief Marshal Sir Arthur, 44
'Harrying of the North,' 37–38
Hastings, Battle of, 36–37
Hathaway, Sibyl, 129
Hawkinge, RAF, 66, 70, 75
Heer
    Army Group A, 50, 51
    Army Group B, 51–52
    Army Group North, 158
    Army Group South, 144
    First Panzer Group, 144
    Third Panzer Group, 155
    Fourth Panzer Group, 155
    Fourth Army, 155
    Fourth Panzer Army, 157
    Ninth Army, 50, 155
    Second Panzer Army, 155
    Sixteenth Army, 50, 55
    5th Mountain Division, 138
    7th Infantry Division, 50
    9th Armoured Division, 121
    22nd Airborne Infantry Division, 120
    35th Infantry Division, 50
    Großdeutschland Regiment, 50
    SS Liebstandarte Adolf Hitler Regiment, 50
Heraklion, 138
    see also Crete
Hereward the Wake, 38
Hermes, HMS, 80
Hewitt, Vice Admiral Henry, USN, 198
Heydrich, Reinhard, 92, 93, 145
Heye, Admiral, 85
Hill 107, Crete, 139

Himmler, Reichsführer Heinrich, 95–96, 172
Hitler, Adolf
   holds back armour at Dunkirk, 18
   admires British Empire, 41–42
   issues Directive No.16, 48
   briefs commanders before invasion, 60–61
   orders preparations to be dismantled, 61
   orders Operation Barbarossa, 62, 142
   demands attacks on London, 75
   approves Plan Z, 86
   abandons German-Polish Non-Agression Pact, 94
   signs pact with USSR, 94
   demands Yugoslavia joins Axis, 99
   demands destruction of Leningrad, 108, 158
   meets King Leopold III of Belgium, 117
   assures Queen Wilhelmina, 120
   meets Marshal Pétain, 125
   accepts need to invade Crete, 137
   publishes *Mein Kampf*, 146
   favours Blackpool, 173
Home Guard, 25–27
Honour, Lieutenant George, 187
Horne, Sergeant Geordie, 179
Horses, 3, 13
Horthy, Admiral (Hungary), 103, 105
Hoses, flexible, for tanks, 52
Hoth, General Hermann, 160
Hughes, Captain J. H. B., 189
Hughes-Hallett, Captain J., 178, 179
Hungary, 103–5
'Hunger Winter,' 123
Hussar, HMS, 192–93

Iceland, 22, 42, 110–11
Identification friend or foe (IFF), 68–69
Ijssel line, 119
Illustrious, HMS, 201
Imperial Iranian Air Force, 64
Infatuate II, Operation, 194
   see also Normandy landings
Invasion of Britain, *Wehrmacht* report on, 1939, 44
Invasion Plans for the British Isles 1940, German, 55–57, 109, 172
Ireland, 23–24, 56, 57
Irene Brigade, 122
Irish Air Corps, 64
Italy, 131–34, 161
   enters war, 20
   surrenders, 102

James II, King, 39
Jarrow, 34
Jason, HMS, 193
Jersey *see* The Channel Islands
Jersey Motor Transport, 129
Jews, 91
   in The Channel Islands, 129
   in Denmark, 112
   in France, 125
   in Great Britain, 173
   in Hungary, 103, 105
   in The Netherlands, 121–22
   in Poland, 96–97
   in Soviet Union, 145, 147, 151
Jodl, General Alfred, 61, 168
Johnson, Group Captain J. E. 'Johnnie', 64, 180
Joyce, William, 44–45, 171
Jubilee, Operation, 176–81
Junkers, Professor Hugo, 146
Jutland, Battle of, 81

Kallay, Miklos, 104, 105
Kampine barge, 47
Kanalkampf, 69
Kanne bridge, 15
Kassa, Hungary, bombed, 104
Kattegat, 1, 5
Katyn Forest, 97
Kauffmann, Henrik, 110
Keller, General Alfred, 144
Kennedy, Joseph, 201–2
Kesselring, Generalfeldmarshall Albert, 75
Von Kesselring, Field Marshal, 144
Kiel Canal, 53
Kiev falls, 144
Von Kleist, Field Marshal Paul, 144
Von Kluge, Field Marshal, 156
Koch, Erich, 144
Konev, Marshal Ivan, 93
Königsberg (cruiser), 7
Kopets, Lieutenant General, 143
Kotor, Gulf of, 100
Kriegsmarine, 3, 7, 44, 45, 84–88
   see also individual ships
Von Küchler, Field Marshal Georg, 159

Ladoga, Lake, 158
Lakatos, General Geza, 105

Landing craft, 29, 47, 187–88
Landing equipment, 214–15
Landing sites, choice of, 50
Laval, Pierre, 124, 126
Lawrence, Pilot Officer Keith, 67–68, 71
Lebensraum, 2, 41
Lee-on-Solent, RNAS, 73
Von Leeb, Field Marshal, 143, 157
Leningrad, battle for, 156–60
Leopold III, King, 116, 117
Lesjeshogen, 8
Ležaky, 93
Lidice, 93
'Lightning War' *see Blitzkrieg*
Lindisfarne, 34
Linzel, Captain J., 194
Little Saturn, Operation, 162
Local Defence Volunteers *see* Home Guard
Logothepoulos, Konstantinos, 102
London Defence Positions, 39
Luftschlacht um Grossbritannien see Battle of Britain
Luftwaffe, 3
    7th Parachute Division, 51, 137, 138
    Erprobungsgruppe 210, 70
    Fliegerkorps XI, 137
    Luftflotte 2, 66, 75
    Luftflotte 5, 70
    see also Aircraft, German
Lutzow panzerschiff, 83
Luxembourg, 16
Lympne, RAF, 66

Macedonia, 99, 100
Maginot Line, 9, 10, 16
Maillé-Brézé (French super destroyer), 9
Malan, Squadron Leader Adolph 'Sailor,' 73
Malcolm III, King, of Scotland, 38
Maleme, 138, 139
    see also Crete
Malta, 20–21, 61, 132, 133, 136, 168
Manchester Ship Canal, 173
Von Manstein, Field Marshal Erich, 159, 163
Manston, RAF, 66, 70, 73, 75
Maps and Communications, *Wermacht* Department for, 55–56
Marcks, General, 150
Margaret, Princess, 27
Marine Nationale, 83, 108
Marinefährprahm, 47

Mass Observation, 2, 199
'Master Race,' 172
McIntosh, Flying Officer *see* Advance Air Striking Force
Mein Kampf (Adolph Hitler), 146
Meindl, General Eugen, 139
Menai massacre, 31
Menzel, Major Hubert, 142
Mercia, 33, 37–38
Meretskov, General, 158, 159
Merkur, Operation, 137–40
Metaxas, General Ioannis, 101
Middle Wallop, RAF, 67, 71
Militarbefehlshaber in Frankreich, 125
Militargeographische Angaben über England, 172
Milorg, 115
Mines, 83
Minesweepers, 183–84
Mobilisation, British, 56
Moerdijk bridge, 15
Monitors, coastal, 52
Montcalm (French cruiser), 8
Montgomery, Field Marshal Bernard, 142, 177
Moravia, 92
Mościcki, Ignacy, 94
Moscow, battle for, 153–56
    see also Barbarossa, Operation
Moseley, Sir Oswald, 171
Motor Torpedo Boats, 195–96
Mountbatten, Admiral Louis, 177
MTB *see* Motor Torpedo Boats
Mulberry harbour, 182–83
Munich Agreement 1938, 4, 92, 103, 199
Mussart, Anton, 122
Mussolini, Benito, 131–34

Naiad, HMS, 140
Namsos, 7
Namur, 16
Národni Souručenstvi, 93
Narvik, Battles of, 7
Navy
    British (*see* Royal Navy)
    German (*see Kriegsmarine*)
Navy, Netherlands, 120, 121, 122
Nazi party, The Netherlands, 122
Nedić, General Milan, 101
Nelson, HMS, 80, 186, 191
Neptune, Operation, 181–92
    see also Normandy landings

Nero, Emperor, 31–32
The Netherlands, 119–23
    forces, 11, 14
    Germany invades, 9, 15
    surrenders, 16
Networks, escape, 119
Von Neurath, Baron Konstantin, 92
Nicolson, Harold, 171
Norman conquest, 29, 35–38
Normandy landings, 49, 175–76, 181–93
North Weald, RAF, 73, 75
Northern Ireland, 57
Northern Lights, Operation, 158–59
Norwegian campaign, 6–10, 82

Oakley, Able Seaman Ken, 188
Oberkommando der Heeres, 49
Observer Corps, 24
Offa, King, of Mercia, 34
Oldenburg naval battery, 55
Operational Training Unit (OTU), 75
Oradour-sur-Glane, 128
Orange, Radio, 122
Orion, HMS, 140
Osprey, USS, 183–84
Ostend, fire at, 195–96
Oster, Colonel, 120
Ostvolk see Volksdeutsche
Overlord, Operation *see* Normandy landings
Ozanne, Marie, 129–30

Panzerschiffe, 3, 53
Paramythia, Albania, 135
Paratroops, 51, 136, 138–39
Park, Air Vice Marshal Keith, 67, 75, 76
Patch, Lieutenant General Alexander, 198
Patton, Lieutenant General George, 93
Paul, Prince, of Yugoslavia, 98–99
Paulus, Field Marshal Friedrich, 160, 162, 163
Pavelić, Ante, 99
Peel-Ramm line, 119
Peniche barge, 47
Pétain, Marshal Philippe, 20, 22, 124–26
    see also Vichy France
Peter II, King, of Yugoslavia, 98
Peter Strasser (German aircraft carrier), 86
Petrograd *see* Leningrad, battle for
Pevensey, 36
'Phoney War,' 12, 124
Pilot numbers, 77

Pionierlandungsboot 39, 47
Plan, German invasion, 49–52
Plan Z, 45, 86–87
    see also Kriegsmarine; U-boat
Plate, River, 82
Plautius, Aulus, 31
PLUTO pipeline, 183
Poland, 1, 2, 94–98
Portland, 34
Pound, Admiral Sir Dudley, 89
Princess Astrid (ferry), 179
Prinz Eugen (German cruiser), 167, 191
Prinz Heinrich naval battery, 55
Propaganda battle, 44

Q-ships, 82
Queen Elizabeth, HMS, 140
Quisling, Vidkun, 113–14

Raeder, Grand Admiral Erich, 1, 44, 61, 84
    see also Kriegsmarine
RAF *see* Royal Air Force
Railways, 53
    in The Channel Islands, 130
Rallis, Ioannis, 102
Ramillies, HMS, 186
Ramsay, Admiral Sir Bertram, 184–85
Ravensbrück concentration camp, 93
Rawalpindi, HMS, 82
Red Cross, International, 102, 131
Regia Marina, 136, 159, 168
Reichskommissariat Niederlanden, 121
Reichsmarine, 3
Republica Socialiste Italia, 134
Retimo, 138
    see also Crete
Reynaud, (French) Prime Minister, 124
Von Ribbentrop, Joachim, 92, 171
Ring, Operation, 163
Rjukan heavy water plant, 115
Roberts, HMS, 185, 194
Roberts, Major General J. H., 178
Rochester, battle near, (Roman conquest), 31
Rochford, RAF, 74, 75
Rockets, 189, 190
Rodney, HMS, 80, 186
Rokossovsky, Lieutenant General, 163
Roma (Italian battleship), 133
Roman conquest, 29–33
Romanian Army, 161–62

238   Operation Sealion

Rome, 133
Rommel, Field Marshal Erwin, 136
'Rommel's Asparagus', 188
Rotte, 72
Rotterdam, 16, 121
Royal Air Force
   10 Group, 67
   11 Group, 66, 67
   12 Group, 68, 76
   19 Squadron, 76
   32 Squadron, 66
   56 Squadron, 66, 74
   74 Squadron, 73
   111 Squadron, 68
   151 Squadron, 73–74
   234 Squadron, 67, 71
   242 Squadron, 76
   253 Squadron, 66
   263 Squadron, 192
   266 Squadron, 192
   302 Squadron, 76
   303 (Polish) Squadron, 75
   310 Squadron, 76
   320 Squadron, 122
   501 Squadron, 68
   611 Squadron, 76
   616 Squadron, 180
   617 Squadron, 71
   see also Tactical Air Force, Second; Aircraft, British; individual stations; Fleet Air Arm
Royal Family, 27
Royal Marines, 79, 179–80, 194–95
Royal Naval Reserve, 79
Royal Naval Volunteer Reserve, 79
Royal Navy, 46, 79–84, 88–90
   see also individual ships; Fleet Air Arm
Royal Oak, HMS, 81, 167
Royal Regiment of Canada, 180
Von Rundstedt, Field Marshal Gerd, 43, 143, 190–91
Russia, invasions of, 141
Rutter, Operation *see* Jubilee, Operation

Sachsenhausen concentration camp, 96
Salamander, HMS, 193
Salerno, 133
Sark *see* The Channel Islands
Sas, Major, 120
Scapa Flow, 46
Scharnhorst (German battleship), 10, 82, 167, 191, 204
Schellenberg, Colonel Walter, 51, 170
Schwarm, 72–73
Scotland, 32, 34, 57
Scylla, HMS, 190
Sedan, 16
Seekriegsführung gegen England, 85
Senate House, London, 169
Service du Travail Obligatoire, 128
Seyss-Inquart, Artur, 121
'Shetland Bus', 115
Shingle, Operation, 133
Shipping, merchant, 114, 121
Shirer, William, 59
Siegfried naval battery, 55
Sikorsky, Igor, 146
'Sitting War' *see* 'Phoney War'
Sitzkrieg see 'Phoney War'
Six, Dr Franz, 171
Sixteenth Army, German, 50
Skagerrak, 1, 5
Slovenia, 100
Śmigly-Rydz, Marshal Edward, 95
Smith, Pilot Officer Irving 'Black', 73–74
SOE *see* Special Operations Executive
Southern Vectis bus company, 26
Soviet Union, 2, 52, 142–45
   see also Barbarossa, Operation
Spanish Civil War, 13, 24
Spark, Operation, 159
Sparrowhawk, HMS, 7
Special Operations Executive, 111, 115
Spending, military, 88
St Brice's Day massacre, 35
St Petersburg *see* Leningrad, battle for
Stalin, Joseph, 142, 144, 151
Stalingrad, 104, 105, 153, 160–65
Stamford Bridge, Battle of, 35
Stay behind teams, 27
Student, General Kurt, 137, 138
Submarines, midget *see* 'X' boats
Suda Bay, 136
Sudetenland crisis, 1, 92
Suez Canal, 61, 136, 168
Surcouf (French submarine cruiser), 85
Sweyn Forkbeard, (Viking) King, 35
Sweyn II, King, of Denmark, 37–38
Szálasi, Ferenc, 103, 105
Sztojay, General Döme, 105

Tactical Air Force, Second, 183

Tactics in the air, 71–73
Talbot-Booth, Lieutenant Commander E. C., 80
Tangmere, RAF, 68, 73
Tanks, 48, 213–14
Taranto, 136, 200
Tavronitis River, 139
Terboven, Reichskommissar Josef, 113
Terror, HMS, 185
Thatcher, Prime Minister Margaret, 200
Theresienstadt, 112
Thomas, Major General Georg, 88
Timoshenko, Marshal Semyon, 152
Tirpitz (German battleship), 86, 167, 204
Todt Organization, 54, 107
Torch, Operation, 126, 132
Toulon, French ships scuttled at, 108–9
Trans-Siberian Railway, 154
Traps, tank, 27
Trenchard, Marshall of the RAF Sir Hugh, 77
Tripartite Pact, 99, 103, 132
Trondheim, 7, 8
Tsolakoglou, General Georgios, 102
Tulle, 128
Tyne Bridge, 173

U-boat, 3, 81, 85, 87
Die U-Bootswaffe (Karl Dönitz), 87
Ukraine, Battle for, 164
Ultimatum, French and British, to Germany, 1
Unification, German, 200
United States 27, 182
Units
    British (*see* Royal Air Force; Royal Navy)
    German (*see* Heer; Kriegsmarine; *Luftwaffe*)
Uranus, Operation, 161
*Ustřední vedení odboje domácího (*UVOD), 93
Uxbridge, RAF, 66

V-1 flying bomb, 112
Varangéville, 179, 180
Vatutin, Lieutenant General N. F., 162
Vega, SS, 131
Veldwezelt bridge, 15, 18
Veranius, Quintus, 32

Versailles, Treaty of, 2, 92
Vian, Admiral Philip, 190
Vichy France, 22–23, 43, 108, 109, 125
    see also Pétain, Marshal Philippe
Victor Emanuel, King (of Italy), 132
Viking landings, 29, 33–35
Vlaamsch Nationaal Verbond, 116
Vlasov, General Andrey, 93, 158
Volksdeutsche, 91, 108
Voroshilov, Marshal, 157
Vroenhoven bridge, 15, 18

WAAF *see* Women's Auxiliary Air Force
Waalhaven airfield, 15
Waffen SS, 14
Wagner, General Eduard, 172
Walcheren Island, 193–94
Wales, 31–32
War, United Kingdom declares, 1
War of the Century (Laurence Rees), 142
Warmwell, RAF, 67
Warspite, HMS, 7, 8, 140, 184, 186, 194
Wartheland, 95–96
Weather, 48, 177
Wedmore, Treaty of, 34
Von Weichs, General Maximilian, 161
Weserübung, Operation, 5
Weston, Sergeant Frederick, 194–95
Wilhelmina, Queen, 116, 120, 121, 122
William, Duke of Normandy, 35–38
William of Orange, 39
Windsor, Duke of, 169–71
Wing Leader ('Johnnie' Johnson), 64
Wintringham, Tom, 26
Women's Auxiliary Air Force, 66

'X' boats, 186–87

D'Yeu, Île, 126
Ypenburg, 15
Yugoslavia, 98–101
    see also Albania; Croatia; Greece

Zhdanov, Andrei, 157
Zhukov, General Georgy, 154, 156